The Pure Theory of Politics

Bertrand de Jouvenel

THE

Pure Theory

OF

Politics

BERTRAND DE JOUVENEL

Foreword by Daniel J. Mahoney

LIBERTY FUND

Indianapolis

© 1963 Cambridge University Press.
Reprinted with permission
Frontispiece: Ulf Anderson/Gamma Liaison

04   03   02   01   00   C   5   4   3   2   1
04   03   02   01   00   P   5   4   3   2   1

Library of Congress Cataloging-in-Publication Data

Jouvenel, Bertrand de, 1903–
The pure theory of politics/Bertrand de Jouvenel.
p.   cm.
Originally published: New Haven:
Yale University Press, 1963.
Includes bibliographical references and index.
ISBN 0-86597-264-8 (alk. paper)
ISBN 0-86597-265-6 (pbk: alk. paper)
1. Political science   I. Title

JA71 .J67 2000
320 — dc21   00-020493

Liberty Fund, Inc.
8335 Allison Pointe Trail, Suite 300
Indianapolis, Indiana 46250-1684

HELENAE

. . et oculi illius in ea sunt a principio
anni usque ad finem ejus

Contents

Foreword to the
Liberty Fund Edition

The great, recurrent theme of Bertrand de Jouvenel's work is the capacity of "men to move men." In many cases this capacity is for the good through the cultivation and maintenance of a community of free people. All too frequently, however, men move men to tragic consequences—as the cataclysmic politics of the twentieth century give ample and disturbing testimony. Throughout his writings, Jouvenel developed this theme of the intrinsically "dynamic" character of political life, a dynamism accelerated by the ideological and mass-driven character of modern politics. The French political scientist Pierre Hassner has rightly observed that this subject is explored *historically* in Jouvenel's best-known work, *On Power* (1945), with its searching exploration of the development of unprecedented state power in modern times. The subject is then explored *normatively* or philosophically in *Sovereignty* (1955), with its articulation of the notion of the common good appropriate for an open, dynamic society. Finally, the subject is explored *analytically* in Jouvenel's most difficult and austere work of political philosophy, *The Pure Theory of Politics* (1963).

The reader might at first be confused by Jouvenel's claim that *The Pure Theory of Politics* aims at a merely "representative" and "descriptive" account of the elementary building blocks of human and political action. After all, Jouvenel had ended his previous work of political philosophy, *Sovereignty*, with the claim that "Political Science is a moral science" or more precisely that "Political Science is a natural science dealing with moral agents." That great work was subtitled "an inquiry into the Political Good." A mere eight years later, in a book that is self-consciously a sequel to *Sovereignty*, Jouvenel appears to echo the language and argument of behavioral or value-free social science. Strikingly, he claims in *The Pure Theory of Politics* that his is a "strictly non-normative" approach that rigorously attempts to separate description from prescription.

The first part of this book, "Approach: Politics as History," develops Jouvenel's argument for a genuinely descriptive political science. In the first chapter, "Configuration and Dynamics," the author argues that the study of the statics or relational configurations of politics must be supplemented by attentive consideration to its movement or dynamics. A consideration of the ways in which human beings act upon each other and thus shape the future is absolutely necessary for understanding political life from the point of view of the engaged political actor. This is the case because "the future is present to the mind of acting man."

Pure Theory not only points backward to *Sovereignty's* emphasis on the dynamic character of modern society, it points forward to Jouvenel's subsequent work as a "futurist" or forecaster of the development of modern societies. This scientific concern with social "prevision" is most fully articulated in *The Art of Conjecture*, published in the United States in 1967. In fact, Jouvenel's attempt to map the evolution of modern societies was always civic as well as scientific, and reflected his deeply held conviction that social science should clarify and inform the choices facing citizens and statesmen.

Already in the first chapters of *Sovereignty*, Jouvenel had defined as "pure politics" those basic human activities which establish coherent "aggregates" or social and political wholes. In *Pure Theory* he widens that definition from a somewhat narrower emphasis on the founders and preservers of aggregates to include the broader processes by which individuals "instigate" and "respond" to human action. He is always careful to emphasize the volitional character of human responses to political initiatives and hence the limits of efforts to manipulate masses of men. He is also careful to avoid "hero worship" or to admire action (or "instigation") for its own sake.

Jouvenel does not deny that political philosophy ought to play a salutary role in moderating and civilizing the actions of men upon men. Far from it. In his chapter "On the Nature of Political Science" he movingly compares traditional political science to the Catholic bishop of the "dark ages" who used his considerable moral authority to tame and even convert barbarians. But Jouvenel believes that the salutary *ought* proposed by traditional political philosophy needs to be supplemented by a detailed analysis of the *is*, namely, the elementary or raw forces that are the foundation of all political order. Such attentiveness to the behavior of political life is, of course, necessary in order to clarify the subject matter of politics as a science. But it is also necessary if political science is to be of practical use to the statesman whose vocation it is to conserve the political community while accommodating and governing political change. In Jouvenel's view, "Wisdom" or political philosophy needs to pay greater respect to the claims and activities of practical men. The themes of political science must move beyond an inordinate consideration of the "best regime" or even of political institutions and forms to a full consideration of all the "material" of practical life. Only by entering fully into the rough-and-tumble of political life, by learning what acting men already know in their bones, can political theorists avoid abstractions and engage politics from the point of view of political actors themselves.

But Jouvenel's approach also entails an implicit critique of the behavioralist political science that was regnant when he wrote. The behavioralists dogmatically denied that reason could state anything authoritative about the moral dimensions of political life. Behavioral political scientists limited their horizon to the study of "weak" behaviors such as voting patterns or the judicial process, in other words, to those behaviors readily available for observation in established democratic regimes such as the United States or Great Britain. Consequently, during an age that produced Hitler and Stalin, the behavioralists ignored the capacity of statesmen and tyrants to stimulate human passions as well as actions on a grand, even unprecedented, scale. In contrast, the observation of a "political milieu . . . rife with political occurrences" afforded Jouvenel his material. To understand the drama of twentieth-century politics, Jouvenel turned to the works of Thucydides and Shakespeare, two classic authors considered hopelessly antiquated by the adherents of a "scientific" approach to politics.

As a result of this approach, Jouvenel articulated one of the few intellectually and morally serious "behavioral" interpretations of politics in our time. Whether analyzing the social framework of human freedom, the ways in which a few men such as Cassius inspire others to great or notorious deeds (as was the assassination of Caesar), or contemplating the disruptive effects of determined minorities on democratic societies, Jouvenel illustrates the elementary foundation of political action in the capacity of some human beings to move other human beings. He thereby provides the basis for a realistic political science sensitive to the "Machiavellian" machinations of those who seek to subvert civilized political communities. Jouvenel himself suggests that his description of "pure politics" is at the service of inoculating defenders of liberal civilization against unguarded optimism or liberal naiveté. The great political dislocations, historical tragedies, and human passions described so luminously in the narrative of Thucydides or the political dramas of Shakespeare are to Jouvenel everpresent human possibilities. The experiences of the French Revolution and of totalitarianism in the twentieth century, in particular, reveal the vulnerability of a politics of civility to disruption by illiberal, tyrannical forces. This is the theme of Jouvenel's elegant and searching conclusion to the final section of *Pure Theory*, "The Manners of Politics."

Bertrand de Jouvenel was, in the self-description of Alexis de Tocqueville, "a strange kind of liberal" who—like his declared inspiration, Tocqueville—eschewed historical optimism because he wisely feared the ever-looming prospect of political tragedy. He was, therefore, a conservative-minded liberal who knew that the regime of liberty is never achieved once and for all. He deeply admired Anglo-American institutions of political liberty, but he also marveled at the bloody and tyrannical episodes that dominated English politics in the centuries before the Glorious Revolution of 1688. He believed that the moral agency of human beings is the most fundamental fact of social life even as he feared the propensity of normative political science to resort to a priori notions of the political good in abstraction from the messy contingencies of real political life. In our age of unprecedented political pathologies, marked by totalitarian ideologies, an excessive readiness to violence, and a general decline in personal restraint and political consensus, Jouvenel encouraged partisans of liberal democracy to come to terms with the full range of political experience. As he stated in his 1980 essay "Pure Politics Revisited," "I believe that one must return to elementary political phenomena, in their raw state, in order to learn how to polish them."[1] This simple observation explains how Jouvenel combined an understanding of politics as a moral science with an effort to confront its elementary phenomena without any a priori moral expectations or evaluations.

The Pure Theory of Politics is a difficult and demanding but wonderfully rewarding book. Jouvenel aims to make his readers, in David DesRosiers's apt formulation, "principled but chastened guardians of the body politic." In the process, he gives his readers a feast for the mind. With the publication of Liberty Fund's edition of this book, Jouvenel's trilogy of political philosophy, beginning with *On Power*, followed by *Sovereignty*, and closing with *The Pure Theory of Politics*, is again available for full consideration by the English-speaking reader. There is no contemporary introduction to politics that is as ample and instructive, or as elegant and enticing, as the political reflection that *The Pure Theory of Politics* completes.

DANIEL J. MAHONEY
Worcester, Massachusetts
1999

---

1. See Bertrand de Jouvenel, "Pure Politics Revisited," *Government and Opposition*, Summer/Autumn 1980 (Vol. 15, #3/4), p. 434.

Preface

Every political situation is complex and original. The hasty mind, however, seizes upon some single feature because of which it assigns the given situation to a certain class of situations, previously formed, and in regard to which the mind has passed judgement once for all. Thus, for instance: "The situation envisaged involves centralization; I am in general for (against) centralization: therefore my stand is as follows. . . ."

It seems inevitable that such work-saving procedure should be commonly resorted to: which implies a permanent demand for ideologies — taxonomic devices constituting wide classes and inspiring general judgements, allowing us in short to take a stand on problems we have not analysed.

The procedure outlined above gives no inkling as to the mode of appearance and the chances of development of a situation. Convenient as we may find it when we only want to assess, it is radically unsuitable if we wish to explain or foresee. We then need to investigate processes, and this cannot be a joint venture unless we use a common set of elementary concepts.

I gratefully remember the care taken by the teachers of my childhood to familiarize me with the simplest possible relations in each field, such as the attribute of the subject, the dependent variable, and so forth. The geometry master took me forward from the humble triangle; the chemistry master made sure that I grasped the combination H_2O before moving by degrees to the intricacies of the protein molecule; the law master began with *Spondesne?* . . .

The acquisition of such elementary notions was then, and surely is now, regarded as the indispensable first stage in any discipline.

We speak naturally of more or less "advanced" study, implying that the most modest learner has travelled some way along the trunk road on which others have gone much further, and from which pioneering research branches out in various directions. This in turn implies that anyone who has been trained in a science holds the keys to any message conveyed by its leaders or researchers: he may find it very difficult to understand the message but there is no risk of his mistaking it, the notions are unambiguous—they have been chosen for that virtue.

Political science offers a contrast. The field has been settled by immigrants from philosophy, theology, law, and later sociology and economics, each group bringing and using its own box of tools. Moreover, political words are widely circulating currency, and so tend to lose neatness and acquire emotional associations: politicians are not interested in using them properly but in using them for effect.

Whatever the reasons, political science stands alone in its lack of agreed "elements." There are no basic concepts, simple enough to allow of only one meaning, therefore conveying exactly the same signification to all and confidently handled by everyone; there are no simple relations, acknowledged by all to form the smallest components of complex systems, and commonly used in the building of models devised to simulate the intricacies of real situations.

Does such a deficiency pertain to the nature of this discipline? I do not believe it. Should it be remedied? I thought so and therefore embarked upon the undertaking here offered to the reader. I shall be rewarded enough if it is adjudged inadequate but necessary, if it evokes not approbation but emulation.

While the book must speak for itself, there are a few points which require an early mention.

The adjective "pure" in the title is used by analogy with the contrast between "pure" and "organic" in chemistry. Just as "organic" bodies are far more complex than those to which the student is first introduced in the beginner's course of pure chemistry, so are the situations and relations of actual Politics far more complex than those examined here. Therefore the reader should not complain that the whole of reality is not encompassed.

Because my purpose is to come down to the greatest possible degree of simplicity, political phenomena appear essentially as relations between individuals. This does not imply an "atomistic" view of society, it simply follows from the tautology that the simpler elements are the "atoms." More importantly my emphasis upon the relation "man moves man"[1] throws me open to the misconception that I deem it a great and admirable thing to move others and am prone to worshipping "political heroes."[2] As it happens my disposition is quite radically the opposite: naturally distrustful of power, I distrust it at its very source. But this work has a descriptive, not a normative, purpose.

This brings me to elucidate the meaning of the word "theory" in my title. It is used to denote what goes under that name in disciplines other than political science. Observations by themselves are of course meaningless: to make sense out of

1. I have recently found that my friend Edward Shils emphasized it as early as 1939.
2. This misconception has already appeared in one important critique of my *Sovereignty.*

them, one must formulate a hypothesis which can account for them, that is, one must choose concepts between which one assumes some relations of dependence, thus elaborating a "model" which simulates reality. This activity of the mind is habitually called "theorizing" in sciences other than the political. Models thus obtained perform a representative function: they have no normative value.

What is called "political theory," on the other hand, offers "models" in the quite different sense of "ideals." Rousseau's model of a democratic assembly is one wherein all those who will be subject to a decision participate in taking it; each one of them in so doing is moved only by concern for the good of the whole, and trusts solely to his own judgement, uninfluenced by the opinions of others. This obviously is not meant as a description.

There exists of course a logical relation between representative and normative models, if one holds the view that any observed shape is a mere accidental deformation of one true shape capable of being known immediately by the mind, and though not open to our observation, the only "natural" one. From this view it must follow that observable patterns in their unending variety are not interesting, while the only one worthy of our attention is that of which all others are corrupt copies. But this view implies special philosophical tenets.

The present attempt, solely based upon observation, aims at representing observable phenomena. In other words it is strictly non-normative. This certainly does not mean that I reject preceptive political science, but only that describing and prescribing are distinct tasks of which I have here chosen the former.

Quoting is very pleasurable; moreover it gives a scholarly look: in this case it would have been deceitful, a borrowing of respectable authorities to cloak the foolhardiness of my venture. It seems more honest to admit that observation has afforded me my material. Born in a political *milieu*, having lived through an age rife with political occurrences, I saw my material forced upon me. For its marshalling, I found my best guides in the geniuses who have immortally portrayed the drama of Politics: Thucydides and Shakespeare. While instances from contemporary events crowded my mind, I have avoided referring to them whenever possible because there is lack of agreement on their interpretation, while every reader has in his mind the great scenes from the classics. The very fact that these could — with the advantage of inimitable expression — serve as substitutes for contemporary instances, testifies that political activity remains fundamentally the same.

Whoever talks of Politics calls to the minds of different listeners different experiences and different doctrines, and therefore the same assemblage of words assumes a variety of subjective meanings. The nature of my purpose obliged me to guard as best I could against this danger. "Elements" are useless if they do not preclude ambiguity. It seemed to me that focusing upon "political activity" offered the best chance of a self-contained exposition, capable of being developed, without too much interference from pre-existing states of mind.

This exposition begins in part III and is pursued systematically to the end. If I have been at all successful in my attempt, it should present the same significance to the erudite as to the beginner.

Why does the exposition begin only in part III? As I am dealing with the action of Man upon Man, it seemed necessary to stress that this occurs in a social setting, whose importance and influence is sketched out in part II.

Part I is of an altogether different character. It does not really pertain to the body of the work but constitutes an extended and somewhat difficult introduction. While in the body of the treatise I have, or hope I have, traced a path, step by step, part I discusses my reasons for tracing this path. Readers who are impatient, or who are not political scientists, are advised to bypass part I: returning to it after going through the work may then explain the author's intention or help to track down the reasons for the reader's dislike of the treatment.

Many a time, during six years of effort, I have grown doubtful about this work. Doubts have been especially fostered by those of my friends who have disapproved of my purpose of describing rather than prescribing. The high value I set upon their opinion has weighed upon my mind. On the other hand, since my first version was completed at the end of 1957, a number of events have occurred, the pattern of which was so close to the patterns here sketched that one might think I wrote after the event instead of before: and this has confirmed me in my purpose.

I have been greatly helped in this endeavour by the opportunities which were generously afforded to me to try out these elements. At the kind suggestion of Professors Brogan and Postan, the Master of Peterhouse, Professor Butterfield, invited me to give three lectures on the subject in Cambridge. The discussions which followed helped me greatly to re-shape these elements. Then came from the Dean of the Yale Law School, Professor Eugene Rostow, an invitation to give the Storrs Lectures at Yale. This honour was once again the occasion of very profitable critiques. In essence this treatise is an expanded version of the Storrs Lectures. The expansion, however, has been considerable.[3] A chance to find out whether I

3. The Storrs Lectures corresponded to part II, part III and part of part IV.

had devised an introduction to Politics acceptable to under-
graduates was offered to me when the Chairman of the Political Science Department of the University of California, Professor Charles Aikin, invited me to teach at Berkeley during
the fall term of 1960.

I am most grateful to the Relm Foundation for the financial
help afforded to me during 1958. I am obliged to *The Yale Review, The American Political Science Review,* and *The Journal
of Politics* for allowing me to use chapters which they have
printed.

English-speaking readers of this book are sure to find its
mode of expression lamentably fallen from the high standards
of style to be found in *Power* and in *Sovereignty.* The present
work I have written in English,[4] while its predecessors owed
their elegance to my admirable translator and very dear friend,
J. F. Huntington: it seems suitable that I should, in the last
words of this preface, refer to the wit and grace and fundamental nobility of my departed friend.

B.J.
ANSERVILLE
May 1962

4. I want to thank the Cambridge University Press for their kind revision of my
English, and also to acquit them of any responsibility for the many barbarisms, sole-
cisms or infelicitous expressions which I obdurately maintained against good advice.

PART I

Approach: Politics as History

—————— CHAPTER 1 ——————

Configuration and Dynamics

Our mind strives towards statements of configuration and statements of consequence. Configuration is "where different things stand in relation to one another." Consequence is "how successive events arise from one another." We grasp far more easily disposition in space than process in time; further, an incomplete "geographic" account can be valid as far as it goes, while an incomplete "historic" account can be highly misleading. The difference in difficulty and reliability between "where" and "how" statements is at a maximum in Politics. It is therefore not surprising that political science should have dealt mainly with configurations.

The baggage borne by a student of Politics returning from a Grand Tour of many countries is apt to consist of maps exhibiting the "commanding heights" of the lands visited. First let us picture our student beginning with a pilgrimage to Athens. There he ascends the Acropolis; here the gods were worshipped, here also was the residence of the erstwhile monarchs; next he ascends the hill of Ares, where an aristocratic tribunal made its decisions, grown more important after the overthrow of the monarchy; lastly he ascends the Pnyx, and evokes the Assembly of the People. These three hills respectively suggest the authority of the One, the Few and the Many, as depicted by Aristotle.

They assist our imagination in conceiving the shift of authority from one eminence to another, but also in conceiving mixed forms of authority which combine the voices issuing from different hills. The same tangible assistance to imagination is afforded in Washington by L'Enfant's skill in posing the Capitol and the White House upon confronting hills. But even where such physical aid is lacking, we are sharply aware of commanding heights. Thus our student, in London, visits the Houses of Parliament, Downing Street, and casts an eye upon Buckingham Palace. In Paris he views the Palais-Bourbon, the Hôtel Matignon and the Elysée. He will thus carry away a series of raised maps of the seats of decision and authority. If he is at all shrewd, he will note what is written in stone beyond what is written in the Constitutions. Thus in Washington he will pay attention to the proliferation of buildings housing executive departments and agencies. Nor will he neglect the mansions erected by unions and other non-governmental bodies.

There is ample material here for a comparative and critical geography of seats of authority or influence. Ground plans suffice to show, for instance, that the dependencies of the Legislative have nowhere kept pace with the dependencies of the Executive, that indeed they have been developed only in the United States, hardly in Britain, not at all in France. Discrepancies may thus be brought out between relative attributions of authority and relative means of implementing attributions.

Mapping the configuration of authorities is a natural and necessary concern of political science. While theoretical writers have ever been interested in advocating this or that ideal map, derived from some principle, practical politicians have ever needed accurate and detailed knowledge of the actual map, as a guide to efficient action. The importance of configurations is great but adequately recognized, and they are dealt with more than adequately by other authors. Therefore it has seemed to me that a different approach to Politics might be tried.

Let us fancy that we visit Athens in 415 B.C. just before the decision is made to send an expedition against Syracuse. As ignorant foreigners we ask our hosts three questions.

First: to whom does it pertain to make the decision?

Second: is it right and advantageous to undertake the expedition?

Third: in fact, will it be decided and undertaken?

The first question is one of constitutional competence, which any Athenian can and must immediately answer in the same manner with complete certainty: the decision belongs to the Assembly of the People which will also, if it makes an affirmative decision, elect the generals. This falls in the realm of configuration. The second question is one of political Prudence: I use the capital P to stress that I have in mind not the skimpy notion of prudence obtaining nowadays but the classical notion of Prudence as the virtue of giving the right answer in specific circumstance, a virtue which we may find in some of our hosts and not in others. The third question again falls in a different realm. It calls for a statement of fact concerning a future event.

Let us then consider briefly our foreknowledge of future events. There are a great many future events which we take entirely for granted, else we could not conduct our daily lives. Upon examination it appears that most such *certa futura* are mere manifestations of configuration. That the sun will rise tomorrow is an event only from an extreme subjective point of view. Stable natural configurations allow us to expect, indeed to produce, "events" with no doubt as to their occurrence. Further, stable social configurations lead us to expect some events with hardly less assurance (e.g. a presidential election will be held in the U.S. on the second Tuesday of November 1964): while for the philosopher there is a great difference in nature between these two assurances, for the practical man there is a very slight difference in degree. But the political event we are now considering, the decision of war or peace to be made by the Athenian Assembly, is one which by definition depends upon the free choice of men between alternatives. And here we know for certain that we can have no certain foreknowledge of the outcome. If we could have certain foreknowledge of the use which other men will make of their freedom to choose, we should be possessed of what theologians call *scientia libera*.

However impossible it is for us to say for certain what other men will do, when they manifestly have a choice and are visibly hovering between alternatives, none the less it is quite possible to state that a given alternative seems to us the more probable: such a statement may indeed be required. Supposing that we are envoys from Syracuse, our first duty is to plead with the Athenians, seeking to dissuade them from attacking our City; but surely that is not our only duty: we must also guess what the decision will in fact be. On our return to Syracuse, we shall be accused of a disservice to our City if we have failed to convey advance information that the Athenian decision was going to be war. It will then be a quite inadequate defence to argue that we could not know what the Athenians would decide as long as the decision was open: though it is strictly true that we could not have certain knowledge, we should have formed a true opinion of the future event.

Surmising is essential to the conduct of human affairs; a mistaken surmise can be disastrous. Napoleon surmised that Grouchy would and Blücher would not intervene on the field of Waterloo. The tragedy of *King Lear* turns upon erroneous surmises: examples thereof are not hard to find in our time. Within one year Chamberlain made three major erroneous surmises: that Hitler would be satisfied with the Munich settlement; that he would be intimidated by the giving of a guarantee to Poland; that Stalin would join hands with Britain and France.

Surely an interest in Politics implies an interest in surmising. However important it is to describe a configuration deemed static, to recommend attitudes wholesome and virtuous, it is important also to foresee what men will do and what will happen.

Indeed when we discuss Politics, not in the character of political scientists but as mere men, we are apt to speculate about some future event. Thus in September 1960 one may well say: "I believe that Kennedy will be elected in November." The speaker, asked the reasons for his statement, may answer: "I could not really say." But this is a natural reaction of defence against a challenge to considerable intellectual effort. It is difficult to state the reasons for a surmise, but self-examination might bring them to light. It would then appear that the mind supposes certain dynamic relations; because of certain past events, people of certain dispositions will prove responsive to a certain call and act in a certain way. The chain of conjectures may be very weak in itself and it may be perceived only faintly by the speaker, but none the less it exists in his mind.

While people are most unwilling to work out their chain of suppositions leading to their expectation of some future event over which they have no control, or only a very insignificant share of control, the same people will carefully work out their chain of suppositions when they propose to bring about that which they ardently desire and conceive as largely dependent upon their own actions. Latin has a convenient duality of words for those two kinds of events: the masculine *eventus*, with its connotation of outcome, can be taken to designate the event which I propose to bring about, of which I am somehow the author, while the neutral *eventum* can be taken to denote the event which is utterly out of my hands. For the Foreign Office or the Quai d'Orsay, the Kennedy election is *eventum;* for the campaign team, *eventus.* However hazy we may usually be about the sequence or intermingling of sequences that will bring about an *eventum,* in the case of an *eventus* we bring our minds to bear on the causative sequence far more sharply.

The future is present to the mind of acting man. The great German jurist Jhering discriminated between human action and animal action in terms of *ut* and *quia. Quia* actions are those I perform under the pressure of outside causes, without choice or deliberation. *Ut* actions on the other hand are those I perform in view of a certain result I wish to bring about. They involve a certain vision of a future state of affairs I propose to obtain, and of a "path" to that state.

There is nothing of which we are more aware, whatever philosophers may say, than our ability to bring about certain situations by our choice served by our efforts. I can, if I want to, raise this glass to my lips. When I raise it, I am aware that I am "causing" its new position. But, to speak more accurately, the very notion of "cause," common to all men, is a product of such experiences. From my earliest childhood, I have found that I can change something, however little, in my environment, by my action, and from this microcosmic experience of a relation between my effort and this change arises the general idea of "cause and effect."

This is confirmed by elementary etymology. In Latin, the word *causa* was mainly used when referring to the trying of causes at law. A *causa* was what one of the parties wanted, a meaning conserved in English when we speak of "espousing a cause," "fighting for a cause." The word Romans were prone to use when they meant the bringing about of a certain result was *efficere*, which contains the idea of *facere*, that is *doing*, but which reinforces it and adds the idea of completion, achievement (a sense which has been reflected in the modern word "efficiency"). The well-known formula *causa efficiens* associates the two ideas that something is wanted, *causa*, and is achieved, *efficiens*, into the one idea of operational wanting.

In the case of my lifting this glass, there can be no doubt that if I want it lifted, I can effect this change: it lies entirely within my power (the word "power," let us incidentally stress, denoting the ability to do). Nobody but a madman, or a philosopher (for different reasons), will give thought to an *eventus* which he can so readily bring about.

But as we well know, men do give thought to an *eventus* that they deem both desirable and difficult to achieve. Presumably it was quite a number of years ago that Mr. Kennedy first had a brief vision of himself as President of the United States. Between imagining and achieving this position there was a vast gap to be spanned. The spanning of this gap required a long sequence of actions. This sequence had to be conceived and planned from the outset, even though many amendments were found necessary in the course of the operation. Clearly, planning a shift from the situation of Senator to that of President is very different from planning a move from one room of a house to another. In both cases steps have to be taken; but in the latter case they are literal steps, and the outcome of each is assured: in the more important case, they are metaphorical "steps," that is, "moves" by the actor, and the outcome of each move is uncertain, dependent upon the reactions of other men. Well-calculated steps are those which elicit reactions helpful towards the attainment of the goal. The problem of achieving the wanted *eventus* then calls for correct surmising of responses. The actor's "steps" in fact advance him towards the goal only or mainly by virtue of the actions of others which they spark off. Far the greater part of the energy expended in bringing about an important *eventus* is provided by others whom the designer sets in motion.

The practical politician is well aware that his means for the attainment of any political objective are the contributory actions of other men. Knowing in general how to obtain such actions, and specifically for what, when and from whom he can hope to obtain them, constitutes his familiar lore. The technology of Politics is essentially concerned with dynamics while its science cleaves to statics. If we want to study dynamics we must seek to understand the sparking off of contributory actions.

The word "designing" has, in common English usage, an unfavourable connotation, when applied to a person. Used neutrally, the term conveniently denotes the occupational trait of the politician. He seeks to bring about a certain *eventus* requiring actions from other persons, and therefore he seeks to elicit the adequate contributory actions, and for this purpose makes the moves likely to elicit these actions: all of this constitutes the *design* of the politician, which, on being carried out, constitutes a *political operation*. The political operation is analyzed in the following emphatic self-portrait of a politician:

> Neither Montaigne in writing his essays nor Descartes in building new worlds, nor Burnet in framing an antediluvian earth, no nor Newton in discovering and establishing the true laws of nature on experiment and a sublimer geometry, felt more intellectual joys, than he feels who is a *real patriot*, who bands all the forces of his understanding and directs all his thoughts and actions to the good of his country. When such a man forms a

political scheme and adjusts various and seemingly independent parts into a great and good design, he is transported by
imagination, or absorbed in meditation, as much and as agree-
ably as they: and the satisfaction that arises from the different
importance of these objects, in every step of the work, is vastly
in his favour. It is here that the speculative philosopher's labour
and pleasure end. But he, who speculates in order to *act*, goes
on, and carries his scheme into execution. His labour contin-
ues, it varies, it increases; but so does his pleasure too. The execution indeed is often crossed by unforeseen and untoward circumstances, by the perverseness or treachery of friends, and by
the power or malice of enemies: but the first and the last of
these animate, and the docility and fidelity of some men make
amends for the perverseness and treachery of others. While a
great event is in suspense, the action warms, and the very suspense, made up of hope and fear, maintains no unpleasing agitation in the mind. If the event is decided successfully, such a
man enjoys pleasure proportionable to the good he has done: a
pleasure like to that which is attributed to the Supreme Being,
on a survey of his works. If the event is decided otherwise, and
usurping courts, or overbearing parties prevail, such a man
still has the testimony of his conscience, and the sense of the
honour he has acquired, to soothe his mind, and support his
courage.[1]

Here Bolingbroke indicates that there is: (1) a patriotic objective; (2) a grand strategy designed to ensure the attainment
of the goal; (3) an active and flexible manoeuvring to carry out
this strategy; (4) an intense pleasure inherent in the whole performance. One would like to think that such pleasure depends
wholly upon the excellence of the project, that the scheming
and handling are made enjoyable only by the merit of the goal.

---

1. Bolingbroke, *Letters on the Spirit of Patriotism*, ed. Hassall (Oxford, 1926),
pp. 19–20. (The italics are Bolingbroke's.)

Observation regrettably suggests that the sport of moving men is enjoyed in itself even when the operation is not inspired by a high purpose, or addressed to a salutary end. The worthiest and wisest men engaging in Politics are least apt to experience the sporting enjoyment described by Bolingbroke. The wielding of power or influence must, in a truly good man, be attended by a constant fear of its misuse, by doubts regarding the goal to be sought and scruples concerning the means to be used. This has been expressed by Fénelon: "Indeed men are unfortunate that they have to be ruled by a King who is like them a man, for it would take gods to set them right. But Kings are no less unfortunate, being mere men, weak and imperfect, to have the ruling of a great multitude of sinful and deceitful individuals." [2]

What a contrast between these two statements! Pride colours the one, humility marks the other. Surely we must prefer that which stresses the statesman's responsibility. But if our purpose is to understand the generation of events, then what is relevant is Bolingbroke's picture of the politician's activity.

Our times are marked by a precipitous course of events and an attendant instability of configurations. Political maps and constitutions are highly perishable commodities.[3] Every New Year, there are countries where foreign diplomats have to shift their compliments from the authorities of yesterday, now outlawed, to the outlaws of yesterday, now in authority. Those parts of the world where only small events occur within an unchanged framework have shrunk relative to those where major events

2. Fénelon, *Directions pour la conscience d'un roi*, published long after they were composed for the instruction of the Duc de Bourgogne (Paris, 1748).

3. The average life-span of a map of Europe since the beginning of the century has been fifteen years. Germans since 1914 have lived under four regimes, the French under four already since 1938.

shake and transform the framework. The character of the times therefore focuses our interest upon the event.

Some minds are so secure in their *a priori* understanding of future history that for them great events fall into place within a preordained scheme. Those of us who do not think so sweepingly regard each event as posing a problem, calling for an analysis of the many factors which have entered its composition.

The smallest identifiable component of any political event, large or small, is the moving of man by man. That is elementary political action. In what follows, the man who seeks to elicit a given deed from another is called "instigator"; in so far as he strives to obtain from different people different actions contributing to an *eventus* he wants, he is called an "operator"; and in so far as he builds a following habitually responsive to the same voice, or a voice proceeding from the same place, he is an "entrepreneur."

This should not be taken to imply a "great men" view of history. What I wish to stress is not that things happen "because" of an instigator, but that they occur "through" a relation instigation–response, that this is the simplest and basic link in complex chains. *Eventum* has no identifiable author: it arises out of the meeting of many chains wherein the phenomena I am concerned with figure as basic constituents. I concentrate upon them because it is my purpose to seek out in the complexity of Politics those elements which are simple and present *semper et ubique*.

The spirit of this study would be completely misunderstood if I were thought to offer a grand simplification of Politics considered globally. Such is not my intention, nor is it an intention I sympathize with when it inspires other authors. Politics seems to me extraordinarily complex: attempts to reduce it to simplicity I regard as misleading and dangerous. It is precisely because political phenomena are so complex that I attempt to reach down to simple components. But the picture I shall try to offer of the elements should not be "blown-up" to serve as a picture of the whole.

It may be useful to display, by means of a fable, the place of an elementary phenomenon, such as I mean to study, in the coming about of an *eventum*.

Macedonia wants political information about Megalopolis. We shall assume that no Macedonian understands or can learn the Megalopolitan language but that three observers can be made invisible, and endowed with the means of immediately reporting what they see. Observer *A* is set up in a balloon high above the city, observer *B* in another balloon much nearer to the ground, observer *C* roams in the streets. *A*'s altitude is such that he discerns nothing but the buildings and the general layout of the city; in short, configuration. This he maps out carefully: it may be a long task but when it is completed he has nothing more to report. Surely the analogy with the description of a Constitution is obvious.

B hovers at a height which allows him to study traffic; he notes streams, the density of which is variable; after some time he recognizes that density at given points fluctuates within the day according to a recurrent pattern; he also finds patterns of longer span: days of abnormally low density (e.g. Sundays) immediately preceded and followed by some increase in density; seasonal variations and possibly a long-term trend to increase: indeed he may note growing pressure upon bottlenecks. Even if *B*—who calls to mind the sociologist—notes a building up of pressures over time, his observations offer but little variety as soon as he has mastered the patterns.

It is otherwise in the case of *C*, who, moving on a level with the individual inhabitants, witnesses an inexhaustible variety of incidents: while A ceases transmission when he has conveyed the map, while B transmits only in the case of a departure from pattern, a scrupulous C transmits all the time a succession of minor scenes.

One day, however, A is shaken from his calm. He has seen a major building of Megalopolis, call it the Palace, going up in flames. This he hastens to report and receives from Macedonia the answer: "Thank you. This confirms our previous information." What previous information? Some time earlier B has communicated that a great mass of people were moving towards the Palace and breaking up a thin line of guards. To this communication, however, he also received the answer: "Thank you. This confirms our previous information."

Why? Because C was on the spot and saw how it all started. He witnessed the formation of the "push," which was noticed by the student of the Constitution only when it had produced its effect. C is the earliest and most sensitive indicator. Also, however, he is the least reliable.

What exactly has the street observer seen? At the beginning a man holding forth, gesticulating, attracting a crowd, and, within this crowd, an increasing agitation. This is the event at its birth, the small beginning from which, by an increase in mass and acceleration, the tidal wave will arise. But let us remember that not every such beginning culminates in such achievement. Our man may well have formerly witnessed and conveyed scenes of this type out of which nothing has come. The decipherers at the receiving end are apt to remember that they have already received a number of descriptions of this kind; and while this nth instance may be momentous, they are not prone to suppose so. Any man who has had occasion to convey warnings is aware of the incredulity which greets them; nothing indeed is more unwelcome to the routine of the staff man than the fever of the field worker.

It is only under the impact of successive information, pouring in more and more rapidly, that increasing notice will be taken of a possible event, to which the receivers will come to allow a growing degree of probability. Of course the event will not be held certain until it has been completed: only postdiction is assured, never prediction. The initial piece of news then presents over the description of the culminating havoc a great chronological superiority but a great inferiority of assurance. This touches upon a problem well known in the press. A reporter cannot forgive his editor for failing to publish the dispatch noticing "the first step" of a revolution; but this the editor acknowledges as effectively the first step only when the revolution has unmistakably occurred. And the reluctance of an editor is nothing to that of a Foreign Office: newspapermen are functionally prone to believe in events, diplomats are functionally prone to disbelieve them.

The illustration used points out both that an elementary political action stands at the start of the large event, and that a large event may or may not follow from this elementary action. Even if not all acorns turn into oaks, it is important to know that all oaks arise from acorns. If we notice only oaks, and not acorns, then we shall not understand oaks.

Should political scientists address their attention to dynamics? A negative answer is plausible. It can be argued that standards of scholarly accuracy can be sustained only in description and classification of given states of affairs, and that standards of logical deduction can be sustained only in deriving prescriptive arrangements from clearly enunciated ethical principles. While it cannot be denied that we do in fact attempt to understand by what process certain events have come about and to guess what will occur, it is easy to point out that our assessments of past causes are controversial and our conjectures of future events highly adventurous; and therefore it may be held that we should not be so bold as to seek an understanding of the political process in the course of time. But such a negative answer would singularly restrict the scope and advisory capacity of political science. The statesman, even the mere "boss," resorts daily to some empirical understanding of operational relationships: can we not elaborate such understanding?

In the foregoing tale, an *elementary action* has given rise to a major event, presumably because this action was part of a *design* the carrying out of which was favoured by a *situation*. Why is the example chosen that of an upheaval? Possibly because upheavals are so common in our day. But there is another reason besides this. Periods lacking in great and tumultuous events are not necessarily so for lack of primary drives, the social field may be rife with instigations but these are then so evenly distributed, and addressed to such various ends, that they do not build up to a grand dramatic impulse. Tragedy occurs when processes, naturally diffuse throughout the body politic, acquire a concentration, an intensity, a polarization which affords them an explosive power. Nothing then is more important to the guardians of a body politic than to understand the nature of these processes, so that they may be guided to irrigate and precluded from flooding.

CHAPTER 2

Wisdom and Activity:
The Pseudo-Alcibiades

One of Plato's dialogues is entitled *Alcibiades*. It is presented as the report of a conversation between Socrates and Alcibiades, occurring in the youth of the latter and just before he had reached the age enabling him to address the Assembly of the People. This is an exemplary conversation, an artifice used to develop an argument: the argument is a warning of Wisdom (Socrates) to Ambition (Alcibiades). The opening attack by Socrates can be summarized as follows:

(1) You have the highest possible opinion of yourself. You deem yourself the strongest and the most handsome, and indeed you are such. You can look to powerful support from your family on both the paternal and the maternal sides; you enjoy the privilege of having been the ward of Pericles, who is all-powerful in this city, whose dominance stretches all over Greece, and extends indeed into barbarian realms. Moreover you are of the wealthy, which helps, but this can be held the least of the many assets which cause your valuation of yourself to be widely accepted.

(2) I am well aware of your great expectations. You feel that as soon as you have stepped forward to address the people of Athens, you will obtain from them a consideration even higher than that afforded to Pericles or any foregoing statesman; and on such basis, you look forward to making yourself all-powerful

in the city, and, once that is achieved, throughout Greece and also among the outlying barbarians.

(3) Indeed you are impatient to come to the Assembly and give your views to the Athenians. Now suppose that, just as you were moving forward to do so, my hand were laid on your arm, and I asked you: "Alcibiades, what of the subject which Athenians are now debating? Have you stood up because it is a subject upon which your knowledge is superior to theirs?"

This opening poses the problem. Alcibiades is eager to lead, his assets are such that his chances of being followed are very great. But what of his chances of leading well? This query drives Alcibiades to claim that he will speak as one who knows, advocating the best decision.

Having taken that stand, the aspiring politician is now subject to successively increasing pressure from the sage, and finds himself forced back step by step. First, he is forced to admit that he lacks the expertise required for the settling of specific problems; then, having taken refuge in the larger issues, he is made to confess that he is muddled about justice or the public interest.

The admission elicited from him then allows Socrates to exclaim: "Ignorance is worse, the more important the matter. But in any matter the supreme ignorance is not to realize that one does not know. Alas! what a sorry situation you are in, as we have found you, by your own words, convinced of supreme ignorance in the most important matter! And thus you rush into politics without knowledge! A situation indeed in which you do not find yourself alone, but which prevails among those who concern themselves with the affairs of the city, with the exception of a few, among whom we may probably range Pericles."[1]

1. Notwithstanding the quotation marks, this is not a literal translation from Plato: it is the gist of what Socrates says.

In other Platonic dialogues, and also in Xenophon's *Memorabilia*, Socrates is shown throwing this same challenge to various eager and impatient youths: "Do you really think that you know and understand enough to offer a valuable opinion, profitable to the city?" But surely the lesson is pointed by taking Alcibiades as the butt. He bears a major responsibility for the disastrous sequence of events which drove Athens down from her position as the most honoured and powerful city of Greece to her shameful surrender of 404 B.C., to the abasement of receiving a Spartan occupation force, to the irretrievable moral ruin of civil strife, of which indeed the trial of Socrates was a by-product.

Alcibiades was the evil genius who brought about the resumption of hostilities after the honourable and satisfactory peace negotiated by Nicias in 421. It was Alcibiades who, in 415, engaged Athens, against the advice of Nicias, in the great venture against Syracuse, a venture the outcome of which was the utter destruction of the Athenian force, the massacre or enslavement of a large part of Athenian youth. Alcibiades again, having left the Athenian army in high dudgeon at an accusation brought against him, went so far as to join and advise the Spartans, and he it was who contrived to afford them the alliance of Persia against his native city. Yet, when Athens was in 411 ready for peace which could still be had on acceptable terms, Alcibiades, by an astonishing about-face, managed to earn the acclaim of the Athenian soldiery, and, against the wish of the city's magistrates, led them to a renewal of hostilities. Restored to a position of prestige in the city, he was able to cause the Assembly to reject the overtures of peace made by Sparta in 410, to reject this ultimate chance of stopping short of disaster and shame.

An extraordinarily gifted and, by all accounts, an irresistibly attractive man, Alcibiades can be called the author of Athens' great fall from glory. These events were fresh in the memories of those whom Plato addressed *c*. 380. The force of the Socratic argument must then have been enhanced in the minds of the listeners by the knowledge of the harm Alcibiades had wrought, and which the city might have been spared, had he heeded the warning of Socrates. Though the dialogue as it has come down to us is of course a work of art, its first listeners could well believe, and we have no good reason to doubt, that some such warning was in fact given by the historical Socrates to the historical Alcibiades.

The *Alcibiades* is altogether more forthright than other Platonic dialogues. Whatever further depths of meaning may be found in it, it conveys a simple and plain message: political activity, undirected by wisdom, is dangerous. Surely this is what all aspirants to Politics should be told. Surely also, if political philosophy forcefully utters this warning, if it thus seeks to generate a hunger for political wisdom, it must stand ready to impart it, a task incomparably more difficult than conveying factual knowledge. Thus the *Alcibiades* teaches a moral lesson not only to aspiring politicians but also to political authors. This lesson is in no way impaired by the considerations which follow.

Apart from the moral lesson it teaches, the dialogue, when taken in the context of historical events, suggests, in the non-normative realm, another lesson, altogether sadder: that political activity is not highly sensitive to the teaching of wisdom.

Socrates, known as "the wisest of men," was born not later than 469 and began teaching when Athens stood at the height of her prosperity, glory and power: when he was killed, at over seventy years of age (399), the city had plunged to its disaster. This was not due to the deep-laid plans of wily and powerful enemies: Thucydides makes it clear enough that Lacedaemon embarked upon war unwillingly and was frequently disposed to peace: he leaves us the clear impression that Athens' undoing was Athens' own doing. Thus the City was most unwisely governed even while it had in its midst the wisest of men. And many of the actors of the drama had been frequent associates of Socrates: one such was Alcibiades; another was Critias, whom we find as the moving spirit of "the Thirty Tyrants"; yet another was Charmides, similarly involved.

Therefore we must conclude that the very admirers of Socrates profited little from his teaching and showed little trace of it in their political activities. This is a regrettable fact, but a fact none the less. Noting this fact does not diminish our ardour for the acquisition of wisdom, but induces us to regard another pursuit as also of some importance: that is, seeking an understanding of what people actually do in Politics. The present treatise is in fact addressed to the latter purpose.

To stress the contrast between political philosophy and political activity, I have resorted to a device which may well be regarded as a desecration. I have presumed to write a sequel to the *Alcibiades*, in the form of a further dialogue between Socrates and Alcibiades. It will be unmistakably clear to the reader that this spurious sequel is not written in anything like the spirit of Plato, but I would not like the reader to think that it is imbued with my own feelings. This *Pseudo-Alcibiades* should be thought of as written against Socrates by a secretary of Alcibiades.[2] Thus while the *Alcibiades* is the warning of Wisdom to Ambition, this is meant as the politician's retort. That it should be made in the name of such a rogue, suffices to acquit me of any sympathy for the point of view presented. But its being unpleasant does not make it any less important in fact.

---

2. This excuses the fact that Socrates is here represented as somewhat weak in argument (as some critics have remarked): an inevitable outcome of my not being Plato.

The imaginary conversation which the *Pseudo-Alcibiades* purports to report is placed some sixteen years after that which Plato relates. It occurs when Alcibiades stands at the height of his influence in Athens and just before he moves the Assembly to decide the ill-fated expedition against Syracuse.

Alcibiades. I have sought you out, Socrates, because a discussion we had many years ago has come to my mind. This occurred while I was still in my teens, eagerly awaiting the hour when I could try my hand at influencing the affairs of the city. Many admirers already upheld the confidence I had in my abilities. Then came your discourse, admonishing me that I was unfit to address the Assembly of Athenians, and exhorting me to acquire the moral wisdom whereby alone I would be enabled to give my fellow-citizens the right advice. Are you aware, Socrates, that you almost stopped my career? If my inner urge had not soon dispelled the impression made by your words, instead of being now predominant in the city, and indeed the most important figure in Greece, I might still be one of those I see in your company.

Socrates. Would that I had made a more lasting impression! I well remember the occasion. I feared that you would move the policy of Athens in a rash manner, and events have confirmed my fears. You did the city a great disservice by your successful efforts to break the peace happily negotiated by Nicias.   .

Alcibiades. However unwillingly, you pay me, Socrates, a deserved tribute. It is true enough that I seized the occasion of the Argive defiance of Sparta to induce Athens into an alliance with Argos which was (although many did not immediately perceive it), incompatible with the peace of Nicias. This alliance was not easily achieved, the Argives doubted that they could obtain our support, I had to send to them secretly inducing them to address an embassy to Athens; its requests might have been rejected when the Spartans sent a counter-embassy to remind us of our obligations. I had to trick the Spartan envoys by promises that they would have full satisfaction upon Pylus if they forbore to tell the Assembly that they had full powers of negotiation; and when I had pushed them into denying their full powers, I turned against them, advising the Assembly not to listen to them under such conditions. It was a cleverly conducted operation, and one difficult to achieve in the face of the prestige enjoyed by Nicias, and at a time when the Athenians were tired of a long war.

Socrates. I blush for you, Alcibiades, that you should boast of such disreputable conduct!

Alcibiades. Are you concerned for my reputation, Socrates? It stands very high with the Athenians, so high indeed that now I can dispense with such deceptions as I practised in my earlier days. By now my political fortune is so well established that I can by the mere force of my speech move them to follow my policy. Soon you will see a striking illustration of my influence.

Socrates. I have heard it rumoured that you want us to send a major expedition against Syracuse, and expect that the Assembly will decide in this according to your counsel. I do hope that either you will give up this foolhardy and unjust project, or that Nicias will prevail against you to have it rejected.

Alcibiades. I shall not give it up and Nicias will not prevail against me. Can you not realize, Socrates, that I have grown even more proficient than Pericles in the handling of the Assembly?

Socrates. Woe then to Athens!

Alcibiades. Do you indeed, Socrates, feel so strongly against this expedition?

Socrates. Assuredly I do.

Alcibiades. Then, Socrates, allow me to offer you a suggestion. Do not leave it to Nicias to oppose me in the Assembly, but do yourself rise and persuade the Assembly against me!

Socrates. You are being unfair, Alcibiades. I am not expert at addressing crowds. My life has been spent in private conversations, whereby I hope I have helped others, and myself, to think more clearly. This, as you know, I regard as a duty in Man: since the gods have blessed him with the power of thinking, he shows himself worthy of that honour only in so far as he uses and develops this power. We would deem it a loss if a man with the limbs and disposition of an athlete did not exercise in gymnastics. How much greater a loss not to exercise our minds! And this is no idle exercise: we can devote our efforts to more or less deserving objects, and the most deserving is the acquisition of wisdom. You are well aware that I have never attempted to assemble an audience for my conversations, I have been content to speak with whoever was willing to speak with me. I made no sacrifice of earnestness to capture attention. Indeed there have been some who have found my mode of conversation tedious, and these I have not sought to retain. Further, those who have persisted I have not sought to best in argument, but it has been my purpose by questioning them to make them discover for themselves the incoherence of their views and therefrom to grow angry with themselves and gentle to others; and thereafter to attempt the setting of their own house in order.

Alcibiades. You do not have to remind me, Socrates, of your method of dialogue and of your purpose.

Socrates. But then, Alcibiades, you must be aware of the contrast between my approach to individuals and the popular orator's approach to crowds. Addressing a gathering of thousands involves holding their attention — that is, angling for unwilling hearers — which I have not done, and the purpose of the speech is to cause these thousands to veer to your side, as against your opponent's. In short it involves the collecting of listeners, and the driving of these listeners to some action you have in mind.

Alcibiades. Thank you, Socrates, for putting it better than I would have. It is true that I speak for the purpose of getting some immediate and definite action from those spoken to. My ability to generate such action is power, would you not say?

Socrates. Definitely it is.

Alcibiades. And you enjoy no such power.

Socrates. I do not. Indeed I might not even get the opportunity of addressing the Assembly.

Alcibiades. You are a citizen.

Socrates. So are thirty thousand others, maybe forty thousand. In any important debate, there are some five thousand present, all of whom have the same right to speak, many of whom are eager to exercise this right. It is clear that in a debate which lasts from sunrise to sundown, only a few can in fact speak, and it is those who enjoy an established political standing who can reach the rostrum.

Alcibiades. True enough. I am one of these.

Socrates. You are. And I am not.

Alcibiades. Well now, Socrates, you have been telling me about this ability to generate decisions, and this personal standing which is a requirement for the exercise of the ability. Would you grant me that these are to be called political standing and political efficiency, and that the acquisition of this standing and the development of this efficiency constitute the craft of Politics?

Socrates. I regard the man who possesses such standing and ability and who does not know what is just and good for the city, as a most unhappy and dangerous man, and that is why, Alcibiades, I so urged you to acquire wisdom before rushing into Politics.

Alcibiades. And so I might have done, Socrates, at your persuasion. If so, I would now presumably still be one of your followers, diligently engaged in the acquisition of that understanding of the good which you so advocate. But then if some other Alcibiades were urging what I am now urging, I would be just as impotent as you find yourself to stop him from his endeavour. It may be that I have only acquired a part of statecraft, but it is the efficient part. It may be that you possess the more important part, but it is an inefficient part. Shall we speak further of this Syracuse expedition?

Socrates. It is better to talk about it before than after.

Alcibiades. Do you realize that if, as I feel sure, the Assembly approves my suggestion, many ships will have to put to sea, which is costly, and thousands of Athenians will embark upon a venture in which not a few will lose their lives?

Socrates. I know this only too well.

Alcibiades. This getting people to perform costly and dangerous actions is an art in which you must confess that I excel, while you, Socrates, are ignorant thereof. How much easier it would be to persuade the people against spending all this money and venturing all these lives, and even this you cannot do! Indeed I can offer you a simpler and more striking proof of your inefficiency. While I was still a youth, trailing after you and awed by your wisdom, you tried to persuade me to do something which was easy indeed: you wanted me to remain for a few years occupied at your side with the problems of wise government; even in this modest effort you did not succeed.

Socrates. It is my purpose to offer opportunities for wisdom, not to drive people to actions of my own choice.

Alcibiades. My purpose is that which you refuse: it is to induce in others actions of my own choosing. And you must grant me this proposition: "Alcibiades knows how to influence the decisions and actions of the Athenians."

Socrates. That is all too obvious, alas!

Alcibiades. Well then, you must grant me that I possess a form of knowledge which you lack. You must also grant me the proposition: "Socrates does not know how to influence the decisions and actions of Athenians."

Socrates. I refuse to speak of this skill as knowledge.
Alcibiades. But you must, Socrates. And you must recognize that it is valuable knowledge. Think how pleased you would be if you now found yourself possessed of it, and able to prevent this expedition to Syracuse, of which you think so ill! You love the city, Socrates, and you are a fighter. Well do I remember how you saved my life on the field of Potidea; it is known that you were a tower of strength on the unfortunate day of Delion, when you saved young Xenophon. Such a man as you proved yourself to be on those occasions would not lack the courage to challenge a popular view in the Assembly.

Socrates. I would not.

Alcibiades. As a citizen you should oppose the proposition which you deem harmful to the city just as stoutly as you withstood the enemy.

Socrates. No doubt.

Alcibiades. And you regard the expedition to Syracuse as harmful to the city?

Socrates. I do.

Alcibiades. Then if you could stop me from swaying the Assembly in its favour, you would. You lack neither the judgement, nor the will, nor the courage to do so. What then do you lack? I will answer for you: you do not know how to do it. I have carefully laid the ground for the reception of my proposal about Syracuse. All this designing and preparation leading up to the decision and move I want constitutes a political operation. Intelligent as you are, Socrates, you should be able to set up a contrary operation. But you lack the knowledge.

Socrates. Surely, Alcibiades, you have not forgotten how often and clearly I have expressed my dislike of the arts of persuasion. You may remember my discussion with Gorgias. Boasting about his art, he illustrated it by occasions on which he goes with his brother, the doctor, to the house of a patient. "It may happen," said Gorgias, "that the patient will not take the medicine prescribed by my brother, but if I intervene, the patient is persuaded." I then asked Gorgias whether he knew by himself whether this was beneficial or harmful medicine, and he admitted that such knowledge does not pertain to his art. I then taxed him with having evolved procedures apt to make people who do not know what is good for them, trust a speaker who knows no more than they. They attribute to him a knowledge which he does not possess and therefore he may persuade them to their undoing. In the same manner you, Alcibiades, do not know whether it is good to do what you advise. Therefore the greater the scope of your art, the more dangerous it is.

Alcibiades. You are free, Socrates, to spurn the art of handling and moving people, and the understanding and knowledge required for that end. But then, Socrates, all your thinking about what is for the best is bound to be by-passed by the actual movement of politics, sparked off by those who, like me, have sought the knowledge and cultivated the skill you despise.

Socrates. I do not despise it. I dread it. I would want those who are possessed thereof, as you are, to walk in constant fear of the harm they may do, a fear which can be laid low only by the cultivation of the knowledge of what is for the best.

Alcibiades. You wanted me to dwell upon the latter before I developed and exercised the skill of moving people.

Socrates. I had indeed hoped that you would attain the high standing you now enjoy, but that you would have acquired the wisdom which you lack.

Alcibiades. In short you wanted me to be two men in one, Alcibiades plus Socrates: to combine the influence I have acquired with the wisdom I might have gained in your company. You warn me that Alcibiades by himself is unwise, but you have to confess that Socrates by himself is powerless. Perhaps you would be content if we were to combine forces. Have you not said that "whoever as a private man possesses the capacity of advising another who rules over a realm should be called master of the knowledge which the ruler should have?" This points to alternative possibilities: Alcibiades, enjoying his influence over the Athenian people, either has acquired the wisdom of Socrates, or takes counsel from Socrates.

Socrates. The first alternative is the better.

Alcibiades. Perhaps also the more unlikely. Be that as it may, in any case your idea is that he who rules men in turn should let himself be ruled by wisdom.

Socrates. Well said, Alcibiades! If only you would bow to the force of your own formulation!

Alcibiades. But, Socrates, according to this formulation, the ability to influence men, which Alcibiades possesses, is to be a mere instrument in the carrying out of the counsels of wisdom.

Socrates. It is indeed instrumental, a mere means.

Alcibiades. I know you think so. But do you deem it probable that those who are past masters in this art would be willing to regard it as subordinate? Let us talk of craftsmen, as you, Socrates, have ever liked to do. It was a current joke among us, in the days when I was of your followers, that we, who came of the best families to learn wisdom from you, constantly heard about cobblers and skin-dressers, carpenters and smiths, and other such.

Socrates. True enough.

Alcibiades. Shall we talk about weavers? Have you not likened the statesman to the weaver who binds together the warp-threads of many individual lives and conducts, weaving them into a harmonious pattern?

Socrates. I have.

Alcibiades. Wherein does the skill of the weaver reside? Shall we say that he is deft at inserting the woof-thread by means of which he binds the warp-threads, or shall we say that he has excellent taste in the designing of patterns? If he has this deftness without this taste, shall we not still call him a weaver?

Socrates. Without question.

Alcibiades. But if he has this excellent taste but is quite clumsy in the handling of the woof-thread and indeed incapable of binding his warp-threads together, then is he a weaver?

Socrates. He is not.

Alcibiades. If we now turn to the political weaver, shall we call it wisdom to devise an excellent pattern and skill to handle the woof-thread and bind the warp-threads? And shall we say that the first is the talent of Socrates, but the second the talent of Alcibiades?

Socrates. This is the first sign of modesty I have ever seen in you, Alcibiades.

Alcibiades. And this, Socrates, is the first sign of hasty judgement I have found in you. For you mistake my conclusion. To go on: if the warp-threads lie ready to the hand of the weaver, and passively let themselves be spread on the loom, it takes but indifferent skill to insert the woof-thread; the weaver then need not concentrate upon it, he can give his attention to working out an excellent pattern, and if he is incapable of such good designing, he must humbly let himself be guided by another who can, since the facility of his job does not entitle him to preen himself on his talent.

Socrates. I agree.

Alcibiades. But in Politics, Socrates, the warp-threads are individual men who are very far indeed from lending themselves passively. Each warp-thread is opinionated and elusive; therefore casting just one woof-thread to bind all these individuals in a common action takes a spell-binder. I am one such, Socrates, and know the difficulty of binding men to my woof-thread, a difficulty enhanced by there being rival spell-binders attempting to cast their spell upon the same threads. And have you not noticed, Socrates, that craftsmen, who are willing to converse with you while doing their job if it is easy, turn unwilling if it is difficult?

Socrates. True.

Alcibiades. The political weaver, whose warp-threads wriggle like serpents, cannot be patient with you. Nor can he feel modest about his achievement, nor can he believe that he must subordinate his talent to the fulfilment of your design. He is carried away by his doing and deaf to your telling.

Socrates. Alcibiades, you are foolishly proud of your spell, and I fear that your binding may shorten the threads of many lives.

Alcibiades. Socrates, you imprudently despise the art of winning an Assembly, and you may regret it, if ever you are subject to a public accusation, and thus forced to defend yourself in public.

Socrates. Should I be unjustly condemned, the shame thereof would not be upon me.

Alcibiades. But upon the Assembly?

Socrates. Indeed.

Alcibiades. And thereby upon the people of Athens, upon your beloved city. Thus, for want of the art I praise, you would be an occasion of shame to Athens.

Socrates. Most unwillingly.

Alcibiades. Not quite unwillingly, since you might have willed the acquisition of the art which might have prevented this. And shall I tell you, Socrates, why you are unwilling to acquire it?

Socrates. Have your say.

Alcibiades. We know that men want, decide and do what seems to them good. Now if there were no difference between what seems good and what is truly such, your whole activity would be idle, since it has consisted in driving men away by argument from their crude view of the good. This driving away, however, you have conducted in personal arguments, now with one, now with another, which seems to imply that even with the help of your questioning, individual men have to make a personal effort to overcome their disposition to see the good where it is not. Now the politician who desires to obtain of great numbers, at short notice, a certain decision or action, must perforce appeal to their present view of the good, such as it is; precisely that view which it is your purpose to change. The views of the good which are presently held are the politician's data which he uses to move people as he desires. That is the way the game is played, and you are not interested in the game.

Socrates. True.

Alcibiades. The politician conjures up some image of the good to be achieved by the action he recommends, and the constituent parts of this image are made up of the ideas of the good which are current among the people. For instance I shall explain to Athenians that the Syracuse expedition will so raise our reputation and add to our forces as to amaze Hellas and intimidate Lacedaemon.

Socrates. While in fact the expedition may prove fatal in terms of its avowed purpose. Mere lack of success would dash our reputation, disaster would waste the best of our forces. A dangerous gamble, and, if successful, what is the gain? Is it a wise purpose to grow more formidable in the eyes of our neighbours? Will it not increase their envy, fear, and potential enmity? The good you seek is twice doubtful: it is not sure that it will be attained, it is not sure that it is a good.

Alcibiades. But I am sure that I see it as a good, and am confident of its attainment. And I am sure that I can induce my compatriots to want it with my own keenness and will it with my own assurance. See this hand which I eagerly stretch towards Syracuse! This same eagerness shall arm twenty thousand hands when I have spoken! Socrates, how could you understand me? You have never experienced the response of the many! You do not know what it is to stand in front of a crowd, send out not only words from one's lips, but heat from one's eyes and fingertips, reaching out to that fellow far away who was idly scratching his ear and shifting his foot, and who now is coming to stare like a man in a trance, with all my warmth working within him, soon to explode in a great shout of approval! This is the happiness of the politician, that the feelings he expresses become those of these many others out there, come back to him multiplied thousands of times by the great living echo, which thus reinforces them in himself. Brave echo, which not only returns my words, but turns them into deeds!

Socrates. In short, Alcibiades, your true volume is not that which I see with my eyes. Applause, it seems, swells you out, so presumably you shrink for lack of it.

Alcibiades. You are joking, Socrates. Still you are right about the hunger for response which grows with the habit. One need not be without it, ever. One has a number of faithful followers anyhow. Moreover I am sensitive enough to tell when I am failing to carry them with me; I can then shift to commonplaces they like to hear and await a more favourable occasion.

Socrates. In all you say I see no Knowledge of the good to be sought nor any effort to extend such Knowledge to others.

Alcibiades. Knowing and getting others to Know is your pursuit, Socrates. Doing and getting others to Do is mine. This is where we differ profoundly. Were I trying to get others to Know, I should have an uphill task which would interfere with my getting them to Do, and had I myself pursued this Knowledge you advocate, I would have divorced myself from the feelings of those I seek to move.

Socrates. But your not knowing, Alcibiades, will cause you to bring disaster to Athens.

Alcibiades. If so it is a disaster which your wisdom, Socrates, is unable to prevent, since you cannot get the people to do other than I recommend.

Socrates. Are you content to risk the ruin of the city?

Alcibiades. Frankly, Socrates, I do not believe your forebodings. You would have us feel that we are blundering blind fellows unless we go to you for the opening of our eyes, a difficult and lengthy process. This is really somewhat offensive. I do care for the good of Athens, and my compatriots whom I address are not bereft of judgement.

Socrates. Obviously if such seeds were not present, it would be idle to call upon politicians to take a grave view of their responsibility, and idle to cultivate the judgement of the people. You have been busily explaining to me that the craft of Politics consists in building up your standing, and developing an ability to move people, which itself makes use of the people's perception of what is good. You have also been taunting me with my lack of such craft. Now, as I tell you that such craft may lead to disaster, you suddenly bring in the assumption that somehow there is a floating sense of what is for the best, in you and also in your fellows whom you address. But this brings us back to our first talk, many years ago, in which I convinced you of ignorance precisely in this respect.

Alcibiades. True enough. Perhaps I conceded too readily.

Socrates. Or perhaps you have now come to be too flushed with your craft of moving men to consider its dangers sanely.

Alcibiades. Well, Socrates, it is an absorbing game, which brings out the best as well as the worst within us. To those who have played it, this is Politics, teeming with opportunities and hazards, and the understanding of this game is the understanding of Politics. This is how history is made.

Socrates. A tale of adventures and misadventures, full of sound and fury. . . .

Alcibiades. A tale of men. Understand, Socrates, that men need and enjoy this stirring of the blood which occurs when I call them to action and make them confident of its outcome. When I lend them my imagination and they lend me their forces, then are we together a joyfully striding giant. . . .

Socrates. Striding where?

Alcibiades. Always your question marks, tripping up our resolution! We grow weary of them. Provide us instead with some noble vision of an ideal city to be achieved, a goal at which we politicians will aim. . . .

Socrates. Aye, and a lever to move men.

Alcibiades. That also. It lies in the nature of Politics that whatever is proposed as an end to be served, serves as a means to move men, and that the noblest dreams figure jointly with lower motives as the inputs available to us movers of men. No matter that my imperial conception of Athens' good seems to you paltry, still it will do as an illustration. It is true that I regard the conquest of Syracuse as a good to be sought, it is no less true that this image serves to build up my following: a goal but also a means; and there is nothing which does not become a means in our hands.

CHAPTER 3

On the Nature
of Political Science

Political activity is dangerous. Arising inevitably out of men's ability to influence each other, conferring upon them the benefits of joint endeavour, an indispensable source of social boons, it is also capable of doing great harm. Men can be moved to injure others or to ruin themselves. The very process of moving implies a risk of debasement for the moved and for the mover.[1] Even the fairest vision of a good to be sought offers no moral guarantee, since it may poison hearts with hatred against those who are deemed an obstacle to its achievement.[2]

No apology is required for stressing a subjective dread of political activity: the chemist is not disqualified as a scientist because he is aware that explosives are dangerous—indeed that chemist is dangerous who lacks such awareness.

This feeling of danger is widespread in human society[3] and has always haunted all but the more superficial authors: very

1. "Tel se croit le maître des autres qui ne laisse pas d'être plus esclave qu'eux," says Rousseau in the first lines of the *Social Contract*. He elucidates in *Emile*: "Domination itself is servile when beholden to opinion: for you depend upon the prejudices of those you govern by means of their prejudices."

2. It is a sobering exercise to count the expressions of anger (as against those of good will) which occur in the speeches or writings of political champions of this or that moral cause.

3. Different voices denounce the encroaching State, overbearing Lords, an Established Church, tentacular unions, or the dominant party: yet such voices, however

few have, like Hobbes, brought it into the open; it has hovered in the background, exerting an invisible but effective influence upon their treatment of the subject; it may be, to a significant degree, responsible for the strange and unique texture of political science.

There are no objects to which our attention is so naturally drawn as to our own fellows. It takes a conscious purpose to watch birds or ants, but we cannot fail to watch other men, with whom we are inevitably associated, whose behaviour is so important to us that we need to foresee it, and who are sufficiently like us to facilitate our understanding of their actions. Being a man, which involves living with men, therefore involves observing men. And the knowledge of men could be called the most fairly distributed of all knowledges since each one of us may acquire it according to his willingness and capacity.

As Politics consists of nothing other than human behaviour, we could expect its knowledge to have made successive strides through the accumulation, comparison and systematization of observations. If Politics is understood restrictively as the conduct of men in offices of authority and the consequent movement of public affairs, then all those who, in the course of time, have held office have found out something about political behaviour. I hold the view that we should regard as "political" every systematic effort, performed at any place in the social field, to move other men in pursuit of some design cherished by the mover. According to this view, we all have the

discordant, all express distrust of some form of established power. In the same manner, emergent power is deemed frightening by some when an agitator musters a mob, by others in the case of a rising dictator: though one may turn into the other. The same feeling crystallizes on different stems.

required material: any one of us has acted with others, been moved by others and has sought to move others.

It is clear of course that mere "facts" can never compose a knowledge unless they are marshalled, and their marshalling always calls for a "theory" which seizes upon certain similar appearances, assigns to them common names and supposes processes which bring them about. The processes we assume constitute in the mind a sort of model of what occurs in observable reality; a necessary attempt to reduce phenomenal diversity to intellectual simplicity. Such "theory" has a "representative" purpose; it guides us in the collection of facts: these in turn call for amendments to our theory in so far as it cannot account for them. We move from initial simplicity to increasing complexity in our theory, until a possibly quite different one is offered which achieves the representative function with greater elegance and accuracy.

Theory of this kind progresses with time, accounting for an ever-increasing store of observations. All this is trite; but it then comes as a surprise that political science should offer no such "theory": what is called "political theory"[4] is an altogether different thing. In the theory of astronomy there is no place for Ptolemaeus, in the theory of chemistry no place for Paracelsus: not so in political theory. The theory of any science is an integrated whole from which past theories have been discarded. Political theory is a collection of individual theories which stand side by side, each one impervious to the impact of new observations and to the advent of new theories. This can be the case only because political theories are normative (that is, are doctrines) and not meant to perform the representative func-

---

4. Discussed in Arnold Brecht, *Political Theory* (Princeton, 1959), and in Eric Weil, "Philosophie politique, théorie politique," *Revue française de science politique*, vol. XI, no. 2.

tion which the word "theory" evokes in the case of factual sciences. Why is political science rich in normative theories, deficient in "representative" theory? Only a fool would opine that the masters of the past were incapable of establishing the latter: they must have been unwilling. And why? The reason may lie in the sense of danger which I noted at the beginning.

Libido sciendi is a noble passion: it is inherently incapable of debasing the man it possesses, and the delights it affords do not wait upon the possession of the object pursued but attend its very pursuit. This *libido* is indispensable to the making of a scientist,[5] and it seems also sufficient. Yet if one studies the personalities of the great scientists, one finds that their *libido* was habitually associated with one or both of the motives expressed in Bacon's timeless sentence: "for the glory of God and the relief of man's estate."

The word "understanding" denotes the grasping of a pattern which underlies the waywardness of phenomena: the scientist finds beauty in such a pattern, and loves it the more the higher its aesthetic quality. The word "discovery" signifies the unveiling of what was both present and hidden. Such terms reveal that ancient inquirers into "the secrets of Nature" (another telling expression) assumed the existence of an "order": and what better warrant for it than the belief in creation? If everything that is comes from the divine planning of a Supreme Intelligence — "Dieu est géomètre" — then the design which stands at the source guarantees that far lesser intelligences, partaking of the same reason, can grasp some parts of the design.

Such was the language of scientists in the deist age of the seventeenth and eighteenth centuries, who felt that the displaying of some lineaments of the universal order was a new

5. Cf. Michael Polanyi, *Science, Faith and Society* (London, 1946).

publication of God's wisdom. Few scientists would today speak in this manner:[6] they now state that their patterns are "made up" and disclaim that they "make out" the "true" structure of things. Subconsciously, however, they hardly doubt that their "made-up" patterns are in some way representative of a true structure. Nor do they hesitate to choose between two equally "serviceable" models that which is the more beautiful; and, though careful to explain that this is a mere preference, in fact they act no differently from their predecessors who would have said that the more elegant model was the most true, as the worthiest of God's sapience; indeed every day scientists resort to metaphysical convictions, such as the Malebranche-Maupertuis principle of least action.

Turning to the second part of Bacon's sentence, it is true that scientists have ever taken pride in the practical results afforded to their fellows by their findings. Just as there has been a high tide of the first Baconian theme (Newton) there has been more recently a high tide of the second, arising from the very advance of technology. Science and technology have not always been wedded. For a long time practical advances were achieved more often by practical men[7] than by scientists, whose minds moved on a different plane. But the social impact of technology affected science, which rapidly became what it is today, the great source of material innovations.[8] Even when scientists are furthest from any specific concern for practical applications, they cannot lack awareness that the high esteem

6. Nor was this language so natural to a more theological age: it fits especially well with deism.

7. Cf. *A History of Technology*, by Singer, Holmyard and Hall (Oxford, Clarendon Press, beginning 1954).

8. Science now "changes the world": not so in Chinese civilization. Cf. Needham, *Science and Civilisation in China* (Cambridge, beginning 1954). Question: if science does so, is it not because of an urge which arose outside the scientific community and challenged it?

in which they are at present held is derived from the general opinion that the increase of knowledge promises an increase of power:[9] so much so that the sciences which hold out no promise of practical applications are put on a starvation diet.

The sole purpose of the foregoing rough indications is to stress that two powerful motives in general reinforce the zeal of the scientist for systematization of observable facts: these same motives, however, assume negative values for the student of political phenomena. He has no occasion to delight in the discovery of a seemly pattern, and every reason to distrust practical applications of his findings.

While the student of Nature can rejoice in the fundamental harmony he discovers beneath disorderly appearances, such aesthetic enjoyment is denied to the student of Politics. Never was there any such thorough-going apologetic of universal order as that of Leibniz. And never was a sharper blow dealt than Voltaire's *Candide*. Trust this prince of controversialists to seek the weak point of the system he attacks: and where does he find it? Voltaire carries the discussion away from the harmonies of Nature to the distempers of human affairs.[10] There is nothing here to evoke a reverent appreciation of the course of things, there is no pattern to be found ("a tale told by an idiot . . . signifying nothing"). And whenever our mind can rest in the acknowledgement of "sufficient reason," this is but an uneasy repose: what is explained is not justified, *causa efficiens* is neither *justa causa* nor visibly at the service of a plausible *causa finalis*.

9. Hobbes's view: "The end of knowledge is power . . . the scope of all speculation is the performing of some action, or thing to be done." (Opening of *De Corpore*.)

10. This choice of ground is the more remarkable in that Voltaire, who originally subscribed to Leibnizian optimism, was shaken out of it, so the scholars tell us, by a natural event, the disaster of Lisbon. Yet he chose the ground of human affairs for his attack. Note that even on this ground, Voltaire had previously illustrated Leibnizianism (in *Zadig*, as stressed by Hazard). But in so doing he must have felt the difficulty and thus when he declared war upon the system this was the battlefield he chose.

We are inevitably more exacting when investigating human affairs than in the case of natural phenomena: regarding the latter we may be content to find an order, whatever it may be; in human society, however, we are not content to find some pattern, we want it to fit our idea of justice.

The deist apologetic of universal order has exerted upon the social sciences a most powerful influence, displayed to the full in economics. Each man's striving for his own advantage results in a social optimum: this has been taken as axiomatic, and whatever went wrong was attributed to "artificial" obstacles: restraints upon trade and competition were first named; much later "property" itself came to be questioned as an artificial restraint.[11]

However questionable the philosophic foundations of economic science[12] they had one great empirical virtue: economists could accept unquestioningly the motives of economic actors, since a good outcome was expected from the vigour of desires. Economists may take exception to my statement, but I feel that the "ethical neutrality" which has served them well has been made possible by a teleological optimism.[13] It is thanks to this promise of good outcome that intellectual doctors[14] could move to the business of understanding eco-

11. This theme appears in J. S. Mill and in our day has been fully developed by Maurice Allais.

12. These have been less discussed than one would wish. See, however, W. Stark, *The Ideal Foundations of Economic Thought* (London, 1943); G. Myrdal, *The Political Element in the Development of Economic Theory* (English edition, London, 1953); L. M. Frazer, *Economic Thought and Language* (London, 1947); J. A. Schumpeter, *History of Economic Analysis* (London, 1954); but above all, Vilfredo Pareto, *Manuel d'economie politique* (Paris, 1909).

13. Openly stated by Adam Smith, and underlying Pareto's great work.

14. I have been advised that my use in this paragraph and elsewhere of the terms "actors" and "doctors" might give rise to misunderstanding, since such general terms are now commonly used to denote specific professions. I am, however, unwilling to give up the logical employment of these terms, which are most convenient for the sorting out, in any field, of those who are engaged in Doing, and causing others to Do:

nomic activity, away from a centuries-old attitude of upbraiding acquisitiveness.

Such a descent from a moral pulpit has occurred only quite recently in political science [15] arousing ardent controversy.[16] There are strong intellectual reasons to applaud this descent and call it belated; there are strong prudential reasons to deplore this descent and call it treason. Light can be cast on the matter only if we reject the fiction that the scientist can and should be soulless. It is not because the economist is an ethical eunuch that he can envisage phenomena with ethical indifference but it is because he expects a desirable ethical outcome regardless of the ethical concern and enlightenment of the actors; his short-term or atomistic indifference is warranted by his long-range or overall optimism. The proof thereof lies in the revival of moral passion regarding economic behaviour in the most scholarly economists as soon as they find reason or occasion to question the assumption of overall maximization. Now in Politics such an assumption seems untenable.

The postulate that economic activity is not to be feared and that the more of it the better is allegorized in Dupont de Nemours' picture of a giant in chains, with the caption: "Otez-lui ses chaînes et le laissez aller." [17] But in those countries where political freedom has been most prized and practised,

---

Actors; and of those who are engaged in Knowing, and causing others to Know: Doctors.

15. This is most clearly recounted in Robert A. Dahl, *The Behavioral Approach in Political Science*, Report for Fifth World Congress of the International Political Science Association.

16. The most authoritative attack is that of Leo Strauss, "What Is Political Philosophy?" in *Journal of Politics* (August 1957). See also Irving Kristol, "The Profanation of Politics" in *The Logic of Personal Knowledge: Essays Presented to Michael Polanyi* (London, 1961).

17. I allude to the frontispiece of Dupont de Nemours' pamphlet of 1788, *Réponse aux observations de la chambre de commerce de Normandie*.

see what attention has been devoted to the formalization of political activity, and to the imbuing of political actors with a public philosophy.[18] We may hold the view that economic activities tend to combine harmoniously: we cannot hold it in the case of political activities. Indeed, Hobbes devised a model displaying the chaotic outcome of political activities running wild. Rousseau subscribed to the Hobbesian picture in his very refutation, since he found it necessary to base his opposite picture upon the supposition of a tiny, closed and static society.

The barbarians are coming, big men with a cruel laughter, who use the conquered as playthings, dishonoured and tossed about. Our knees shake at the very thought of them. Our bishop, however, goes out in state and, bearing the Cross, he stands in the path of the fierce captain. Our town then shall be spared. The strange chief with the awesome mien will indeed become our sovereign; but, guided by the man of God, he will be a just master, and his son will, at an early age, learn from the bishop the finest examples of wise kingship.

The bishop, in my apologue, is political philosophy: its function is to civilize power, to impress the brute, improve its manners, and harness it to salutary tasks. In dealing with our wild chieftain the bishop will often say bluntly: "You cannot do this." That is not a factual statement; the very motive for the utterance is that the power-bearer can in fact do this thing. What lies in the bishop's mind, behind the simple statement, is far more complex: "He wants to do this and has the means therefor; I cannot convince him — nor am I certain — that from this bad action some harm will come to him that he can rec-

18. It takes an observer foreign to Britain and the United States to note the extreme formality attending the least political move (e.g. the decorous conduct of the most insignificant meeting) and to notice the fundamental orthodoxy which underlies all political differences.

ognize as a harm. He must be prevented from doing this, the moral prohibition therefore has to be made in his imagination a hard, concrete obstacle. 'Hence: You cannot. . . .'" This manner of speech is required for preceptive efficiency.

Similarly, when teaching the ruler's turbulent child, the bishop accumulates examples of princely virtue: "That," he says, "is what is done." He means of course: ". . . what is to be done." Not all that has been done by past rulers is relevant to his purpose, but only those praiseworthy attitudes and actions that can contribute to the forming of a noble image which, being firmly implanted in the youth, will exert its pull upon the conduct of the grown man. Deplorable instances are adduced only if they can be joined with a tale of ensuing disaster. Not until the love of virtue has been firmly established will the pupil be faced with the hard saying: ". . . there be just rulers to whom it happeneth according to the work of the wicked; again there be wicked rulers, to whom it happeneth according to the work of the righteous."[19] It is the test of virtue that this bleak truth be accepted by the mind, yet serenely spurned by the soul.

The political learning which I sought to describe by means of an apologue turns upon two sentences: "You cannot . . ." (ideal of law) and "This is what is done" (right example). Such lessons are designed to edify: strange indeed that this word should have fallen into disrepute, since it means "to build up"; and surely it is important to build up the virtue of the men who rule, whether it be One, Few, or Many.

And here we come to the difficulty attending a factual science of Politics: by its very nature it pulls down what the preceptive science endeavoured to build up. Where the preceptive science stressed "You cannot," factual science is bound

19. Ecclesiastes viii. 14.

to observe that "You can"; and what the preceptive science indicated as "What is done" is denied by the findings of factual science: actual doings are very different. A factual science in this realm is therefore dangerous medicine for weak moral constitutions.

Imagination, properly cultivated and addressed, imparts a magic prestige, the loss of which is a public disaster.[20] Madame de Staël helps us here with two pictures:

> The Constituent Assembly ever believed, erroneously, that there was some magic in its decrees, and that all would stop in every way at the line it traced. But its pronouncements can be compared to the ribbon which had been drawn through the garden of the Tuileries to keep the people at some distance from the palace; while opinion remained favourable to those who had drawn the ribbon, no one dreamed of trespassing; but as soon as the people wanted no more of this barrier, it became meaningless.[21]

> The grenadiers marched into the hall where the representatives were assembled, and hustled them forward by simply advancing in solid formation from one end of the room to the other. The representatives found themselves pressed against the wall and had to flee through the window into the gardens of St. Cloud in their senatorial gowns. Representatives of the people had already suffered proscription; but this was the first time that political magistrates were ridiculed by the military;

20. This seems to be the main lesson which Necker has drawn from the great events he was so well placed to witness. It impregnates the two main works he wrote in his years of retreat: *Du pouvoir exécutif dans les grands etats* (2 vols., 1792, no place of publication), and *De la révolution française* (4 vols., 1797). Strangely enough, in view of the very important political role played by the author, these works enjoy a very limited reputation. But a preoccupation which imbues the whole work of Necker is sharply revealed in the two vivid paragraphs written by his famous daughter, which are here quoted.

21. Baronne de Staël, *Considérations sur les principaux evénements de la révolution française* (3 vols., Paris, 1818), vol. I, p. 416.

and Bonaparte, who wished to establish his power on the deg-
radation of bodies as well as of individuals, delighted that he
had been able, in this first moment, to destroy the reputation
of the people's representatives. As soon as the moral power of
national representation was destroyed, a legislative body, whatever it might be, meant no more to the military than a crowd of
five hundred men, less vigorous and disciplined than a battalion
of the same number.[22]

Indeed the law is a mere ribbon; but traditional political science has been at great pains to make it seem an impenetrable
wall. Indeed the body of representatives is incapable of standing its ground against a battalion, but traditional political science has been at great pains so to raise its prestige that battal-
ions may never challenge it but always obey. The danger of the
factual approach is that it may deflate these salutary prestiges.

The dangers of the factual approach are not yet manifest
because studies of this kind have been addressed to "weak" political behaviour, such as voting. I speak of weak political behaviour since it is precisely a finding of such studies that voters
do not care very much. Strong political behaviour is that inspired by a strong passion,[23] and into which men throw themselves wholeheartedly. The picture of Politics which is apt to
emerge from the analysis of strong political behaviours[24] may
be nefariously suggestive.

However little the scientist thinks of practical applications,
whenever they come to his mind it is with a favourable connotation: the gain in efficiency to be expected from the in-

---

22. *Op. cit.* vol. II, pp. 240–41.

23. E.g. militantism in its moderate and extreme forms (conspiracy, terrorism).

24. "Behaviours" is throughout used in its technical sense of the sequence of a
given individual's actions in the course of time, which is of course different for each
individual.

crease in knowledge is a good thing. No such optimism is allowed in the case of the "technology" which may be derived from increased factual understanding of Politics: political efficiency may be a bad thing. Knowing how men are won over and induced to lend their energies is knowledge which can be used for good or evil. Indeed it is more likely to be used for evil. A good man is humble and therefore advances his views with some diffidence; he respects his fellows and therefore is not likely to be an aggressive salesman. It is the presumptuous, over-bearing man who is most prone to exploit the technology of moving men for his purpose.

This thought is very disquieting. And it might suffice to turn the scholar away from a quest for knowledge which may be ill-used, if the technology of Politics waited upon his discoveries. But such is not the case: the technology has been mightily developed outside political science during the last half-century, and developed by the very men to whom the prudent scientist would like to deny it. Naturally enough those who are least sensitive to the aesthetic and ethical appeal of traditional theory have broken away from its restraints and guidance; while those with finer feelings are victims of processes which they cannot grasp. In such a position all the harm which a factual science of Politics can do is already let loose, and it can come as a useful warning.

It has been suggested here that recognition of the dangers inherent in political activity may have held up the progress of scientific inquiry in Politics; but however important this factor, it can hardly serve as a full explanation. A useful complement is suggested by comparison with medical science: a comparison current since the days of Plato.[25]

25. The two sciences are of equal antiquity. Hippocrates was born c. 460 B.C., between Socrates (c. 469) and Plato (c. 427).

What is the purpose of medicine? The health of the body. What therefore is the knowledge required in a doctor? The knowledge of health. This seems a reasonable approach to medicine: it leads first to the primacy of hygiene,[26] but secondly to envisaging any disease as a derangement of a natural harmony.[27] Hence for instance Themison's classification of diseases: they arise from an undue constriction (*strictum*), from an undue relaxation (*laxum*), or from a combination of both (*mixtum*).[28] In a case of *strictum*, antispasmodic, sedative medication is indicated; in a case of *laxum*, tonic, roborative remedies. This is very attractive, so much so that economic prescriptions of our own day are "Themisonian": if there are congestive areas in the economy, relieve the pressure of demand by the sedatives of deflation (including if necessary *saignare*,[29] the removal of excess buying power), and if there is laxity in the market, administer stimulants.

However reasonable it seems to take the satisfactory state of affairs as the axial concept, it has not paid off well in medicine: the concept of health led neither to a close study of diseases attuned to their specificity, nor to a far-reaching physiology.[30] It is amazing that the emphasis laid upon the proper function-

26. "For the worshippers of Hygeia, health is the natural order of things, a positive attribute to which men are entitled if they govern their lives wisely. According to them, the most important function of medicine is to discover and teach the natural laws which will ensure a man a healthy mind in a healthy body." (René Dubos, *Mirage of Health* (London, 1960), p. 113.)

27. Galen said that the duty of the doctor is to conserve the natural condition, to reestablish it when perturbed, and to restore what is lacking as far as feasible. (From F. J. V. Broussais, *Histoire des doctrines médicales et des systèmes de nosologie* (4 vols., Paris, 1829), vol. 1, p. 200.)

28. *Ibid.* pp. 107 ff.

29. Kitchen-Latin for "blood-letting."

30. Dubos stresses that the broad point of view of orthobiosis leads to "the danger of substituting meaningless generalities and weak philosophy for the concreteness of exact knowledge." (*Op. cit.* p. 137.)

ing of the body should have sparked off so little curiosity about this very functioning. Physiology can hardly be said to start before Harvey (b. 1578), when medical science was twenty centuries old; and it took wing only with Haller (b. 1708). I regard it as encouraging for my view of political science that the microscope proved so important an instrument of physiological knowledge, and finally led to the discovery that many illnesses are not mere derangements of natural harmony but arise from the intrusion of minute agents.[31]

When resorting to analogy, one should always stop to note contrasts between the systems compared. There is a most striking contrast between the object studied by medical science, the body of man, and the object of political science, the body politic. In the former case, only the integrated whole has value in our eyes, the component cells are expendable: not so in the case of the body politic, where the whole is justified by its components, real persons. But the contrast goes further. Human bodies are built on the same model, not so political bodies. The health of the human body is therefore a clearer and more distinct notion than a state of health in a body politic. The anatomy of the human body is a datum, political anatomy changes. Therefore, if anatomy is already inadequate knowledge in the former case,[32] how much more inadequate it must be in the latter!

31. The word "microbe," now a popular term abandoned by scientists, was introduced as late as 1878.

32. Claude Bernard wrote: "Descriptive anatomy is to physiology what geography is to history, and as it is not enough to know a country's topography for the understanding of its history, it is not enough to know the anatomy of organs for the understanding of their functions. An old surgeon, Méry, compared anatomists to those messengers who are to be found in great cities, and who know the layout of the streets, and the numbering of buildings, but do not know what goes on inside. Indeed, in tissues, in organs, vital physico-chemical phenomena occur which mere anatomy cannot reveal." (*Leçons sur les phénomènes de la vie commune aux animaux et aux végétaux* (2 vols., Paris, 1878), vol. I, pp. 6–7.)

The "healthy body politic" is an attractive starting-point but one which leads to little progress of knowledge. If the body politic wherein we find ourselves is accepted as being at present healthy,[33] we are not given sufficient provocation to look into the minute day-to-day processes which keep it so. If we regard it as now distempered, we are apt to go back to some past moment of "health" with great chances of substituting our fancy for the true past, and slight chance of understanding what has changed, where, how and why. Even worse is our picking upon some body politic distant in time and using it as our model of health. This leads for instance to the ludicrous mistake of the French Jacobins who wanted to build a Sparta, ignoring that it had rested upon extreme social inequality, its renowned "equals" forming but a minute fraction of the whole population.[34]

The notion of healthy political body leads to pseudo-restorations of which the Germanic "Holy Roman Empire" is a striking instance.[35] It leads to transpositions which have never worked out very well.[36] It ceases altogether to be relevant if it is recognized that one has to meet new needs by means of new institutions, or if one cherishes the fancy of building up such a body politic as has never been seen before. In

33. This complacency is a most uncommon attitude.

34. Again when one takes Athens as a model, one forgets that in its age of extreme democracy (which did not exclude slavery) the notion that "aliens" could not become part of the body politic was so fundamentally embedded that Pericles himself was the author of a law which struck from the registers a large fraction of the citizenry: men who could not prove that they were descended from both an Athenian father and an Athenian mother.

35. Though why the Roman Empire should have been looked back upon as a healthy political body is beyond my understanding.

36. For instance the transposition of the United States constitution in Latin America, or for that matter the transposition of the Westminster model in Continental Europe.

either case, one must form some idea of the probable working-out of new arrangements. And such an idea cannot even be formed unless one has acquired as much basic knowledge as possible about the elementary forms of behaviour which are to be dovetailed in a new combination. Thus we always come back to inquiry into elementary political behaviour.

PART II

Setting:
Ego in Otherdom

CHAPTER 1

Of Man

Man appears, a screaming bundle of flesh, the outcome of mating. He is utterly helpless, his existence hangs upon the nursing he receives. A plant develops autonomously from its seed; in much the same manner the lowest forms of animal life are capable of locomotion and self-nourishment from birth: not so the higher forms of animal life, Man least of all. "Exposing" an infant amounts to killing it, since it cannot live without the care lavished upon it by the mother, or a substitute. In the case of Man, the capacity to survive is not inherent in the new-born: the means of survival must be provided to him by others. Since no new-born can grow up without such provision, some form of organization for the care and protection of children is a vital condition of Man's existence: there would be no men but for the family; whatever its form a fostering group is essential.

Not only is such a fostering group essential for the survival of the children, and therefore the production of a new generation of men, but the newcomers require for their development an attention continuing over many years. Man is slow in reaching adulthood. There seems to be a correlation between a higher degree of biological organization and a slower pace of maturation: this in turn requires that the fostering group should endure. No matter how small, there must be a lasting society to afford protection and food to the newcomers in their prolonged period of physical helplessness or weakness. The natural necessity of protecting the children makes the mutual protection of adults more necessary than it would be, but for these cherished impediments: a man can flee from danger more easily than a family. Basic traits of human society derive from the cherished helplessness of the offspring. Most animal species whose young require some period of care display a rudiment of social organization (a herd) within which there are some means of communication. Obviously if the young are all born simultaneously and brought to adulthood in a succeeding season, the "league of parents" may dissolve after the "turning-out" of such a new generation; not so if new births are all the time occurring while older children are still being attended to: the establishment must then be permanent, the social organization and the means of communication can develop.

Man's prolonged physical dependence upon his begetters is a great boon, the *sine qua non* condition of his humanity. Living for many years in the shadow of adults, he learns, partly by spontaneous imitation and partly through systematic coaching, whatever skills they possess, such forms of mastery over Nature as they owe to their own experience or to tradition. He does not have to find out for himself what is common knowledge in his group.[1] The simplest human societies care not only for the immature but also for the superannuated, who provide the "public library" of primitive life.[2] The process of educa-

1. Pride all too often impedes us from recognizing that what we have "found out for ourselves" constitutes but an infinitesimal part of our knowledge, almost all of which has been given to us by society. And indeed this is the more true the higher the state of knowledge in our society.

2. The rearing of children is the "investment" indispensable for the continuation of mankind. One may think of the preservation of the elders as the first "investment in progress" through the procuring of "memories."

tion, which occurs in any human group, embraces the acquisition not only of skills but also of moral notions. Pufendorf noted that if Man attained the fullness of his physical powers at the age of 18 months, he would be a wild and dangerous animal. It is thanks to the length of the tuition period that the innate force of the passions, which drive Man to progress, can be combined with an acquired mastery over these passions.

Men have been found living in tiny hordes of a few dozen souls with a specific dialect: it is easy to picture some such group manifesting a superior ability to ensure the survival of its offspring, thereby swelling its population. If it succeeds in keeping descendants together, its social organization becomes more complex, its language more elaborate,[3] and eventually it absorbs a number of less prolific groups.[4] Proficiency in the rearing of children must have been the first principle of political selection and social evolution.[5] While extensive rearing must have been in the distant past an essential condition of progress, intensive rearing is its permanent hallmark: we find the period of tuition longer as our eye moves from a lesser to a higher civilization, and within the latter as our eye moves up the social scale.[6] The more accomplished the human product sought, the longer its "period of production," the duration of Man's dependence. Individual pride should be dashed by recognition that only dependence has made us what we are.

---

3. Language is of course essential to any progress in co-operation and advancement of knowledge. The present dependence of advanced societies upon tangible means of communication is but a faint image of the general dependence of social development upon language.

4. Which may either be fully integrated or find themselves for some time in a position of social inferiority.

5. Cf. L. Krzywicki, *Primitive Society and Its Vital Statistics* (Warsaw, 1934).

6. A long period of tuition for all is now regarded as a goal of every advanced society.

Man is to be regarded as arising out of group protection and group tuition: but for the former he would not live, but for the latter he would not acquire the traits of humanity. Such obvious remarks should suffice to dispel the fantasy of Individual Man striding about in Nature and deciding deliberately to come to terms with his fellows. This is an intellectual monstrosity: it assumes a certain agent, full-grown and competent to fend for himself, while assuming away the conditions of his production. This agent freely joins forces with others: what forces? Those due to nurture within the social nest.

"Social contract" theories are views of childless men who must have forgotten their own childhood. Society is not founded like a club. One may ask how the hardy, roving adults pictured could imagine the advantages of the solidarity to be, had they not enjoyed the benefits of a solidarity in being throughout their growing period; or how they could feel bound by the mere exchange of promises, if the notion of obligation had not been built up within them by group existence.[7] Indeed the most ancient of contracts, the exchange of brides between two groups, is a commutative reception into the group: of the brides in person and of their kindred in principle.

Many intellectual delusions dissolve if one cleaves to the simple truth that we begin our lives as infants. Man is not born free but dependent. He does not renounce rights when entering into society but he owes his very existence and the features of his developed being to the fostering group. Instead of speaking of *homo sapiens* we should speak of *homo docilis*, who reaches a condition of more or less sapient manhood thanks to his unfolding within a primary social nest. Our claim to knowledge rests upon our ability to learn, far the greater part

---

7. The question "Why do men feel bound by their word?" is very properly raised by G. Davy, *La foi jurée* (Paris, 1922).

of which is a receptivity to teaching. It has been shown that chimpanzee and human infants, for some eighteen initial months, display much the same receptivity to teaching, after which such receptivity drops off sharply in the ape as compared with the human being.[8] Assume in the individual of the species a great talent for "finding out" but a low receptivity for registering what he is told about the "finding out" done by others: the species would then progress in knowledge far less than it would do with a lower individual talent and a considerable receptivity.

These points are obvious. But I find it useful to stress Man's dependence upon the social nest and his receptivity to teaching. The more so as I propose to deal with simple relationships between individuals.[9] I shall have no occasion then to underline that they are not independent atoms, therefore it is well to emphasize here that they are deeply rooted in social soil.

The infant is born into a humanized cosmos. The sharply unpleasant sensations of cold and hunger are relieved by human agency: the mother brings a rug or gives her breast. However little we know about the beginnings of awareness, there can be no doubt that the first "events" of which the infant grows aware are caused by human actions, though not recognized as such. One of our earliest steps in our exploration of the universe is to discover, behind an occurrence, a person: this being our earliest perception of cause, we long remain prone to identify the notion of cause with that of person, a trait often underlined in the case of primitive people.

8. Cf. W. N. and L. A. Kellogg, *The Ape and the Child* (New York, 1933). The question "What happens when you hit the limits of receptivity to teaching?" (which are now assumed to be much lower in some men than others), is raised by Sir George Thomson (*The Foreseeable Future*, Cambridge, 1955: "The future of the stupid").

9. From Part III onwards.

As the child has to be sheltered and is near-sighted, the screen of human actions which constitute his immediate environment is more important to him than what lies beyond. And therefore "the way things are" is first and foremost "the ways of our people." These ways form a pattern and constitute for the individual a "structured environment." If this individual later in life moves far away from the group within which he was reared, no matter where he moves, again he will inevitably find a structured environment. Just as the individual starts his life in a condition of dependence, he starts his operations in a previously structured environment. "Man is born dependent," "Man operates in a structured environment," have the force and value of axioms.

I find it much better to speak of a structured environment than of a society, not only because, in our day, any actual environment is much smaller and more specific than "society," but also because I am anxious to avoid the unwarranted personification implied in such expressions as "society and the individual." Society is what Leibniz called "a being formed by mental aggregation, owing its unity to our mind," [10] and if we want to see things clearly we had better think of a complex of people tied together by a pattern of behaviour. Such is the setting within which the individual man (henceforth called Ego) exercises his freedom.

That Man is free is an unquestionable axiom. "Is," not "should be": it is not here a legal right claimed but a natural datum acknowledged. Acknowledged by the tyrant himself when he throws fear in the balance of choice. Whenever we pray, advise, exhort or command a certain man to do (or not to do) a certain thing, we thereby acknowledge that the man can

---

10. Cf. *Correspondance de Leibniz avec Arnauld*, ed. George Le Roy (Paris, 1957, Lettre xx), pp. 168–69.

do this or not; otherwise our effort to influence him would be absurd. This simple proof of Man's freedom (a third axiom) implies a fourth axiom: that man is susceptible to promptings. Men forever inciting each other, with varying degrees of success, to actions desired by the prompter: that we shall find essential to Politics.

We may take as a fifth axiom that Man is forward-looking. The word "project" is formed from a verb (*proicio*) denoting the action of casting ahead: and indeed it is a casting of the mind into some future moment of time, where the imagination raises a picture which becomes a fixed point attracting our actions. Picture it as rope which the climber flings up to some outcrop towards which, when the rope has caught, he will haul himself. Developed and equipped by education, operating in a structured field, conceiving desirable goals and calling on his fellows to help him to their attainment—such is Political Man. These are trite remarks but necessary steps.

CHAPTER 2

Home

During his pre-natal months, Man is enclosed and protected in the maternal womb; thus also in his early years, he is enclosed and protected in the familial womb. Psychologists now tell us that the impressions received in Man's early years are far the most important. If so, the understanding of Political Man calls for the study of the attitudes acquired in childhood.

Parents give, the child receives. From parents to child, there is a downward flow of services and goods, without return. What the parents do for the child is not in fulfilment of a contract passed with it, or in expectation of a *quid pro quo*. At all times, in all societies, parents attend to and provide for their children, feed, protect and cherish them: any exception arouses scandal. Indeed the human being is never so diligently served as while he is incapable of "bargaining" or "standing up for his rights." Naturally, therefore, we carry over into our existence as grown men some remnant of the expectation to be liked, humoured and helped which was fostered in our childhood.

This expectation is overlooked in those pictures of society which seem to assume a club of celibates: here human relations are all bargaining, making and carrying out of contracts, observance of commutative justice. It seems forgotten that mankind could not go on if there were no giving; that the boon is more essential than the exchange.

No idea of a "return" due for the kindness received enters the child's mind. Proof of this assertion is easily adduced: if parents unwisely seek to foster such a notion, they surprise and antagonize the child.[1] He takes for granted the role of the parent. On the other hand he quite early begins to mimic that role in relation to some toy, pet, or younger child. He thus displays his ability to think himself into a part: the first which he tries out, that of mock-parent, is highly significant. It denotes that a non-circular flow of free services underlies in any society relations of exchange. The child will never "repay" his parents for the free gifts received from them, but will, in due time, provide similar boons to his offspring. The role of mock-parent, a shadow of things to come, is tried out very soon and then laid aside, to be resumed in earnest much later in life.

However useful it is that commutative justice should obtain between those who travel side by side in the stream of time, they could not have started on their journey without a waterfall of liberality at its origin, and they must in turn be the head of another waterfall of liberality. That is essential, and any view of society which does not bring it to the fore must be misleading.

As it is necessary that Man should at one stage of his life receive without returning, and at another stage give without a return, it is hardly surprising that his attitude towards his fellows should display traces of both his child-role and his parent-role, some expectation to be taken care of, and some disposition to take care of others. These two propensities are surely present in every one of us but in very different proportions. The role of parent implies taking care of a very few others: therefore it is not easy to impart to this propensity a very large span, and only a few tend to become "a tower of strength"

---

1. It seems that this mistake is made by parents, only when and if *quid pro quo* has been impressed upon them as the basic pattern of relations in society.

to many; while the habit of having one's needs attended to by others dies hard, and the demand for "protection" remains widespread in a generation of adults, an important political datum.

The child grows up in the shadow of towering adults. They have forces he lacks, the ability to do what he cannot.[2] Power properly means nothing other than ability to do. The adults who can do what the child cannot, have superior power. In his eyes, they are Great Powers. As such they are impressive: hence a propensity to obey them. I deny that the child's obedience is rooted in fear. An assured voice falling from a great height has a momentum of its own, without any implied threat. If a child has never suffered the infliction of the parent's strength, he does not imagine its being turned against him and, when this occurs, feels amazed.

There are of course huge differences in parental attitudes towards children, a matter of social fashion as well as of individual character. Anthropologists report attitudes far milder than those related by Latin authors. Xenophon's example has been too little followed: we need studies linking education to political *mores*.

But even where parental attitudes are far more repressive than we now like them to be, the Great Powers at whose feet the child plays are primarily helpful and beneficent.[3] The more so in the earliest childhood, since then the main figure is the mother. The Great Power is constantly available to remedy any difficulty experienced by the child. The infant places itself in real or fancied jeopardy, calls out, and is unfailingly rescued. This relationship persists as the child grows up.

2. The emphasis is upon "cannot": there is no question here of "may not."
3. Since this was written I have seen the interesting paper of Robert D. Hess and David Easton, "The Child's Changing Image of the President," *Public Opinion Quarterly*, vol. XXIV, winter 1960.

Indeed the very fact that the child survives and develops testifies to the protective efficiency of the Great Powers. Such experience accustoms Man-in-formation to regard Authority as accessible to his calls, prompt to intervene in his favour. However essential the difference between the superior power of the parent (which inheres in the person, is due to his being a fully developed adult) and the superior power of the governor (which is made up of the obedience of his equals in natural powers), the notion of an attentive, responsive, and helpful superior power tends to be transferred from one to the other. Such an expectation relative to Authority is satisfied much better, in adult life, by the "Boss" who "will take care of my problem," than by the magistrate who has no regard to persons and merely "follows the law." Those who dwarfed us when we were "small" proved accessible and helpful: this we expect as adults when we feel "weak" or "in trouble" from those who tower above us in positions of Authority.

Parents are naturally stronger and more knowledgeable than we are, and naturally inclined to procure our welfare. It is a great convenience for the government of men that we are prone to assume these same traits in our rulers, however often experience proves our assumption to be ill-founded (which usually leads to no more than a transfer of our expectation).

The child lives in a stable universe: this stability is diligently maintained by that shock-absorbing agency, the family group. No matter what waves hit the group, as far as possible the child's quiet pool is preserved from their impact. For the child a patch of certainty is secured in an uncertain world, and therefrom an expectation of continuing orderliness in human society.

The familiar formulation "law and order" reveals a juristic origin. A psychologist would no doubt emphasize that the notion of order is much prior to the idea of law. Order is what we expect; and laws are features thereof which we find it possible to pick out and express. In the sciences of Nature, of course, we proceed from a general postulate of order to the spelling out of some specific regular relations. Surely the first human laws were derived in the same manner.

Ask a child to describe "the ways of the home": if he can be induced to the intellectual feat implied, you will find that the result looks somewhat like the "Twelve Tables" of the Roman law. The child will have picked out the way some things are done "when they are done right." His statements could be pretentiously described as sociological observations restricted to favourable cases. It is very probable that the first laws formulated in human societies were of this kind, and probable moreover that the effort of formulation was made because of the accession of aliens who had to be told what the members of the group were aware of.

The contrast drawn by philosophers between the descriptive "laws of Nature" and the prescriptive "laws of the City" may be narrowed down, if we go back far enough. Primitive laws are simultaneously descriptive and prescriptive: "this is the way things *are* done by our *good* people, and *must* be done by *all*." Like the laws of Nature, they describe courses which have been observed; but the courses of men are not as uniform as those of Nature. The statement: "this is the way things are done by good people" of itself carries a strong suggestion, which may well suffice; but in times of perturbation, when Ego comes to doubt whether others will follow the "proper" course, the imperative intervenes to restore his confidence. Thus while primitive laws as well as the laws of Nature start as assertions of facts, in the case of the human law its purpose is not only to make the facts known, but to make them *more true:* or in other terms to combat the frequency of departure from the pattern stated.[4]

---

4. Therefore periods of legislative activity tend to occur in times of trouble.

The child needs a reliable environment. So, to a lesser degree, does the grown man. In the case of the child, there is an agency for the provision of a reliable environment: the enfolding family group. In the case of the man, reconciliation of reliability with freedom and change poses the most difficult problems of Politics.

Man appears within a family, and in time forms a family. But the family he forms as an adult is then only a special and privileged segment of his human contacts, while at the outset all his human contacts are within the family which fosters him. We are "home-made" and derive therefrom certain expectations concerning our relations with our fellows, which are more or less sharply disappointed when we move out of the home; their vigour is attested by our readiness to espouse the ideal of a nation-wide or world-wide family.

The urge to collectivism is present to some degree in most men, whether consciously or not, stemming from the experience of our childhood. The more definite its wording, the more clear it becomes that the picture is drawn from the model of the family. "One for all and all for one, from each according to his capacity, to each according to his needs": these are the "natural ways" of the home.

It is not my purpose here to discuss whether a social edifice comprising tens or hundreds of millions can be built on the same lines as one which comprises only a few individuals. Galileo's law should be kept in mind, stating that a structure, solid and serviceable at a given size, cannot stand if one seeks to reproduce it in a different order of size; that the much greater edifice has to be built on different lines.[5]

But it is relevant to note that primitivist nostalgia, widespread

5. Galileo's law is expressed in his *Discorsi e dimostrazioni matematiche, intorno à due scienze nuovi* . . . and is thoroughly discussed in that most admirable book by D'Arcy Wentworth Thompson, *On Growth and Form* (Cambridge, 2nd edition, 1942).

in classical literature and strikingly displayed by Rousseau, must be granted some factual foundation.[6] Very early societies comprising a few dozen members did have the character of "large families": the child growing up therein could look upon all elders as "uncles" or "aunts," and the playmates of his early years were the fellows of his manhood.[7] The man born into such a society, in fact, never "left home." The setting of his infancy was also that of his maturity, and the social lore of the household remained valid in the city. Under such conditions, the development of the individual did not proceed very far, but his affinity to his fellows was very strong. Surely the affinity between two persons taken at random in such a society is far stronger than between two persons taken at random in our modern society? Whatever the merits of the large, open, heterogeneous society, it bears the psychological handicap that *average* bilateral affinity is weak.

The material benefits afforded by a large society are conditional upon uprooting and mixing processes which thrust Ego into companies characterized by a low degree of mutual affinity. This is one of the main causes of the unease or anxiety which is so commonly attributed to modern man: the feeling indeed seems the more pronounced the more "advanced" the society. That Ego should find himself with uncongenial fellows is, given the conditions, the most probable situation, but not one to which Ego is condemned. The open society affords him opportunities of finding congenial associates, with whom he can achieve an affinity much higher in quality than that which is naturally given in the small, closed society. Dis-

6. On primitivism, cf. A. O. Lovejoy and G. Boas, *Primitivism and Related Ideas in Antiquity* (Baltimore, 1935) and G. Boas, *Essays on Primitivism and Related Ideas in the Middle Ages* (Baltimore, 1948).

7. An immense and entrancing literature exists on family relationships in *Naturvölker*. What I say here of "uncles" and "aunts" is of course a brutal simplification, but all that is needed for my purpose.

satisfaction with the haphazard cluster in which Ego finds himself and the eager search for more suitable companionship are basic attitudes which have their impact on the political plane: if inadequate harmony with one's given environment can be imputed to some specific institution, if the search for affinity can be channelled towards companionship-at-arms in a movement, important political phenomena are generated. It does not affect their generation that the military comradeship proves transitory and the removal of the institution incapable of establishing the desired harmony.

The child survives thanks to services which natural affection inspires. The grown man goes through life requiring affection, and is fortunate indeed if he obtains it from worthy persons whose expectations spur him on to achievements. Geniuses, it is said, can do without such a climate, not so ordinary men. We are affective creatures, and moved by our affections.

Working upon men's affections is characteristic of Politics. Followers are won, not hired. A man's services can be obtained in exchange for something which he wants, and this is basic to economic relationships. In that case the man does not want to do what he is doing, but he does it for the sake of a quite different desire of his own; therefore it is rational for him to pay the least possible price for what he wants. Political urging, on the other hand, is a stirring up of a man's own passions, and what he will then do in the direction suggested depends upon their vigour.

Man is capable of love, devotion, admiration, respect, resentment, fear, envy, anger, vengefulness, cruelty. His passions are essential to Politics, and therefore we are justified in drawing attention to their early shaping within the home. The development of the child should receive a great deal of attention from students of Politics — the form of adult activity wherein the traits of childish behaviour are best preserved.

CHAPTER 3

Otherdom

A "new boy" stands in the courtyard of the boarding-school to which his father has just brought him. He is lost in uncharted territory, among an alien people: he feels a solitary intruder in a strange cosmos, the parts of which have no name or meaning for him, and in which he has no place or significance. He is exposed to the queries, demands and commands of "the others" who, at first, appear to him as a many-voiced and many-limbed giant, unaccountable and over-powering. How can he single anything out, when behind so many surrounding windows are unknown rooms, and behind so many faces unknown characters? He perceives only an ancient, all-pervading and omnipotent presence to which he must bow. This subjective appraisal I denote by the expression: "Ego in Otherdom."

I could say that the child is an immigrant in an established society. But here I shun the latter term, because it suggests a form of knowledge which pertains to the observer, not to the subject. When we look down upon a human cluster from a position of intellectual vantage, when we treat it as an object of thought whereof we consider the fundamental structure, then what we hold under our eyes can properly be spoken of as a society. But the new boy enjoys no such detachment, can achieve no such masterful vision. From his humble point of entry, he gropes forward almost blindly, feels his way by methods akin to the sense of touch, venturing and then drawing back when he encounters a check. His knowledge, empirical and subjective, extends irregularly in different directions by reason of the contacts achieved: it is no more than a growing familiarity with certain places, paths, and persons. Society known in this manner, from the viewpoint of the individual experimentally coming to terms with it, I call Otherdom.

The word is so chosen as to convey the feeling, immanent in the knower's approach, that what he moves in is the realm of the others, wherein he is subject to the demands of the others. Which others? All the others, and this is the important point.

By one whose attention is focused upon government, a school may be described as a monarchic *Rechtsstaat*. Bound by fundamental laws and inspired by a more or less clear view of the benefits which should be afforded to the subjects, the Principal has legislative and judicial powers and is Chief Executive. His ministers in executive offices, whether his agents or junior partners, whether appointed by himself or by the same superior who appointed him, may as a Senate of Professors, or House of Lords, share to different degrees his decision-making, or simply assist him with their advice if and when sought. Whatever the various combinations possible in theory and practice, the Principal is the supreme authority within the school. And it is to him that the father entrusted his boy, to him that the father will utter whatever protest he may eventually feel inclined to make. Indeed the father feels that the boy has become, for a time and a purpose, a subject of a Master, owing obedience to the Principal's rules and decisions.

However suitable this may be as a formal definition of the child's situation, it utterly fails to convey his position as he experiences it. The child is exposed to pressures which are not, by any means, confined to the rules and commands of school authorities: requests and promptings proceed in far greater number from his fellows, who form a complex company, with its common customs, its rival clans, its competing leaders.

"Those first days [at school], like your first days in the army, were spent in a frantic endeavour to find out what you had to do."[1] Practically everything I wish to say is packed in that sentence. Awareness that there are things you have to do, ignorance as to what they are, fear of failing to do the right thing or of doing the wrong thing, extreme responsivity to directions, which makes you a ready prey for malicious misdirection,[2] incapacity to discriminate between the various promptings: indeed at this initial stage, any and every voice is deemed an expression of Otherdom's collective will.

The new boy painfully finds out that marching to this or that bidding has brought him under this or that fire, and instinctively seeks an equilibrium path[3] between pressures the diversity of which he comes to realize. Such a path is indeed very different from mere obedience to formal authority; and if the father has instructed the child to submit in all cases to established authority, the boy will find, by incurring the mockery

1. The sentence quoted is from C. S. Lewis, *Surprised by Joy* (p. 74 of the Fontana edition). In that beautiful book, two chapters, "Bloodery" and "Light and Shade," describe the encounter of the boy Lewis with the "tribe" of the Wyvern schoolboys. They constitute an entrancing anthropological analysis of "tribal" customs; but, even more to my point, they recount the experiences of "finding out," illustrating the approach here designated by the expression "Ego in Otherdom." While I can think of no more impressive treatment of the subject, I am aware that the theme "new boy at school" occurs in many works of literature. In our day of sociological studies, it would seem worthwhile to make a collection of such accounts, the comparison of which would yield lessons.

2. Cf. the misdirection by one Fribble in C. S. Lewis, *op. cit.*

3. A line of advance which presents such features that there is no sufficient reason to stray to its left or right.

and indignation of others, that this is not the optimal course, the tracing of which is altogether more complex. What to do, when, with whom, and how, is learned by a process of interaction with the collective, a process whereby the boy acquires a worldly prudence attuned to this specific Otherdom. Man finds himself similarly in a maze when he enters a profession, is recruited into a firm, is received in a military body, takes up a situation, is admitted to a club or into a circle. The new member of parliament is in no very different situation from the new boy at school: he hardly feels at once one of those who share equally in the existence of a body, rather he senses at first that he comes alone into an ancient and exacting presence. He stands before the Sphinx, doubting his ability to answer the riddles. Problems of behaviour in a new environment are indeed riddles to a newcomer, who is intimidated, ill at ease, and consequently sensitive, and easily resentful. He suspects that he may be making a false step, fears to be laughed at or penalized.

This feeling of being a solitary junior, exposed to ridiculous or disastrous mistakes,[4] affects even the elderly and more or less famous man who has just been elected to the French Academy. Every man is at some time, and maybe several times, a raw newcomer in a pre-existing company. Bonaparte himself was a bewildered "new boy" at Brienne, and one might mark out, in the career of this most forceful of men, successive critical moments when he had to find his bearings in new environments.

Each man begins operating within a field already settled, wherein he finds prior occupants, and an established complex of relations and manners. Such priority of Otherdom relatively to the individual should be remembered as the basic datum of political science.

4. Cf. Balzac, *Un début dans la vie*.

The psychological position of inferiority which I have stressed is not at all conveyed when one says that Ego becomes a member of "society." This word, borrowed from the juristic vocabulary, has retained juristic connotations which are misleading. Just as *socius* means a companion you have deliberately chosen, one with whom you have contracted an alliance, *societas* means an association you have entered upon by an explicit meeting of wills, a contract. Indeed jurists have commonly used the term society to designate, not only the situation arising from a given contract, but that very contract.[5] Thus when the complex of human relations had been (as I believe, unsuitably) designated by the name fitting a voluntary and terminable partnership, by a natural association of ideas it was assumed that a "social contract" must underlie it.

All this suggests an agreement reached by Ego on a footing of equality with all the other members figuring in the agreement, *ut singulis*. But if one insists upon thinking in terms of contract, the subjective impression of Ego is that he signs on the dotted line, as one weak, solitary party, subscribing willynilly to the conditions laid down by all the others together, which appear to him to make demands with the collective force of one powerful body. And while this is nothing but Ego's fancy, it is none the less operative.

If I may digress for a moment, the idea of social contract entered literature in the guise of what we would now call a government contract. In any political doctrine it is recognized that the ruled have obligations towards the rulers and the rulers obligations towards the ruled. This can be represented as an

---

5. Thus Domat: "La société est une convention entre deux ou plusieurs personnes" (Jean Domat, *Les loix civiles*, livre I, tit. VIII, sec. I: folio ed., Paris, 1735, p. 82). Thus Ferrière: "La société est un contrat du Droit des Gens . . ." (*Institutes . . .* avec des *Observations*, livre III, tit. XXVI, ed. Paris, 1701, vol. V, p. 144).

On the ambiguity of the word *société*, cf. my article on "Société: Contribution au dictionnaire des termes fondamentaux de la philosophie et de la pensée politique," *Revue internationale de philosophie*, no. 55 (1961), fasc. I.

implicit exchange of promises: indeed it can give rise to an explicit exchange of promises.[6] This view of things is quite advantageous to freedom since civil obedience to the governor is now conditional on his keeping the promise he made. Presumably it was in order to erase reference to a ruler that the idea was shifted to that of a contract of each with all: little did the liberty-minded authors of this shift suspect that thereby a commutative contract was changed to a leonine one. For I can break my contract with the ruler if he has not observed its clauses, but I cannot break off from "all the others" if I deem myself misused.

You can tell me that the social field in which I find myself has rules and customs which I would be foolhardy to infringe, that I shall arouse enmity if I show no deference to the values current therein, that I shall suffer if I do not meet the demands made upon me; that moreover I should cultivate my affection for my fellows and thus become chary of offending them; that I should also seek to understand what is established so that my conforming shall come from rational assent rather than from timorousness; but it is too much to tell me that I have of my own free will entered into an association with men most of whom I shall never know, and signed a contract rife with clauses which I can in fact discover only bit by bit. This is equivalent to producing an endless document in illegible

---

6. Sir Ernest Barker puts it very well: "Feudalism generally was a system of contract, under which each man could say to his lord: 'I will be to you faithful and true . . . *on condition that* you keep me as I am willing to deserve, and all that fulfil that our *agreement* was, when I to you submitted and chose your will' (*sic*). It was part of this general system of contract that the feudal king, at his coronation, entered into an explicit contract with his feudatories when he exchanged a coronation oath, pledging him on his side to good government, for their reciprocal oath of homage and fealty." (Introduction to *Social Contract* in the World's Classics edition.) Note the resemblance with the "contract" between leaders and militants in a party of today. If the leading team does not keep its promises in the judgement of some fraction of the militants they are justified in a withdrawal of their loyalty.

print to which my signature has been faked. Non-conformity thereby becomes forfeiture. My dependence upon all the others seems in itself enough to bind me down without the forging of my signature.

Indeed Otherdom encircles and constrains Ego. It can be sensed as more or less oppressive. Consider a mathematician thrown in with a company of horsemen: he feels baffled because he does not understand what he is told, because he lacks the skill to do what is expected of him; but these handicaps of unfamiliarity might perhaps be overcome; more fundamental is his lack of affinity with the company: he does not ardently desire to become a good horseman, has no respect for the values here prevailing, and is deeply offended by the spurning of his values. He might accept being laughed at during the period of clumsiness preceding his earning acceptance, but he cannot tolerate contemptuous rejection of what he holds dear.

Such a situation is quite common in advanced societies: it is inconceivable in a primitive society. Here is no sharp contrast between "home" and "otherdom": in fact here is no "Otherdom": the society wherein the adult will move is no more than the extension of the family which reared him. He is destined to live with his "peers": peers not in the narrow sense of different men with equal rights, but in the true deep sense of men with similar tastes and principles.[7]

7. Note that I need not "stand on my rights" when I am in a company of like-minded people. There, I cannot be eager to step forward when I have nothing to contribute, nor will my companions ever hold me back if I have something to contribute. As "mine" and "thine" do not matter in marriage except when divorce occurs, "rights" become valuable in proportion to the loss of affinity between Ego and his environment. Just as a man moving in deep water or in outer space needs an insulating suit to preserve his organism from an unfavourable environment, so does Ego, in similar social conditions, need the protective armour of his "rights." Indeed this train of thought leads to the suggestion that individuals are not in need of "equal" armour, but the more different the individual is from the environment the heavier the armour he must have. The "deviant" is smothered by pressure unless he obtains special protection.

Being thrown as an unknown into a company where one knows nobody and the manners of which one is unaccustomed to is an experience common to modern Man, but this never happens to the primitive. His birth has been noticed by a variety of kinsfolk and practically the whole village; as he begins to run around he accomplishes his "Grand Tour" of the human cosmos which is to be his life-setting. All his seniors participate, to different degrees, in his education, which is a continuous, informal process, teaching him to meet the actual situations of daily life, in his people's way. Here the cosmos of the adult is congruent with the cosmos of the child, the behaviour which will be expected of the adult is that which he has observed and mimicked as a child.

There is no call for any sudden and painful adjustment. Yet many societies of this kind have their *rites de passage*, ordeals and ceremonies of graduation, meant to note and consecrate the shifting of children into a teenage class and behaviour, or into an adult class and behaviour. The ceremonies deepen the awareness of the incumbents that a new behaviour is now demanded, the ordeals give them confidence in their ability to meet the standards of the superior age-group. Even though such primitive societies can be encompassed by the eye, even though their every child has from an early age known all the members and undergone a ceaseless process of acclimatization, it is deemed necessary to stress and play up the participant's change into higher gear. Surely this can be interpreted as a once-for-all process of adaptation. Nothing similar obtains in the various circles of complex modern society: the individual entering a new circle is expected to solve by himself the problem of adaptation, a long-drawn-out operation, which he often fails to complete successfully. Modern anthropology seems to confirm that the age of primitive societies was indeed the Golden Age, from the viewpoint of harmony between Ego and his social cosmos.

The situation of "Ego in Otherdom" has been experienced by every man to different degrees; the problem set to Ego, however different its form, is familiar to all; it has given rise to expressions of the widest currency: fitting in, feeling one's way, finding one's place, learning one's way around, or even learning how to get by. All these formulations denote getting used to Otherdom, coming to terms with it, a vital necessity for the individual; since indeed the all-important power in his life is Otherdom (not government).

Various individuals, introduced in a given environment, proceed in very different ways. I find it tempting to venture a rough classification of attitudes, based upon picturing Ego's approach to Otherdom, as a shape. The retiring Ego will assume that shape which subjects it to minimum pressure from Otherdom, filling up less social space than it might, in order to reduce its surface of contact to the minimum. Far the most frequent attitude will be that of the conforming Ego, taking that shape which fits readily into a prepared nook, as a new crystal adds itself to a crystalline structure. The opportunist Ego takes advantage of every cleft and opening in the structure of Otherdom, expanding through infiltration: it will occupy a maximum volume while accepting a strange shape. The solid Ego assumes its own shape coming into conflict with Otherdom; and finally the forceful Ego systematically undertakes modifications in the structure of Otherdom. The third type of conduct is favourable to advancement within an unchanged structure, the fourth and fifth types generate changes in the environment even if eventuating in personal failure.

Venturing further, one might suggest that different attitudes are different compounds of Ego's propensity to expand, and of Ego's propensity to escape pressures, possibly also of Ego's propensity to assume a specific shape. But such simplification is to be shunned when dealing with a situation which manifests human complexity. It takes the sensitivity of artists to do it justice. "Ego in Otherdom" constitutes the very essence of the modern novel. While the art of tragedy enlightens the political scientist because it displays the clash of characters in a moment of crisis, the art of the novel is no less enlightening because it displays the hero's total relationship with his environment. For our limited purpose, we may distinguish two schools of novelists. Authors such as Dostoevsky or Kafka bring out the loneliness and anxiety of the hero, the pressures exerted upon him by his contacts, the wounds he suffers in dealing with others. Other writers, foremost among them Balzac, describe the efforts made by Ego to establish himself successfully in Otherdom; in the latter case, it can be said that "the micropolicies of Ego" play a great part in the novel, often affording it its visible thread. Thus Balzac shows us Rastignac successfully upgrading himself in his new Parisian environment while another provincial, Rubempré, also launched in the great city, goes from initial success to final disaster. Stendhal leaves us in no doubt that his heroes are "micro-imperialists," following a Napoleonic archetype.

Such writers have offered us unforgettable pictures of individuals oppressed by the environment or swimming therein with vigorous opportunism. These pictures are essential to the understanding of political dispositions. Men who are ill at ease in an environment are susceptible to the offers of a patron who promises to fit them in or of a leader who proposes to pull down the edifice to which they remained alien and to build another more suitable.

The anxiety experienced by Ego when inducted in a new Otherdom is a global feeling impervious to analysis. But the outside observer can note the various factors which intervene eventually for its removal, and therefore *a contrario* assign a variety of causes for its initial existence.

Otherdom is bewildering to the freshman by its mere unfamiliarity. This is an environment about which he has no information, where events occur around him, and to him, in what seems a random manner. The pressures to which he is exposed come as surprises, so do the reactions evoked by his actions or attitudes. He has no store of precedents to draw upon, whereby he might say: "At this time, that. . . . Under such conditions, this. . . ." He has no key to the messages which reach him, can neither decipher them nor assign to them relative weights. Such a condition of no-information is intolerable and utterly paralysing: how can Ego do anything when he cannot at all foresee what will come of it? But such a condition does not last, the initial dizziness will be dispelled as Ego accumulates information, as noise turns into meaning, and movements fall into a pattern. Ego will come to know where he stands, and what is expected of him. Indeed it takes very little time to learn some paths and some routines.

The condition of such learning, be it noted, is that the environment should be reasonably stable. The newcomer would be "at sea" if the environment had no enduring consistence and regularity. Returning to our schoolboy, suppose that his classmates were changed every day, and the hours and places of classes, his bewilderment could not be overcome. This yields us one obvious remark: Ego requires an environment about which he can rapidly acquire reliable information, therefore an environment with a low degree of entropy.

This condition is of course fulfilled in a human cluster pervaded by routines. It is the less easily fulfilled the more the members of the cluster depart from routines. Whenever Alter departs from the course which Ego assigns to him on the basis of precedent, this is a perturbation in Ego's Otherdom. The stability of Otherdom, necessary to Ego, is made up of a general adherence of individuals to typical behaviours, the concatenation of which forms an environment capable of being known.

Let us fancy Ego shrunk to the size of an atom and projected into a world of atoms. Because their courses are random, Ego would have zero foresight, could never know what would come of any action of his, could not decide on any action; his will would be useless, and his consciousness merely a source of misery.[8]

I am inclined to stress this point because of late certain mathematicians have taken frequency of departure from predicted behavior as an index of freedom. It should be noted that, as the degree of such departure increases, the conditions of purposeful behaviour by Ego are impaired.[9] Therefore the more individuals may depart from predicted behaviour, the more necessary it is that "negentropic"[10] agencies, some moral, some concrete, should be at work, to maintain the reliability of Ego's environment.

Ego may learn about his Otherdom and still not like it. He now knows what is expected of him in his present position, but the obligations are to him painful. The "price" (e.g. attitudes, performances) which he must pay for being accepted in that position seems to him heavy. This does not imply that the price is "objectively" high: Alter, in the same position, may find that the attitudes and performances called for are no burden at all,

---

8. The idea is borrowed from Erwin Schrödinger, *What Is Life?* (Cambridge, 1948).

9. Any imaginative behaviour by Ego rests upon the assumption of routine behaviour by Alter, as can be illustrated by a simple tale. Daphnis and Chloe, living in somewhat distant homes, are wont to meet under a certain tree which stands in between. On a certain day, the ardent Daphnis starts early and decides to intercept Chloe on her way to the tree. But Chloe has also started early, and has wanted to deck herself with flowers; with this intention, she goes to the trysting-place by way of meadows where she picks flowers. Thus the boy languishes at his post on the path she has not taken, and the girl is desolate under the tree to which Daphnis has not come.

10. The term is borrowed from Léon Brillouin, *Science and Information Theory* (New York, 1956).

indeed he may enjoy them. Again Ego may feel that the perquisites of his present position are very unsatisfactory; he may look up to another position, which seems to him desirable. There is also a "price" (in achievements) required for the attainment of that preferred position: but this "price" he is unable to pay (let it be for instance, in a school, proficiency in some game). Ego then has both a feeling of being burdened and a sense of inferiority. This may go no further than generating unhappiness if Ego is unaware of other talents and subscribes to the values of Otherdom.[11] If aware of other talents which are badly priced in this environment, he may realize that his "terms of trade" with Otherdom are unfavourable, and hope for a change in the pricing system. He may be quite slow to pass from that merely wishful attitude to indignant rejection of the prevailing price system.

What I call the "price system" is very complex. Take Shakespeare's Coriolanus. His outstanding valour and generalship have qualified him for the highest distinction in Rome. But in order to attain the Consulate, there is a complementary requirement: let him bare his wounds in public; a braggart might enjoy such display, to Coriolanus it is demeaning. Let him ask his compatriots for the votes he feels due to his deserts.

11. No society could endure if, as is sometimes implicitly assumed, its members became hostile to it by reason of and in proportion to their lowly status within it. Should you so plan a society as to establish and maintain equality in every respect you can think of, there would naturally be a restoration of scarce, desirable positions, by nature attainable only by a minority. You can allot equal time to each member of an Assembly: but you cannot ensure that each will command equal attention. You can chase unequal (more or less log-normal) distributions out of one field after another: they will reappear in new fields. Nor are men so base as to be disaffected from any ordering in which they are low-placed: they are indeed lavish in the precedence they afford to those who excel in performances they value. What exasperates them is a system of qualifying values which seems to them scandalous, a social scaling which jars with their scoring cards.

Coriolanus. You know the cause, sir, of my standing here.
Third Citizen. We do, sir; *tell* us what hath brought you
   to it.
Coriolanus. Mine own desert. . . .

Coriolanus. Well then, I pray, your *price* o' th' consulship?
First Citizen. The price is, to ask it kindly.
Coriolanus. Kindly! Sir, I pray let me ha't: I have wounds to
   show you, which shall be yours in private. Your good voice,
   sir; what say you? . . .

Coriolanus. Rather than fool it so,
         Let the high office and the honour go
         To one that would do thus.[12]

It is not because he is denied the office, but because the price
which he is asked to pay seems to him scandalous, that Coriolanus revolts.

Nothing is more hackneyed nowadays than an attitude of
"revolt against society." This is no place to discuss its gradual
development, which seems to have coincided with the disso-
lution of hard-and-fast customary patterns of behaviour, to
have risen — a troublesome thought — with the very flexibility
of the social price system: as this moves under the free play of
many actions in society, it seems to evoke more protests. There
is of course no one "Big Person" called Society which can be
blamed for it; but such blames addressed to a mythological person are a standing invitation to use governmental powers for
the rationalization of the social price system, though of course
there can be no assurance that the system rationalized in any
one way would meet a diversity of complaints. Obviously public policies are of greater personal (as distinct from patriotic)

12. Act 2, scene 3.

concern in proportion as they are more involved in setting social prices.

I have left for the last the pleasantest part of this exploration of Otherdom. The new environment is one which is initially sensed as hostile, that is where Ego sees no friendly face. His making friends therein is the most important transfiguration of Otherdom. The "I and Thou" relationship[13] is Man's greatest boon under the sun,[14] and Sulla was much mistaken in calling himself *Felix* by reason of his successes, an adjective more suitable in the man rich in mutual affections. The formation of friendships is like the surging-up of hospitable islands in the open sea of Otherdom.

Few men have been so unfortunate as to have never experienced the intense happiness of communion. Those who have missed its most complete fulfilment in true marriage, who have not achieved enriching companionships, have at least glimpsed it in rough cordial partnerships such as those of war.

But the better the thing, the worse its caricature. The community which arises out of love or friendship cannot be contrived by decree, the intensive emotions which it is proposed to extend wear thin. Such is our hankering for union with our fellows that the less we achieve it in our daily commerce, the more we dream of "instituting" it at large — a dream which has proved to generate hate more often than harmony. Also, the network of well-wishers which naturally fosters the happiness of Ego, if used by him in furtherance of some eagerly sought prize, changes in character. The prize-seeker had better recruit a coalition on the basis of common interests or a shared passion, or a spoils-sharing covenant. Then, however, there is no

---

13. As beautifully described by Martin Buber in *I and Thou* and *Between Man and Man*.

14. Ecclesiastes ix. 9.

one-to-one linking, but a banding together: this is self-seeking in company.[15]

I have merely skimmed the surface of the "Ego in Otherdom" theme. This is enough for my purpose. As I plan to discuss Politics at the "micro" level of action of individual upon individuals, I deemed it necessary to stress at the outset that these individuals do not operate in a void, but are situated in an environment.

15. Cf. Martin Buber on conviviality in *Between Man and Man*, pp. 50–51 of Fontana edition.

————— PART III —————

Action: Instigation and Response

---------------- CHAPTER 1 ----------------

Instigation

I propose to consider the simple case of two men, one of whom prompts the other to perform a certain action. Throughout this discussion, A will stand for the speaker, B for the man spoken to, and H for the action suggested. First, A suggests to B the action H, and we call this an instigation; secondly, B performs H and we call it a compliance, or he does not and we call it a non-compliance. An instigation followed by compliance is called efficient, and inefficient if not so followed. That is all I want to deal with at present; but I hope to deal with it exhaustively, thereby laying the foundation for the analysis of complex situations.

This formulation brings the situation within the general class of the stimulus-and-response relationships. The statement made by A is a stimulus applied to the subject B, and to which the latter responds or fails to respond. It is assumed that the response is all or nothing.

It is important that nothing should be read into the foregoing exposition beyond what has been explicitly stated. It comes naturally to clothe in flesh the relation enunciated in abstract terms and to picture A as in some way "entitled" to obtain H, or as in some way enjoying some initial superiority over B. These are possible specifications of the situation studied; but the specifications may be quite opposite: the action called for by A may be a sheer favour which A craves from the superior power of B. Specifications will in time claim our attention, but they should be regarded as circumstantial additions to the formal relation.

For the sake of convenience we shall use the expression: "A tells B to do H": "telling," however, should be thought of as embracing all possible varieties of address from the bluntest bidding to the most humble entreaty. Indeed, the imperative "Come!" can just as well be aimed upwards, by a sinner imploring God, as downwards by a warder ordering a convict. "Give me" may refer to a pure grace as well as to an unquestionable claim. In order to clear the relation of any psychological associations, we would have to say: "That B should do H, is the suggestion of A, to which B responds or not." This very inelegant expression makes it plain that we are studying the relation between the suggestion of an action by one man and the performance of an action by another man.

It is obviously untrue that every A suggestion is followed by a B compliance; also it is obviously untrue that no A suggestion is ever followed by a B compliance. Thus faced with the problem: "There is an A suggestion, will there be a B compliance?" we can recognize it as a formal problem which acquires precise meaning only when A, H, and B are specified, and even then, as we shall see, the question can be answered with certainty only after the event. As a formal problem, ours can be met only with the formal answer: there is an unknown probability of response, ranging between nought and one, and which may be narrowed down by increasing knowledge of the specifications.

It is immediately apparent that the formal problem enunciated, while itself following the general pattern of the stimulus-and-response relationship, has a wide scope of its own, and embraces as special cases many problems commonly dealt with by political scientists. Take civil obedience: in our terms this is the response of the citizen (B) to what (H) he is told by the law-maker or the lawful authority (A). Take sedition: again in our terms, this is the response of the citizen (B) to what (H) he is told by the agitator (A). Surely it is an advantage of our treatment that situations which are fancied to be of different natures should fit into the same procedure of representation: civil obedience is the response of the Bs to the lawful As, sedition their response to other As, which implies lack of response to the former. Incidentally, such lack of response may arise if the lawful As demand an unlawful or inopportune H. But of this more anon.

The formulation offered embraces political relationships but also embraces relationships thought of as non-political. Bs, for instance, may be induced to strike, or simply to adopt a fashion. It is customary to set apart phenomena connected with the attribution and exercise of public authority, but I regard this practice as regrettable in so far as it leads to divorcing them from phenomena of the same character, lacking this connection. What we are engaged upon here is the understanding of some elementary human relations wherever they occur and in whatever context.

Some A suggestions obtain some B compliance. This we know full well from experience. Within a single day we often respond positively to the wants expressed by others, and others to ours. Let us imagine a human universe where no B would comply with any A suggestion: in such a case society could not exist. If I could never induce any other man to lend a hand to my purpose, indeed if I could never induce him to stay his hand when he might injure me, then the proximity of my fellows would afford me no services and offer only dangers. Nor could the resulting state of "war of all against all," linked to the deafness of each to each, be repaired by the institution of Government: since if no *B* complied to any *A*'s bidding, Government would command in vain; but moreover Government could not come into existence, as its very existence depends upon habitual compliance to its biddings. Indeed we cannot drive our imagination to conceive a universe of noncompliance: it would be empty of men, since nothing is more inherent in human nature than the give and take of bidding and compliance.

Here again I must stop to cleanse what is being discussed of undesirable psychological associations. Children, who are told what to do, commonly yearn for the time of life when, as they believe, they will not be told and indeed will tell others, which seems to them a grand thing. Children who have been unfortunate in their upbringing tend to associate compliance with humiliation and therefore attach to it a very unfavourable value judgement. Such childish dispositions are all too often carried through life, implying an inordinate appreciation of "telling" and an inordinate depreciation of "being told."

It seems therefore necessary to stress that the propensity to comply, far from being a sign of weakness, is the most excellent and essential social virtue, the condition and fount of every progress. While we shall say much about the instigator, I want it clearly understood that it is not the spirit of this work to build him up as the social hero. In fact the propensity to comply is a thing good in itself, while the instigation may be bad as well as good.[1]

Moreover it should be remembered that, in the relation between *A* and *B*, while the initiative lies with *A* (by definition),

---

1. If I say no more about this, the reason is that the present work does not deal with moral problems. If I say this much, the reason is that I mean to avoid any possible confusion of my methodological emphasis upon the instigator with "hero-worship," for which I have little sympathy.

the decision lies with B (also by definition). Therefore, while A enjoys a certain form of superiority over B in that the action H is that which A wants (thus what is in question is A's choice), B enjoys another form of superiority in that he may refuse to perform H (thus he holds A's satisfaction in his hands). Nor is B's power of refusal ever blotted out by attendant circumstances. These may be such that it is dangerous for B to refuse, but it is never impossible. Such attendant circumstances are anyhow "accidents" of the relationship; they are not part of its essence, which reduces to a suggestion advanced by A and giving rise to a choice by B. In short, the relation of A with B implies no assumption or connotation of inequality between the protagonists. On the other hand, the formulation does recognize a fact all too often ignored: that in all human relations, what occurs is the result of an initiative by a certain party.

Efficient instigation can be thought of in terms of the action H which results, or again in terms of the agreement reached by A and B. We have analysed the process into two stages: A speaks and B acts, and this breakdown is suitable to our purpose; indeed as we propose to conduct our investigation from the angle of the outside observer, who witnesses a stimulus and a response (or lack of response), it may be inadvisable to break down the process any further. But such further breakdown may serve to shed light upon the spirit of our inquiry. For that special object let us then distinguish four successive stages: A states what he desires, B understands it (receives the message), B agrees to it (sends a Yes signal), and finally B does it. This indicates that there is a moment of agreement between A and B, which follows upon A's initiative.

I regard it as regrettable that the time-sequence between initiative and agreement should so often be blurred or neglected in writings dealing with the social sciences. Consider a committee which reaches a unanimous decision; surely it is less realistic to regard such a unanimous decision as a single indivisible fact than to distribute the occurrences over time. First, a given member moved a resolution, then another one supported it, and unanimity was cumulatively reached: anyone experienced in such things will admit that unanimity in fact reached on a certain decision is no proof that a majority might not have been obtained for a quite different resolution if that had been advanced at the start of the meeting. I have been careful to stress that the relation between an A suggestion and a B response implies no subordination of B to A; what it does imply, however, is a time-sequence between the suggestion of H and its performance: it underlines the role of initiative. This underlining is useful in a day when people are prone to regard collective bodies as moving by themselves: any move of a collective body must originate in the suggestion of some real person.

The last four sections have been devoted to the dispelling of possible misunderstandings. They constitute nothing more than footnotes to the first section, and they would have been unnecessary had it been certain that the initial statements would be taken at face value. But it is not to be expected in the moral sciences. As they deal with ourselves, we find it difficult to follow an argument as dispassionately as if it dealt with angles or atoms. Indeed, in geometry itself some initial effort is called for to divorce the formal notion of line from our empirical knowledge of a stick. Incomparably greater is the effort needed to divorce the formal notion of a relation between suggestion and compliance from our experiences. Perhaps this effort will be lessened as Pure Politics comes to establish itself as a science (the difficulty seems to be overcome in Pure Economics), but in the meantime it must be taken into account, and this explains the many cautionary statements which have been made. Also this difficulty induces us to resort to concrete illustrations as far as possible. This we shall do to illustrate that capital feature of the "political animal," the propensity to comply.

I am driving along rapidly at night on a dark road. Ahead a flashlight is waved up and down. I do not know who is signalling or for what ulterior purpose: all I do know is that someone wants me to slow down or stop; immediately I brake, slow down, and prepare to stop abreast of the flashlight-wielder (note my initial compliance, his — X's — first suggestion has been efficient); now I reach him, receptive to his second, or elaborated, suggestion.

He may be a road-worker posted to apprise me and others of some obstruction on the way, and my slowing down may have been all he required of me. But he may also be a policeman requesting to see my papers, or he may be a stranded motorist hoping to borrow a tool he lacks, or again a tired hitch-hiker wanting a lift. I may be confronted with the victims of an accident needing transport to the nearest hospital, or with a group of roughnecks whom I may be fearful of letting into my car. Indeed, I may be ambushed. A quick judgement by sight may cause me to clamp down my foot upon the accelerator without even listening to the demand: but this will occur only if I am a very timorous man or if the danger is manifest. In most cases I shall stop and find out what the suggestion is. If I am dealing with a policeman, it is extremely improbable that I shall drive away; but it is no less improbable if I am dealing with casualties: in these two cases the motives for my compliance will be quite different but my compliance will be the same. Finally, if I am dealing with hitch-hikers, my response will depend very much upon their looks, and to some degree upon my haste and mood.

This tiny scene from life brings out some features of man as we know him. Ready to obey an imperative signal, he is willing to hear out what is demanded of him, and he is inclined to do it rather than not to do it. His decision will, of course, depend upon the circumstances and his character: but by itself the request exercises some pressure, which bids fair to be operative in the absence of strong motives to the contrary.

These features constitute or manifest what we call the propensity to compliance, which is to be thought of as a cardinal virtue of social man, since all services which man affords to man are derived from and dependent upon this disposition. As in the case of all virtues, its exercise calls for discrimination.

The suggestion-response pattern is, of course, an empty form which has to be filled in with concrete specifications. "How probable is it that B will perform the action H called for by A?": such a question becomes determinate only when we have substituted real terms in place of the signs. Let us illustrate this substitution. I find myself in a friend's office. His telephone rings: he unhooks the receiver, an automatic response to an imperative signal. I do not hear what the caller says but obviously he begins by stating who he is, and then goes on to state what he wants. From my friend's expression, I gather that he thinks highly of A, the caller, and is therefore favourably disposed towards the impending request before he has any knowledge of what it will be. But as the one-sided conversation proceeds, my friend's face grows troubled, and I infer that the suggestion is not to his liking. Finally, I hear him saying: "Well, I shall give it due consideration but I am afraid I will not be able to do it": which, of course, means "No." In this case the subject of the experiment has not responded.

The foregoing example offers a contrast of the *who* and of the *what* factors: the *who* factor militated in favour of compliance, but the *what* militated against: however receptive my friend was to the author of the proposition, its nature did not suit him. Had the action suited him, he would have complied, no matter how indifferent the instigator was to him. Had he been only mildly reluctant to perform the action, his friendly or respectful disposition towards the caller might have sufficed to overcome this reluctance. But in this case the reluctance was such that the prestige of A (whatever its nature) was powerless to sway B. If, however, my friend's reluctance is not very great, he may yet change his mind, if called upon by some other A who carries more weight with him than the first, or again by several As who do not individually carry more weight, but whose independent prestiges add up in some way towards the same outcome. Thus B's response is affected both by the nature of the proposition and the weight of authorship or, to put it more precisely, by his subjective valuations of the proposition itself and of its author.

The valuations are subjective: for different Bs the same A will carry more or less weight, and to different Bs the same H will seem more, or less, suitable. Moreover, different Bs will attach different degrees of importance to the authorship of a proposition as against its substance. This last point is clearly brought out in Shakespeare's *Julius Caesar*, the first two acts of which are the story of an instigation.

The action to be performed (H) is the murder of Caesar. Cassius is the instigator. He urges Brutus: Shakespeare makes it quite clear that the latter is not swayed by his regard for Cassius but by his growing conviction that the action proposed is becoming to Brutus. Brutus states at the outset the condition for his being moved: "If it be aught toward the public good...." Thus H will be performed by Brutus if and only if it is in itself an action he regards as suitable. This we may call a pure

H motivation, meaning that the response owes nothing to the identity of *A.* Such an attitude is most cleverly contrasted with that of Antony, who states: "When Caesar says 'do this' it is performed": this we may call a pure *A* motivation, meaning that the substance of *H* does not determine or affect *B*'s response, caused solely by the identity of *A.* The fellow-conspirators are represented as falling between these extreme attitudes: while inclined towards the murder, yet they need as a decisive touch that Brutus, instead of Cassius, should assume formally the role of instigator. In the great orchard scene, it is Brutus, not Cassius, who bids the others "Give me your hands all over": he has in fact taken over the part from Cassius, or rather Cassius has cast him for it. Why? Because Brutus enjoys a personal prestige which Cassius lacks. This prestige element is most unmistakably stressed when Casca explains the need for Brutus:

> O! he sits high in all the people's hearts;
> And that which would appear offence in us
> His countenance, like richest alchemy,
> Will change to virtue and to worthiness.

Thus, in time, Brutus will stand between the conspirators and the people, his "countenance" winning the latter to the belief that the murderers have done well. But even before this, the conspirators themselves will have drawn assurance from being able to regard Brutus, and not Cassius, as their leader.

Something is asked of me. Who asks it, and what is it? The chances of favourable response are compounded of the credit enjoyed in my eyes by *A*, and of the lure of *H*. But these two weights may be combined in different degrees according to my character. I may be prone, even as Antony in the foregoing quotation, to consider mostly who asks; or as Brutus, what is asked.

It is therefore tempting to form a class of those subjects which are the most impervious to the A factor and look only to the substance of the suggestion, regardless of its author. Such a classification is indeed operationally important. We must be careful, however, not to interpret it in terms of moral superiority. For the class thus formed will be morally heterogeneous. It contains men of strong convictions, indifferent to any personal prestige, and who consider solely whether the proposition fits in with their principles. But also it contains heedless fools, who scoff at their superiors in wisdom, and are ready to fall in with any suggestion which suits their whim or passion. Thus pure H motivation may be associated with extreme levity as well as with extreme austerity; it may lead to very different actions, or indeed to the same actions performed in a very different spirit: it is not unusual to find rogues allied with fanatics in seditious movements.

We do not want to delve into the motivations of responding subjects. It is enough to have pointed out that the probability of response, other things being equal, is a function of the subjective values set upon the author and the substance of the proposition, with different weights attached to these two valuations in the case of different subjects. Such valuations do not only vary from subject to subject but also from time to time, according to circumstances and indeed to moods. Thus there is always some degree of uncertainty about the response of a given man to a given proposal made by a given author. Masters of intrigue have ever boasted of their ability so to time a suggestion that it obtained a response while on any other day it might have misfired.

A moves B. In so simple a statement, B can stand for a stone just as well as for a man. And indeed it is important to mark that instigation is a "push." That B should move as a consequence of a "shove" from A is a phenomenon as fundamental to political science as it is to physics. But also it is important to mark the difference. The "force" which moves a stone is something objective and measurable, not so the "force" which moves a man. Indeed the seat of the force which moves me (a B subject in this instance) when I respond to the instigation of A, does not lie in A, it lies in me. Even if I perform the H action requested, not at all because I recognize it as suitable but merely because I am under the spell of A's prestige, still this prestige sways me only because it exists *for me*, because it is a subjective phenomenon within my imagination. It is vital to remember that "being moved" in the case of a human subject is indeed an *activity* of that subject.

In Racine's tragedy, the pleading of Esther results in a complete reversal of attitude on the part of King Ahasuerus towards the Jews. Should we say that this was due merely to the force inhering in Esther which would have produced the same effect whoever happened to sit on the throne of Ahasuerus? It seems obvious that the personality of Ahasuerus was decisive. In other words, response displays the personality and disposition of the subject.

Napoleon is admittedly one of the most outstanding examples of an impressive personality. On his adventurous return from Elba, he was confronted at Grenoble by a regiment sent to arrest him: he walked towards them alone and they rallied to him in a turmoil of enthusiasm: this is the sheer weight of personality operating; but is it? On the most decisive day of his career, when he seized power, the same man entered the council room of the Five Hundred, and instead of mustering the majority which had been carefully prepared, he was completely discountenanced and the situation had to be retrieved by his accomplices who ordered the soldiers into the room, a move which had not been foreseen as necessary.

There is no simpler (or more important) phenomenon in human relations than that A moves B. But the simplicity of the phenomenon should not induce us to assume the simplicity of the cause, to say that this follows from a quality inhering in A. When A moves B, this manifests a relationship which cannot be tracked down to a single factor. It is a simple event but should not be regarded as the outcome of a simple cause.

It is impossible to foretell that a given instigation will be efficient whoever the subject may be. Further it is impossible to predict with certainty that a given instigation will be efficient in the case of a given subject. Regarding the first point, great is the variety of our dispositions, which have deep roots in our individual past. The lasting impressions made by education and example, the habits contracted, the ingrained beliefs or prejudices, all these enter into our present individual disposition. *Operari sequitur esse:* we act, and react, according to our being, which is a creature of our past. In criminal cases, so much is made of the culprit's past that we need not labour the point. Conversely, we are haunted by images of proper, noble, admirable conduct, and such images can be quickened by present instigation.

When Napoleon presented himself to soldiers in 1815, they were moved by memories, personal or vicarious, of this great general leading the French army to victory, and their orders to seize him seemed absurd. When Bonaparte presented himself to the Five Hundred, even some who had been prepared to accept his accession to power suddenly saw him as Caesar and remembered their admiration for Brutus, which moved them against him.

This underlines the extreme importance of behavioural images implanted in minds favourable to the reception of certain instigations and unfavourable to the reception of others. Whatever one regards as good, it is certain that a "good" behavioural image implanted in the mind is to a "good" instigation almost what the fixed point is to the lever of Archimedes. Almost but not quite. There is a fluidity in our disposition which makes it impossible to predict the response of a given man however much we know about him. In dramatic circumstances, I sought to guess respective reactions to competing instigations in the case of men I knew very well and found myself with a poor score of good guesses.

We have been dealing with instigation-and-response in general. Let us now consider the additional circumstances of a prior commitment of *B*, relevant to the occasion. The simplest case is the following: *A* tells *B* to do *H*, and *B* had in fact previously promised the performance of *H*; obviously *B* is now in a situation quite different from that which would obtain if he were not committed. At this present moment I feel no inclination to perform *H*, nor does the prestige of *A* stand so high with me as to overcome my reluctance. In short, I would not respond to the instigation by itself; still I do perform *H*. My previous commitment can be regarded as the main cause of my action, or again it can be regarded as a reinforcing factor of the present instigation. This latter presentation, which fits into our model, is authorized by an illustration again borrowed from Shakespeare.

When the conspirators meet in Brutus' orchard, Cassius says: "And let us swear our resolution." Brutus retorts: "No, not an oath." Then he explains that if the motives were weak, then the potential performers might well need the spur of an oath: not so in this case. Incidentally he makes the important point that the necessity for an oath might prove the weakness of motives. Thus we are led to regard prior commitment as necessary in human relations to ensure the performance of an *H* action at some future time if it is now deemed that pure instigation may, at that point in the future, lack efficiency. In all societies it happens that A asks B to give his word, to swear an oath, in order to remedy the assumed future weakness of the A instigation.

No doubt what has just been said calls to the reader's mind the public authority which stands surety for commitments between private persons. And it is fitting that the first mention of the public authority in this work should occur in that context. For indeed it is an essential function of any public authority anywhere to hold men to their word. There is no simpler civil suit than that wherein A claims the execution of H by B, consequent to B's promise. But it is far from true that the public authority stands surety for every promise: Law looks to the form and content of the promise. Quite a number of promises are not legally binding, we feel bound by them none the less. An authentication of the promise which affords it the backing of the public authority is an additional surety; but the promise by itself is a bond. Hobbes, in my view, speaks of it all too lightly: "the bonds of words are too weak to bridle men's ambition, avarice, anger, and other passions, without the fear of some coercive power." [2] The bond may indeed, in many cases, prove too weak: but it is by no means negligible, and with some men it is an unbreakable chain: we have all heard of Regulus who, freed on parole by the Carthaginians, came back to deliver himself into their hands.

In fact, forgetting for the moment that some promises have the backing of the public authority, we may state that commitment by previous promise is a factor in the disposition of B at the time of his instigation by A: it belongs to the natural realm of relations between men.

---

2. *Leviathan*, part I, ch. 14 (p. 89 of the Oakeshott edition published by Basil Blackwell, Oxford, 1946).

The same may be true of a prior commitment different in kind; that is, a commitment to obey A. Assuredly no commitment of that nature can be so binding in fact that whatever A happens to demand, B will do it. Even when B has in a way delivered himself into the hands of A by submitting to a hypnotic trance, B will fail to respond to certain commands. But on the other hand, it is a fact of experience that men will feel bound to do certain things because of the allegiance they have promised to some A. This phenomenon is displayed in the conduct of members of Parliament who frequently vote against their own judgement upon request of the Party Whip. Commitment by allegiance reaches a frightening pitch within Communist parties. But within fortunately narrower limits it is a most common social phenomenon. The term of "loyalty to the organization" is current quite outside the field of Politics. It is generally invoked as a reinforcing factor in order to induce B to do something which he does not want to do, or indeed which he should not do; also it occurs when B seeks to justify in the eyes of others or in his own something he knows he should not have done.

Prior commitments may, of course, work against a given instigation just as they may work in its favour. Just as I may, however reluctantly, perform H because I have so promised, or comply with A's demand because I have given him my allegiance, also I may, however reluctantly, deny my compliance to an instigation because it conflicts with my previous promise or prior allegiance. In the latter situation, the instigation may or may not overcome the commitment. For instance, though their heart was with the Allies, the French soldiers in Syria during the last war resisted the appeal to join with the British because of their allegiance to the Government of Vichy. Conversely, in 1815 Marshal Ney, who had sworn allegiance to Louis XVIII, and indeed promised to bring back

Napoleon "in a cage," could not resist the Emperor's instigation and joined him.

The murder of Caesar served in this chapter as a concrete instance of the action H. For purposes of clarification, let us compare the murder of Clarence as described by Shakespeare in *King Richard III*. A brief quotation brings out the contrast:

> *Second Murderer.* Faith, some certain dregs of conscience are yet within me.
>
> *First Murderer.* Remember our reward when the deed's done.
>
> *Second Murderer.* Zounds, he dies: I had forgot the reward.
>
> *First Murderer.* Where's thy conscience now?
>
> *Second Murderer.* O, in the duke of Gloucester's purse.

These men are in no way like the associates of Cassius, who have been won over by him to regard their evil deed as good, who are now driven to it by their own consciences.[3] To them, Brutus can mention "the even virtue of our enterprise . . . the mettle of our spirits," and exclaim: "What need we any spur but our own cause?"

The murderers of Clarence have in no way espoused the cause of Gloucester. He wants Clarence to die, they want money; a bargain is struck, and carried out. The *quid pro quo* relationship between Gloucester and the murderers is utterly different from the relationship between Cassius and his partners. It would be absurd to deny the importance of *quid pro quo* relationships in the political realm, but no greater mistake, I feel, could be made than to regard them as essential to and characteristic of that realm. It is the "moving" achieved by Cassius which is typical of political action.

---

3. Cf. Pascal: "Jamais on ne fait le mal si pleinement et si gaiement que quand on le fait par conscience." (*Pensées*, vol. xxiv, p. 43.)

This is a basic chapter of a treatise on Politics. I deem it important to stress that no mention has been made of the State, of sovereignty, of the constitution or functions of public authority, of political obligation, etc. If some illustrations have been drawn from political history, for the sake of their force, what has been dealt with throughout is the relationship between private individuals. It has been outlined that men seek to move other men to certain actions, that we have a certain general disposition to respond, that our actual response depends upon our subjective impressions regarding the nature of the action suggested and the person of the instigator; that these impressions are in turn subject to our personality, shaped by our past and by our convictions; that some constraints are placed upon our response by our prior commitments relative to deeds or leaders. All this holds true in fields far wider than what is thought of as the realm of Politics.

In fact what is commonly thought of as Politics is merely a natural and necessary outgrowth of fundamentally political relations which spontaneously arise whenever men are brought together and thereby are given the opportunity to act upon one another. There is no difference in nature between social relations and political relations: it is just a matter of relations between men.

CHAPTER 2

Response

The man who speaks to others and carries them to the actions he desires: there is the man who makes history. Yes, but there is one who decides whether our "hero" shall indeed make history: it is the man spoken to.

The landing of William of Orange in 1688 might have been mere anecdote: response turned it into "the Glorious Revolution"; the landing of Bonnie Prince Charlie might have been "the Glorious Restoration": lack of response turned it into an anecdote. In the early twenties of the present century, Hitler met with initial failure where Mussolini had succeeded; and there was a time after the abortive *putsch* of November 1923 when Hitler's chances in Germany seemed weaker than those of a Blue Shirt leader in France called Georges Valois. Response to the latter, however, rapidly fell off, while response to Hitler, after lagging, soared.

Response, there is the king-maker:

> Your nobles will not hear you, but are gone
> To offer service to your enemy.[1]

They will not hear you, and there goes your might. For the might of man is not as the Lord's might, an indefeasible and

---

1. Shakespeare, *King John*, Act 5, scene 1.

permanent attribute: it is an ability to move others, and those others, by refusing to be moved, deny and destroy this might. The king's power seems a thing solid and heavy like a block of ice, but it is capable of running off like water and crystallizing elsewhere. A voice moved men and now it has lost its virtue while another is listened to.

The theme of shifting allegiance runs through Shakespeare's historical plays. The king calls his barons to meet a challenge, and as they shift to his challenger, so does the crown. The stripping away of the king's power by a cumulative process of desertions is most strikingly depicted in *King Richard II*. As Richard lands in Wales, he comforts himself against alarming news with the thought that all will respond to his voice:

> This earth shall have a feeling, and these stones
> Prove armed soldiers. . . .[2]

Yet when Salisbury greets him, the first exchange proves disquieting:

> *King.* Welcome, my lord: how far off lies your power?
> *Salisbury.* Nor near nor farther off, my gracious lord,
>   Than this weak arm . . .
>   For all the Welshmen . . .
>   Are gone to Bolingbroke.[3]

The melting away of the "power" which Salisbury had assembled for the king's service is the beginning of Richard's loss of support which moves him in despair to exclaim:

> Discharge my followers, let them hence away,
> From Richard's night, to Bolingbroke's fair day.[4]

2. *King Richard II*, Act 3, scene 2.
3. *Ibid.*
4. *Ibid.*

The use of the simple image "Richard's night," contrasted with "Bolingbroke's fair day," is most telling, coming only a scene after Richard's brave words, likening his own reappearance to that of the sun:

> So when this thief, this traitor, Bolingbroke,
> Who all this while hath revelled in the night,
> Whilst we were wand'ring with the antipodes,
> Shall see us rising in our throne the east,
> His treasons will sit blushing in his face,
> Not able to endure the sight of day. . . .[5]

The day was then Richard's attribute, and night Bolingbroke's. Now the images have been changed around. What has intervened to justify this change? The king's return has failed to dispel Bolingbroke's following, the king's call has failed to elicit response.

Response is a fact, a hard fact, a measurable fact. This the gardener makes clear to Richard's queen, meeting her distress with pity but her disbelief with sober explanation:

> In our lord's scale is nothing but himself,
> And some few vanities that make him light;
> But in the balance of great Bolingbroke,
> Besides himself, are all the English peers;
> And with that odds he weighs King Richard down.[6]

What a play for kings and rulers! How sharply it brings out the nature of power! It is precarious even as Salisbury's army:

> O, call back yesterday, bid time return,
> And thou shalt have twelve thousand fighting men!
> Today, today, unhappy day too late. . . .[7]

5. *Ibid.*
6. *Ibid.* scene 4.
7. *Ibid.* scene 2.

Let us descend from high tragedy to everyday life. The individual is exposed to suggestions, indeed to competing suggestions, he is called this way and that by different voices. The experience of such a situation is so common that writers have always drawn upon this experience in order to depict vividly the somewhat different situation of a man worried by an internal conflict: the man is represented as struggling against a temptation which is endowed allegorically with external existence, or as hearing out the debate between various motivations, again represented as external voices seeking to sway him. Thus the special case of a man in doubt is described in terms of the more general case of a man subject to different solicitations.

It is not suprising that the individual should be thus besieged. It could be otherwise only if man were useless and indifferent to his neighbour. In fact, as we well know, any Ego can improve his position and further his purpose if he succeeds in causing some change in the attitudes, actions, behaviours of other men. These he therefore naturally looks upon as "means," capable, if he sways them, of contributing to the achievement of his goal. There is almost no goal which Ego may set himself which does not depend for its attainment upon some connivance and contribution from some other men. The scope of Ego's project may be narrow or far-reaching; its character may be sordid or noble: in any case moving other men is a requisite. It would be unrealistically cynical to omit mentioning that Ego may indeed wish to alter other men's behaviour for their own good, but this can easily be fitted into the general picture if Ego's interest is thought of as anything he is interested in, ranging from his own personal advancement to the salvation of his brother's soul. What I wish to stress here is that everyone is naturally a target for beckoning messages.

It must be so since the individual is the ultimate source of energy. We are accustomed to contrast the might of large social bodies with the weakness of the individual: this is partly a delusion. It is no doubt true that even a rich individual's income is paltry compared to that of a giant corporation; but it is also true that the corporation's income depends upon the securing of a great many individual decisions to spend portions of individual incomes upon the wares offered by the corporation. It is even more true that any social might results from the spending of many individual energies in its service, and that the greatest human authority, if it ceases to obtain response, goes out like a candle.

The individual has the alternative of responding to a suggestion or failing to respond; when faced by several suggestions, he has the choice between them. In a very real sense he has the last word; but he is seldom aware of it and the less so the greater the number of individuals to whom the same prompting is simultaneously addressed. Obviously a motor-car manufacturer who responds to the suggestion of his research department that a certain new type of car be put into production is more conscious of making a decision important to others than the customer who decides whether to buy this new type or not. But ultimately the clearly important decision made by the manufacturer is validated or not validated by the apparently unimportant decisions made by the individual customers. In the same manner the most absolute ruler's decision to follow this rather than that advice is subject in the last resort to the test of compliance by the subjects.

Any historical relation must perforce be focused upon "prime movers" who have proved successful in generating streams of actions performed by many. Such concentration on heroes (in the loosest sense) is necessary to procure coherence. How futile it would be to write the history of the sixteenth century without mention of Luther or Calvin! For any deep understanding of the phenomena, however, it is indispensable to explore the dispositions obtaining in the social field, the given propensities to respond.

We may think of instigations as initial investments some of which are utterly lost while a few pay off fantastically. And the story of the former remains untold, while the success of the latter is to a considerable degree due to their harmony with propensities to respond.

People are apt to say that they keep their minds open to any suggestion: this is quite untrue, and fortunately so. If minds were indeed believed to be so wide open, they would be flooded with suggestions of all kinds and from all sources, which would so interfere with one another as to produce nothing but "noise." The human mind may be thought of as receiving, deciphering, appraising messages and deciding appropriate actions: obviously a given individual has a limited capacity of understanding messages, an even more limited capacity of appraisal and a still more limited capacity of taking action. Indeed we know from experience that while we are taking action in consequence of a message which has obtained our sanction, we cannot at the same time deliberate upon another without taking our mind off the action in progress, which leads to miscarriage. Nor can we, while deliberating upon a message received, ingest other messages without loss of concentration, resulting in an ill-considered decision. Moreover, our passing a judgement is made more difficult when our task is not merely to choose between "Yes" or "No" to a given suggestion, but to choose between a number of suggestions. It follows from these rough indications that our intake of messages must be limited. We are protected against an excessive influx of instigations by its being generally known that suggestions of a certain nature would be wasted upon us. The range of suggestions which have some chance of moving us is an important characteristic. We can regard it as a social characteristic that a certain suggestion at a given moment is likely to move only very few people in a given society; we can regard it as an individual characteristic that a given suggestion has but a slender chance of moving a certain person. We can think of patterns of responsiveness, and we can think of "vanishing points," forming the limit between the suggestion which will be accepted by some one person in a society or which has a minute chance of being accepted by one person, and the suggestion without any individual response in society or any chance of response from a given individual.

The foregoing paragraph covers a lot of ground very rapidly. This rapidity does not imply that the subject deserves no greater elaboration but rather that such elaboration calls for more work than we can perform at this stage or with our individual efforts. It is enough for our present purpose to introduce the notions of social and individual "patterns of responsiveness," which can be thought of as ordering suggestions according to probability of response, from one to zero. Suggestions with zero probability of response are those which will not even be considered, suggestions with probability of response equal to one will be acted upon automatically.

At both these extremes suggestions give no work of appraisal and decision, though suggestions which are automatically carried out do give work of another kind. The suggestions falling between these extremes, in the case of an individual, do give rise to an expenditure of time and attention; they are painful.

I attach great importance to the painfulness of decision-making. Decision-making is man's birthright but it is also a strain. There is no more honourable office than that of judge but this is no light task: every man sits as a judge, giving decisions in his inner court, previous to carrying out with his own forces his own sentence. The individual, like the judge, cannot ponder more than a few decisions in a given period of time and therefore it is of the utmost importance that the great majority of the solicitations reaching the individual should give occasion for no deliberation, classified outright in the class One, "to be performed automatically," or in the class Zero, "to be rejected without examination." Nor should one say that in such cases the individual does not manifest his freedom, for built-in criteria of immediate acceptance and refusal are part and parcel of his personality. In cases which call for a debate within our inner court, it is clear that our principles and habits are as helpful to us as law and precedent to the judge. As the judge leans on the law and precedent, so the individual upon the internal structure of his convictions and character.

A judge would be regarded as unworthy of the Bench if his successive verdicts were quite inconsequent, if he gave contrary decisions in similar cases, and denied today the principles he affirmed yesterday. In like manner an individual seems unreliable if his attitudes and actions display no coherence. Dealings with such a person should be avoided: he is, properly speaking, a man of no character, since our character consists precisely in the internal coherence of our behaviour. A man's character is what reconciles his freedom with the predictability of his actions by others. A man who acts according to his character surely acts freely; but also his action can be foreseen by another party who knows his character. Unfortunately the view has arisen in our day that a man's freedom is measured by the disappointment of other men's expectations: such a freedom is nothing but randomness. Each man's character is very much his own; it is not given once for all but grows up as the fruit of his confrontation with Otherdom and consultation with himself. But we do reasonably expect a man of a given society, of a given standing or occupying a given office, to display the character pertaining to this society, standing or office. Such expectation does not imply the individual's thraldom but his virile acceptance of obligations.

All this intervenes to narrow down the range of other men's doubts about a given person's actions, because it intervenes to narrow down that person's hesitations. Nevertheless, it would still be inconvenient for Ego to weigh each solicitation reaching him "on its merits" alone. This has formerly been called "pure H motivation." The difficulties attending it deserve to be stressed.

"Being totally destitute of all shadow of influence, natural or adventitious, I am very sure that, if my proposition were futile or dangerous, if it were weakly conceived, or improperly timed, there was nothing exterior to it, of power to awe, dazzle, or delude you."[8] The exordium of Burke, here quoted, neatly stresses the distinction we drew between the intrinsic appeal of a suggestion (the action, H, suggested has its own appeal), and the super-added appeal it owes to the regard one has for its author, either because of his personality (natural influence) or because of his position of office (adventitious influence).

Were the case such as Burke represents it with somewhat rhetorical modesty, the disposition of his hearers would owe nothing to his authorship, the proposition would be assessed "on its merits" alone: which of course means according to each several hearer's subjective assessment of the proposition's merits. Reverting to the terminology of the previous chapter, while it is the person A who tells the person B to perform the action H, the person B reacts according to his judgement of the action H, taking no account of the person A. At first sight this seems a superior sort of reaction to that which takes A into account.

8. Burke: Speech on "Conciliation with America" (22 March 1775), in *Works* (1808 edition, vol. III, p. 30).

Surely if I decide to do H solely because H seems good to me, the action is more my own than if I do it because it is a certain A who requests or recommends it: this seems very clear. But such apparent clarity is delusive.

Let us first take the problem at a low level, and assume that doing H or not doing it is simply a matter of expediency: for instance it is the problem of the banker deciding to grant or refuse a loan. If it be an unsecured loan with a purpose unspecified, obviously the grounds of acceptance or refusal are afforded by the banker's appraisal of the borrower's character and status; B's response in this case is entirely dependent upon his appreciation of A, not of H. Now let the loan be secured by a mortgage: in that case, the lender's decision will not be determined by the personality of the borrower, but it will be determined by the appraisal of the asset pledged: this appraisal, however, will be achieved by an appraiser; and therefore the banker will in fact grant the loan on the strength of the opinion of another man, the appraiser. Let us go one step further: this time the borrower is seeking funds to carry out a project and the banker will provide the funds only if he is convinced that the project is sound; thus it is only on the merits of H that the decision will be taken; but how will the banker make up his mind about the merits of the project? By seeking expert opinion, and therefore he will be acting on the strength of some other man's recommendation. We can analyse the last-mentioned operation in the following manner.

A_1 asks B to do H; B is determined to take no account of A_1 and to decide upon the merits of H alone; but in order to measure these merits he turns to A_2, an expert. Finally, therefore, he will grant the funds at the "secondary" instigation of A_2. Thus, in the banker's case, the idea of an autonomous appraisal of H dissolves upon examination: B's reaction may possibly be quite independent of any regard for A_1, but it is dependent upon his regard for A_2. From this simple illustration, two important conclusions can be derived: one is that "deciding a case upon its merits alone" may well mean in practice deciding it upon the surety of a third party's opinion, and by virtue of "secondary" authorship, while on the contrary he finds himself launched upon a difficult process if he feels that he cannot even trust to secondary authorship. This last point is most obvious in the case of the banker who could not perform his function if he had to investigate personally the prospects of each loan.

Let us now go to the other extreme: doing H or not is a matter of moral rightness. The action H is recommended to me by A_1; I am quite determined to do it only if it is right. But if I think highly of A_1's moral character, this constitutes in my mind a strong presumption that H is right. Assuming that this presumption fails to determine my decision, I shall naturally seek the advice of other persons whom I deem good judges of ethics. Is it true that by so doing I shall be shunning a personal decision? Not entirely so, since my choice of advisers is quite as personal as my acceptance of principles: my belief in these men as good men is part of my overall beliefs. If these A_2s agree that H should be done, their secondary instigations will reinforce the primary instigations of A_1 and I shall seldom withstand this combination. Note the basic assumptions that I think highly of A_1 and have chosen the A_2s: therefrom results a combined moral weight of primary and secondary authorships, or of authorship and guarantors; obviously there will be no such moral weight if the instigating A_1 inspires me with no respect and if the same is true of concurring A_2s intervening without my having called upon them. Take for instance Luther: he had first conceived a poor opinion of the high dignitaries of the Church in his day, as a consequence of which the coalition of their views against his carried little moral weight with him. The weight of the initial authorship and of the supporting sponsorship taken into account in our assessment of a proposition is, of course, a function of our subjective valuation of the primary and secondary authors.

I wish to concentrate upon the foregoing statement. I am requested to do H and this request originates with a certain A_1 while it may also be backed, more or less directly, by the surety of some A_2s. What has just been said is that the "authorship factor" will be meaningful to me in proportion to my subjective valuation of the authors, primary and secondary. It is a fact that my favourable valuation of the instigating A_1 (and eventually of the supporting A_2s) in itself lends weight to the suggestion. We are now discussing the axiom (or rather the pseudo-axiom) that the best way to make such a decision is to discount such weight: this is unnatural, the fact is that there is such a weight, subjectively assessed by me; but further, I shall show that it is irrational.

My being asked to do something about which there is in my mind an element of doubt poses a problem. To solve this problem I must bring into play all the elements at my disposal. I may find myself ill-equipped with means to assess the worth of the suggestion, while at the same time I find myself equipped with the knowledge (or belief) that the author of the suggestion (or a certain adviser to whom I may turn) is competent to pass judgement upon the merits of the suggestion. My assessment of these individuals is then part of my endowment for the solution of my problem and it makes no sense to forbid myself the use of this part of my means. Indeed, in the great majority of cases I shall find it necessary to trust my judgement of the judgement of other individuals. Consider the case in which I recognize that the chances of my making the wrong decision are equal to the chances of my making the right one; assume that therefore I decide to postpone my decision until I have considerably increased my chances of being right; but such improvement may take a good deal of time, and in most instances this will be practically equivalent to a "No" decision. But this has equal chances of being wrong, and therefore more chances of being wrong than the decision requested or recommended by a person to whose answer I assign a high probability of rightness.

Responding on grounds of authorship is the general and unavoidable practice of mankind. Intellectuals have a strong prejudice against it, which is understandable enough in view of our specific function which is to "make up our minds" on some definite problems, regardless of the effort expended and without any time limit. It would therefore be sheer treason on our part to take short cuts, while they are necessary whenever an immediate or near-immediate decision is wanted. But even in the case of our specific task, we take a great deal for granted on the authority of fellow-scholars.[9]

The word "Authority" has now been uttered. While the term has a great variety of meanings,[10] the simplest is that which is closely linked with the word "authorship": a statement is authoritative by virtue of the credit afforded to its particular author. Should *I* state that there can be a speed greater than that of light, I should provoke laughter; but should Professor Heisenberg say so, his authority would command world-wide attention. Requiring scientists to give an equal chance to the statement whatever its author would be quite unreasonable. It is widely believed that if statements were considered regardless of authorship, there would be more of a chance for novel truths; but this is a mistake. If every one of us assessed state-

9. Cf. Michael Polanyi, *Personal Knowledge* (Routledge, 1958), p. 217.
10. Cf. *Authority*, edited for the American Society of Political and Legal Philosophy by Carl J. Friedrich (Harvard Press, 1957).

ments on grounds of his own judgement, without regard to authority, the great majority of us would not believe that the sun is but one of the most minute of all stars: a statement which is part of our knowledge because we have accepted it from competent authorities. Our modern Age of Science is certainly not characterized by my critical examination of every statement offered to my belief, but on the contrary by my own uncritical acceptance of any statement vouched for by competent authorities.[11]

My mind is stocked with a great number of "is so" statements, of which no doubt some few are erroneous; but on the whole my wealth in "is so" statements is good and indeed necessary: I could not enjoy it if I never accepted an "is so" statement without checking it personally. Let me illustrate this: suppose that I refused to consume any drug until I had analysed it in my own laboratory, to take any food until I had tested its wholesomeness, etc. My life would be made impossible, and moreover the process is at some point self-contradictory: even if I do test everything, the means I shall use for testing are those which have been recommended to me by trustworthy authors; my checking of a given man's affirmation always at some stage implies my relying upon some other man's affirmation. It is entirely beyond my scope to dwell upon the deeper implications of "checking"; for my purpose it is sufficient to point out that any checking implies "costs" which may be so high as to make checking impossible. Our suspicious consumer might find himself starved out; in the same manner a suspicious learner would find himself very poor in knowledge.[12] In the case of "is so" statements, it is equally impossible for us to believe every statement and to

11. Cf. Polanyi, *op. cit. passim.*
12. Polanyi, *op. cit.*

check every statement: therefore, it is a vital necessity that we should accept a great many statements by reason of their source. It is just the same in the case of "should do" statements. Responding to every one is materially impossible; weighing the merits of each places upon us an unmanageable burden; therefore the criterion of authorship is extremely useful, indeed it is indispensable. I certainly do not mean that this is the sole criterion we apply or should apply in our choice of responses, but that it is and has to be a very important factor.

Prejudice and Authority are commonly contrasted with active individual choice. The relationship is in fact of considerable complexity. If, as I do, one regards active personal choice as the supreme manifestation of human dignity, then it follows that one must regard as good the conditions necessary to such activity. This is a costly one in terms of time and attention. Therefore it should not be frittered away on a great variety of objects. A man who carefully shops around to buy the most becoming and cheapest shirts does not thereby display an outstanding capacity for decision-making, but merely wastes decision-making energy on an unworthy object. I have summed up views which seem to me unquestionable, in the three following statements:

> Decision-making is the supreme manifestation of human dignity.
> Decision-making is an expenditure of energy.
> This energy should be wisely spent.

Of these three statements, the first is basic to modern western society, which has derived it from Christianity. When the human mind moved from regarding God as mighty to regarding him as good, the question arose: "Why, in his supreme

Goodness, has he allowed his children to stray into evil paths?" The question[13] can be answered only by postulating that he has willed them to determine themselves freely, that he has set a supreme value on their freedom. And this we all take over from theology. While the first statement made here is basic to western ethics, the second statement has attracted next to no attention. In modern society and thinking, decision-making is always dealt with as an enjoyable right, never as a painful task.

Indeed, there has been considerable acceptance of Gide's extreme view[14] that man's freedom is displayed to the utmost when he acts for no end and out of no motive other than to experience his freedom. While if we consult our own experience, we recognize that, when the occasion arises for us to make a decision, we find it a considerable strain to choose one which we can deem right, whether this "rightness" be one of morality or merely of expediency.

When engaged upon such a process of decision, I sit as a judge. And the more prone I am to make my own decisions on some cases, the more prone I must logically be to throw out of court other cases, to be settled outright on a basis of prejudice or authority. This seems to me quite obvious, but apparently the point has to be elaborated since I have never seen it mentioned. Surely attention is for every one of us a scarce commodity, and in order to devote the proper amount of attention to one question we must refuse our attention to other questions. It is an undesirable position to have to face a great number of questions, as anyone who has held a press conference can testify. Therefore, it may not be cowardice but husbandry to reject or accept without discussion many suggestions in order to concentrate upon those which one regards as justifying

13. The problem is raised most clearly in Bayle's *Dictionnaire* at the article "Pauliciens."

14. Gide's point is illustrated in his famous novel, *Les caves du Vatican*.

careful examination. Consider a man at a desk with a heavily loaded "In" tray: he will give himself most chances of dealing with the items which are both doubtful and important if he gets rid most rapidly of the items which are either not very important or not very doubtful. Indeed, he is a fortunate executive if his secretary does not even put into the tray those queries which by reason of their nature or source deserve acceptance or rejection. The part played by the secretary in this familiar scene is played by the unconscious or by the subconscious in our daily treatment of suggestions received. The choice of response to instigations is a process of decision-making: it falls under the general law of economy which applies to decision-making in general and which we shall deal with at another stage.

"Prejudice" is a word of ill-repute: but this is absurd; it merely means that we have some built-in principles by virtue of which some cases need not be brought up before our court of justice, as the decision of these cases is implicitly given by our principles. This spares us a lot of work, and it spares others who deal with us a lot of conjecture, it allows them to say: "No need to ask: B will refuse" or "If asked of B, it will be done." Again "Authority" is a word of ill-repute; but it takes on another colouring if it is thought of as the surety which B will accept when in doubt about an action.

PART IV

Authority: "Potestas" and "Potentia"

CHAPTER 1

On Being Heard

I wake up in an Arab town. Because inhabitants are tightly packed, I hear many voices; because I am idle, I am aware of them; and because I do not understand the language, my attention is not turned off by a feeling of indiscretion. Therefore I let the tones of voices play upon my mind. It is easy to tell that this voice is recounting events, these two are engaged in bargaining, while children at play near by are taunting each other. But now suddenly a voice is raised, immediately followed by a clatter of feet: in response to that voice, children have assembled. Somewhat later I notice that a discussion is warming up: voices wax loud and angry, others join in excitedly: then a new voice cuts in and the shouting abates. Thus in a short time I have observed, through sounds alone, the immediate efficiency of two voices: the voice which mustered and the voice which appeased. And it comes naturally to call them both "voices of authority."

Both manifest a phenomenon central to Politics: the pressure of words upon the behaviour of others. When the uttering of words by one affects the behaviour of many, this is objective proof that the words have weight. We know in general that if streams of activity are deflected by the intervention of a new factor, this factor effects work, which testifies to its energy. The working of words upon actions is the basic political action. Shakespeare exhibits it in the scene of Mark Antony's oration over Caesar's body: when the orator has done, his listeners move violently in the direction he has suggested; as Antony observes in an aside: "Now let it work. Mischief, thou art afoot."

The scene induces us to reflect that in this case the effect of the speech has gone very far beyond what Brutus expected when he allowed it; and surely Shakespeare meant this great reversal of the citizens' attitudes to come as a dramatic surprise to the public. It is profitable to distinguish the *ex post* observed efficiency of a speech from its *ex ante* expected efficiency. Now if we place ourselves in the *ex ante* position, as outside observers, we do not know what the speaker will say nor the manner of its expression. Therefore our surmise must be based upon the standing of the speaker relative to the audience. This is the initial "capital" with which he starts the operation which will prove more or less productive.

In this part of the treatise, the speaker's capital is the main theme. Obviously this capital is not "a thing in itself," it expresses the *ex ante* relation between the speaker and the audience. The word "capital" suggests an asset, but it should be clear that we are dealing with an intangible asset, which has the nature of a credit valid here and now. The same speaker, facing a different audience at the same moment, might there enjoy a very different credit; and he may in the same setting, over a period of time, increase or lose his credit.

This gives rise to no difficulty. What is difficult is the naming of this capital. The obvious name is "authority": but here we run into semantic difficulties.

I want to use the word "authority" to denote the position in which A finds himself in relation to Bs who "look up to him," "lend him their ears," have a strong propensity to comply with his bidding. This then is something which has dimensions: it has an extensive dimension: more or fewer people may look up to a given A; it also has an intensive dimension: any one of those who has this propensity towards A may have it to a greater or lesser degree. In either of these dimensions, the authority of A is capable of increase and decrease in the course of time.

This use of the word, however, conflicts with the usage of jurists. To them, Authority (I shall spell it with a capital whenever the word is taken in their sense) means the right to command, implying a corresponding duty to obey. Constitutional law delimits positions of Authority and their competence: that is, it seeks to dispel any uncertainty regarding the scope of control and also to narrow down the uses to which such control may be put. Whether a given B is susceptible to the authority of a given A (in my sense) is a matter of observation; not so in the case of a juristic Authority. If the position of a given A is known, then it is immediately known whether a given B lies within or without the field of exercise of this Authority. And no change in the persons occupying the position of Authority makes any difference to its extent. Moreover, though with a far lesser degree of uncertainty, the jurist at least seeks to draw a line between those actions which the person in Authority can demand with Authority and those he may not: of this more later.

Clearly Authority and authority are different concepts: Authority is, and in view of its salutary purpose must be, a static concept; how disastrous for society were the Authority of magistrates to vary ceaselessly! On the other hand authority is a dynamic concept called for to describe the actual process of Politics wherein personalities are forever gaining or losing in "stature" and "weight." I regret that I could not find two distinct words to denote the two distinct concepts.

Words generate deeds: their efficiency is enhanced if spoken with authority, but far more if uttered from a position of Authority. The difference is measurable. For some charitable purpose, an appeal is launched by a group of people who are highly thought of and looked up to: the funds thus raised are minute by comparison with the proceeds of a tax levied for the same purpose by the Authorities. Or suppose that the best medical authorities urge vaccination: the response is by no means equivalent to that obtained when vaccination is required by Authority.

Therefore men who want to generate deeds naturally seek to climb upon existing platforms of Authority from which their words will fall with the momentum imparted by the high place. If successful in such climbing, they will then find it easy to obtain what their bare authority could not have achieved.

And what is needed in order to gain a footing on the existing platform? Let us suppose that this position is filled by the choice of the people. Then our candidate is in fact seeking to move for his election the very same agents whom he feels he cannot move by his bare utterances to the deeds he has in mind. But moving them towards his election is an altogether lighter task. *Ex hypothesi* the position exists, is open, has to be filled. All our candidate needs to win it, is to be preferred to his competitors. His credit with his fellow-citizens must be somewhat greater than that of his rivals. In other words while his authority is quite inadequate to make the people do what he advocates while he remains on a level with them, it is adequate to raise him to the position from which he can command what he has in mind.

Let us take the analysis a step further. Our man is not alone on the platform of command, but a member of a deciding "college." This college has to make decisions: in the deciding process our man can prevail if he has some superiority of authority in the eyes of his colleagues. The important word throughout this description is "some." At the outset our man lacked the weight of authority necessary to generate the deeds he had in mind. Finally he does generate them, thanks to the powers of established Authority, and to succeed therein, all that he needed was a margin of authority over his competitors for the office and then his colleagues in the office.

To illustrate, here is a legislator who has attached his name to a bill prescribing certain behaviour. This behaviour he could not have obtained in his private capacity, not even in his own constituency, not even of all those who have given him their votes. The system of established Authority has proved a formidable multiplier of his will. A system of established Authority can be characterized by the disproportion of the results obtained with the personal authority of the men who operate it. Indeed, I shall have occasion to note[1] that the "authority" required to work one's way up within the system is not only much less than that which would be necessary for direct compliance, but also may be different in kind.

A system of well-established Authority can be run by men of mediocre authority: indeed, I would be tempted to stress that it requires such men, because its multiplier effect is so great as to make it very dangerous in the hands of a man with huge personal authority. It is therefore not unreasonable that there should be a tendency to recruit, into anciently established systems of Authority, individuals with decreasing ability to move people on their own account. But in time this slowly rots the collective Authority of the system, while on the other hand competing authority rears its head outside the system: these combined phenomena finally result in a violent change.

1. Part IV, ch. 3.

The wealth of relationships existing in a society sustains or gives rise to a diversity of authorities. In societies where family ramifications are of great account, the head of a *gens* speaks with great effect when addressing his own clan, and therefore is also listened to with deference when addressing others. Even where the gentilic organization has utterly disappeared, inherited name (e.g. "Roosevelt" in America) can lend a great deal of weight to a speaker. Also, even where religion has been shifted from its central place in Society, an eminent position in a religious hierarchy, which carries great weight with the faithful, also carries some with others. The authorities which have been quoted can be called "subsisting authorities," bound to ancient institutions, and the hearing which they procure is in fact due to established position. Though such positions are of non-governmental character, because the hearing is here assured by reason of place, as in the case of Authorities, I feel inclined to say that here we have not so much "authority" as "quasi-Authority."

What I am concerned to stress here is the contrast between the claim to compliance attached to a given position and the current accumulation of propensities to comply achieved by a man who gradually builds up his credit. In the latter case, we have a phenomenon of "emergent authority."[2]

The building up of authority outside the framework of Authorities can be exemplified by the trade-union movement in the nineteenth century. The first union leaders were not men who sought preference over competitors to fill established positions of Authority. They were men who slowly, by a laborious

---

2. Cases can be cited (e.g. Archbishop Makarios of Cyprus) where such "emergent authority" has been built from the starting-point of a "quasi-Authority." But the case is rare rather than frequent.

process, induced their fellows to an unfamiliar mode of action. Let us follow a founder in his promoting process.

The promoter is a working man respected by his fellows: he broaches his project to those who are closest to him, and as they are persuaded, his status rises in their eyes. In turn, they spread the idea, and as it becomes clear that they cluster around him, this makes him more important in the eyes of those who are successively approached. His first associates are his lieutenants who also form his council. Here is the beginning of a political structure.

Progress must be considerable before a meeting is called. This meeting can be regarded as the equivalent of the initial coming together for the foundation of a commonwealth, in Hobbes and Rousseau. But how different is reality from theory! In theory the meeting is the beginning of everything: not so in reality. How could the meeting even occur if contrivers had not set a place, date and hour? How could it be attended, if the contrivers had not worked to arouse curiosity and interest? What chances of success would it have, if the contrivers had not, by conversations with the men one by one, prepared a disposition which is now to be displayed collectively? Further, however successful the meeting may be, it certainly does not result, as both Hobbes and Rousseau postulated, in a once-for-all commitment of each to behave as subjects to all, in a giving up of individual rights henceforth entrusted to all (Rousseau) or to some (Hobbes). The best that can be hoped for is that a feeling of solidarity is generated, and regard for the promoter enhanced. It is a good meeting if, at its end, the members of the audience are disposed in greater proportion and to a greater degree than before to act upon the word of the promoter: that is, if his authority has increased extensively and intensively.

But the crucial moment will come with the first strike. If it ends in disastrous defeat, the authority of the leader will be impaired or destroyed. If the latter the body will cease to exist: for it has not as yet acquired any durable consistency; it is his creation, and disappears with his authority. If on the contrary the strike can in any way be regarded as a victory, then the authority of the leader is increased and the body acquires more consistency. In time the body will come to acquire the character of an institution. When its leader disappears, the union endures and there is now an established position to be filled. Someone has to be preferred for the filling of that position: it may be one who could not have built the institution, though the contrast is not apt to be sharp at the first succession: it will become sharper in the succeeding choices.

As displayed in the foregoing example, the promoter owes what authority he enjoys to his own efforts: he has proved a valiant, wise, trustworthy leader, and over the years an increasing number of people have looked to him with increasing respect and confidence. The propensities to comply which he can count upon at any given moment are those he has earned up to that moment. If they are thought of as a capital, this capital is the fruit of his labours.

Different indeed is the case of the man who accedes to a preexisting position of Authority. The compliance he can expect is addressed not to him but to the position he occupies: any other occupant would be entitled to the same homage of deference and tribute of obedience. This latter point has been stressed with bitter derision by Shakespeare:

> Lear. What! Art mad? A man may see how this world goes with
> no eyes. Look with thine ears: see how yond justice rails upon
> yond simple thief. Hark in thine ear: change places and,

handy-dandy, which is the justice, which is the thief? Thou
hast seen a farmer's dog bark at a beggar?
Gloucester. Ay, sir.
Lear. And the creature run from the cur? there thou mightst
behold the great image of authority—a dog's obeyed in
office.

Harsh words these. While here it is a dethroned king who
realizes with amazement that all the weight of his utterance
has passed away with his crown and robe, the "dog-in-office"
judgement comes more naturally to a man of self-made authority who is shocked to find that the mere donning of a
mantle immediately affords the wearer a far greater hearing
than he himself has gained by persistent labours.

He is like a struggling *entrepreneur* who feels at the same
time more deserving and less favourably placed than a *rentier.*
These two expressions, borrowed from another field, seem suitable here. I shall indeed make much of the concepts of *political entrepreneurship* and *political enterprise.* Political entrepreneurship I have defined elsewhere[3] as "the activity which
tends to the banding and bunching of men in order to create a
force capable of exerting pressure upon a social field, large or
small." No more need be said about it at present. What I propose to stress here is not only the difference of position between the political *entrepreneur* and the political *rentier,* but,
further, the mutual antipathy which must normally reign between them.

It has been pointed out that the *entrepreneur* is prone to regard the occupant of a pre-existing Authority with feelings of
envy and more or less pronounced contempt. In turn the man
installed in an established position is apt to regard "the new

3. In my paper "Thoughts on a Theory of Political Enterprise," *University of De-
troit Law Journal,* vol. XXXVI, no. 2, December 1958.

force" built by this *parvenu* as a threat. It is a threat to the man-in-office whatever the nature of the "new force." Three possibilities can be shortly considered. In the first case, the new force has an extra-governmental purpose (e.g. a trade union): then it is disturbing to the man-in-office as a molehill which arises in the social field and poses new and possibly troublesome problems. In the second case, the new force is designed for legitimate operations within the established political structure (e.g. a new party): it is aimed at the conquest of existing political strongholds, positions of legitimate Authority; thereby it threatens the tenure of present occupants. In the third case, the new force is of a revolutionary character. It is aimed not at piecemeal conquest of existing political strongholds within accepted rules of the game, but thrown against the whole fabric of the political establishment to bring it down and with it many or most established positions of a social, non-governmental, complexion.

This is meant as a suggestive, not an exhaustive, enumeration. What is suggested is that entrepreneurship offers a challenge to existing Authorities in more ways than one. It seems to me that political science has been prone to consider only what figures above as the second case (e.g. legitimate competition for established offices), eliminating the first category not as unimportant but as falling outside the realm of Politics narrowly defined (i.e. government), and eliminating the third category again not as unimportant but as scandalous, monstrous. . . . No doubt! But surely not to be disregarded in fact.

Established positions of Authority are strongholds controlling the surrounding countryside. Their occupants have some psychological dispositions which are required of them by the very office. They must want the fort to endure and to control the vicinity: this follows from their being its entitled custodians.

Wanting this, they must regard with anxiety any ganging-up which occurs in bush-country, and constitutes a separate company escaping their control. This they have to suspect even if the purpose of the group is not aggressive in respect to their position, if its purpose is quite different from the taking-over of the citadel: the distinctive grouping and the distinct authority are a sort of defiance. The case is much worse if the avowed purpose of the bush-rangers is to assault the citadel, if they propose to raze it and set up something utterly different.

In the former case, it pertains to the duties of office to get the outlying group under control, chartering it maybe if its purpose can be approved. In the latter case it pertains to the duties of office to break up the bush-rangers.

In the framework of democratic institutions, there is a duty incumbent upon the holders of the citadel to permit the operations of an outlying group which proposes to lay siege to the stronghold according to well-established rules of "political siege," it being understood that if the besiegers win, there is no more to be feared from them than the turning out of the present commander and his supersession by the commander of the attacking force.

This is the political equivalent of the courteous, formal and humane war of siege practised in the eighteenth century. These practices which so happily kept down the violence of conflict did not endure for any length of time, and those who elegantly persisted in them went down to defeat before the roughness of the revolutionary and Napoleonic armies.

In time, emergent authority always wins, and its victory goes far beyond a mere replacement of personnel within established positions. Established positions of Authority are the shells generated, captured, extended, destroyed and replaced by the play of political enterprise. History is a museum of broken shells and a workshop of new forms.

The ground which has been covered in this chapter requires more careful exploration of its several areas: but it seemed necessary to take a somewhat panoramic view, in order to stress the importance of emergent authority, the active force in Politics. It may also be useful to deal briefly with a frequent delusion according to which a state of affairs could exist, characterized by the absence of any authority besides established Authorities.

The reasons which render such a state of affairs desirable in the eyes of many involve major ethical issues which I do not propose to discuss here. I address myself merely to the problem of practicability.

There are two ways of achieving a situation wherein there is no authority besides established Authority: one is to discourage and prevent the formation of any authority within the social field; the other is to recruit into the structure of established Authorities any authority which does assert itself upon the social field. Not only is the first course objectionable, but also it involves all the practical difficulties of suppression. The second course seems at the same time far more desirable and far more feasible. At first sight it appears obvious that a system of direct suffrage which calls those subject to a given position of authority to choose its holder[4] must result in the attribution of each position of legal command to the man who *ex ante* commanded the most attention.

Many reasons, however, intervene to balk this result. One of them can be expounded as follows. Cleaving to a leader implies an intensive assent; the majority choice of a man to fill a given position implies an extensive preference. Extensive preference often works in favour of a man incapable of arousing

4. Note that modern democracies fall far short of this supposition, which would for instance imply the election of military officers by their own soldiers.

intensive assent. By definition followers are willing to do a great deal at the call of their leader. Electors on the other hand may well, in picking the occupant of a position from which much can be demanded of them, choose a candidate whom they judge likely to demand little.

A trivial comparison may perhaps cast some light on the subject. A great number of investors have most of their funds tied up, whether they like it or not, in a vast investment fund, and are called upon to choose its manager. Some few of them have enthusiastic confidence in a bold Primus whose advice they follow in the handling of their free funds and whom they would like to put in control of the great fund. But most of the investors are frightened of this daring fellow and their choice will in fact lie between two less colourful personalities, Secundus and Tertius: let the winner be Secundus. After some time, it appears that the management of Secundus has been poor and that the followers of Primus have done well: the prestige of Primus will rise in the eyes of many: an increasing number will abide by his word in the management of their free funds; the discrepancy between established Authority and authority will become extensive.

Even though this example is deplorably trivial, it can serve to introduce another element of the situation. It is improbable that the unorthodox Primus will even find it possible to stand for the position of manager. In the case of any well-established positions of Authority, however open the electoral process may be in principle, there is always some degree of control exercised by "insiders," which in effect screens the candidate. Thus Primus may not only be unable to muster a majority if he stands, he may also be unable to stand.

Therefore, even in a system which would seem likely to fill positions of Authority with the men of most authority, there is a discrepancy, which perhaps tends to become more pronounced as the system ages. It is not our business here to discuss current institutions,[5] but the theory of Politics. What was germane to this purpose was to stress the distinction between established Authority and emergent authority, to underline the great importance of the latter and to show that the two things do not regularly merge, and that they therefore give rise to tensions more or less pronounced at different moments.

5. If we did that, we should have to discuss the new trend towards the choice of a Chief Magistrate with considerable personal authority, and the resulting change in the balance of legal powers.

The Law of
Conservative Exclusion

Instigation was discussed in part III. We posited the "radical" [1] of political action: "A tells B to do H"; and pointed out that the reaction of B is uncertain (which can be signified by writing ABH?), and that the probability of its being positive is a function, on the one hand of his positive appreciation of H, on the other of his positive valuation of A. Now in part IV, attention is focused upon the reinforcing factor of A's speech constituted by his position of relative authority in respect of B (which can be denoted by $A!B$), a relation which can arise from A's occupation of a position of established Authority, or more simply from his having built up, accumulated, some propensity towards compliance on the part of B: authority *simpliciter*.

As we have ever lived in the shadow of established Authority, it seemed necessary to stress that simple authority is a ubiquitous, dynamic and logically prior phenomenon. At the end of the last chapter it was shown briefly that a state of affairs where there exists no authority besides established Authority cannot

---

1. I am anxious that the reader should bear in mind that the relation referred to is "cut out" by intellectual analysis, from complex situations wherein it figures as a basic component. It seems to me that this character is properly denoted by the term "radical," which for that reason I persist in using, although advised that it lacks elegance.

be achieved. Here it will be formally proved that a state of affairs where there would be no established Authority would be intolerable. For this demonstration, we shall assume such a state of affairs at the outset, and from its consideration the necessity of some established Authority will be made clear. Such a demonstration may seem redundant. Almost no one is a consistent anarchist, pursues to its logical conclusion the belief that there should be no command: practically all men take for granted that there must be some pronouncements binding upon everyone. But the very function of a "theory of politics" is to substitute for a hazy awareness an articulated edifice of sharply defined and logically dovetailed notions.

If we clearly perceive how the necessity of command arises from the facts, this will cast light upon the disputes concerning the scope of command. That will become apparent as we proceed.

I shall here take as my starting-point an objection which has been raised against my taking "A tells B to do H" as the radical of political action. It is an objection which I regard with great respect, as coming from excellent minds. Meeting it at this point is not at all out of place, since its discussion will lead us straight into the heart of the subject of Authority.

The objection can be formulated as follows: "What you are doing in this work is discussing in general the moving of man by man, or the attempt to do so. You claim that such a call to move is a very general phenomenon in human relations, and this is not to be denied. But it is too general: calls to move are present throughout the social life of men, and far the greater part of them can, by no stretch of the imagination, be regarded as pertaining to Politics."

I do not deny, on the contrary I affirm, the obvious: that this moving of man by man occurs everywhere within the social field; and I readily acknowledge that far the greater part of such activity is not commonly thought of as "political." What I hold is that a more dynamic understanding of what is commonly recognized as Politics is obtained if this moving of man by man is defined as the elemental, basic political action. The very objection which I encounter will serve to demonstrate that my definition of political action provides a high road of entry into the problems which are generally acknowledged to lie in the field of Politics.

The objection is rooted in the fact that "man moving man" is, and is inevitably, present wherever men are together. So shall my demonstration be rooted.

Consider a cluster of men; it is agreed between us that within this cluster there are at any moment some men who are attempting to move some others. For the sake of simplicity let us reduce the number of "movers" to only two, Paul and John. Before considering whom these movers seek to move, let us concentrate on what they call for. Paul calls for an H_P action and John for an H_J action. These two different calls, uttered by two different callers, may be addressed to two different persons, whom we shall assume to be responsive, and we shall denote them as follows, B_P and B_J.

The situation can be made more concrete if we picture the scene as laid in a primitive village. Paul calls upon one man to come fishing with him and John upon another to give him a hand in felling a tree. The situation gives rise to no difficulty. There may be some difficulty, if the two calls happen to be addressed to the same man: the two actions required of him are incompatible at the level of the individual B; he has to choose, and in so doing may antagonize either Paul or John. But this need not be a serious situation.

Now let us consider the case where Paul and John address their calls to the incompatible H_P and H_J actions to the villagers at large. Suppose that some of the latter respond to the call of Paul, some to the call of John, possibly some to neither. This sorting out of the villagers into Paul-followers, undertaking H_P, and John-followers, undertaking H_J, again creates no difficulty provided that the actions H_P and H_J are compatible at the level of the set.[2] The fact that n_p members go fishing with Peter does not conflict with the fact that n_J members go felling trees with John.

This situation can be described as the uttering of competing signals S_P and S_J addressed to the whole set, incompatible at the level of the individual but compatible at the level of the set. If the actions indicated are compatible at the level of the set, the signals are competing but not conflicting.

The more complex the subject—and we are here entering into complexities—the more familiar the illustrations should be. Let me therefore instance competing but not conflicting signals by two neon advertisements standing side by side on a dark road: one of these calls upon drivers to stop at Paul's restaurant, the other to stop at John's restaurant. These are competing signals but their competition is harmless. Not so if we substitute for these two lighted signs a pair of others, one of which states "Keep Left" and the other "Keep Right." Havoc must result if some drivers choose to comply with the "right" signal and some with the "left" signal. Such signals are incompatible at the level of the set, one of them must be struck down.

This simple observation leads us to the heart of political organization. Any set of people in some way dependent upon one another must have some provision, explicit or implicit, for the elimination of signals which would conflict at the level of the set. Signals which do not conflict at the level of the set may

---

2. The word "set" is used throughout as in mathematics, meaning here the well-defined collection of people to whom the calls discussed can in practice be addressed.

freely compete, but signals which are incompatible at the level of the set cannot be allowed to compete. This is the Law of Conservative Exclusion which is essential to any body politic.

The Law of Conservative Exclusion is not a law in the sense that it operates at all times inevitably. It is not a law in the sense of its having been edicted by some Authority. It is a law in the sense of its being a necessary condition for the persistence of a body politic. Whenever and wherever competing instigations would conflict, from different signals to do, one is selected and the others are eliminated. There is room for only one signal and moreover compliance to this one signal must be enforced. There is a name for this single, monopolistic, obedience-exacting signal: it is a command. The contrast between suggestion-communication and command-communication is stark. In the former case, any member of the set may, with widely different chances, seek to move all or some other members to the action he desires, and any member of the set may choose to respond to this or that suggestion or none. Quite different is the case of command; it squeezes out competing suggestions which would conflict with it, and requests compliance.

The natural basis for the Law of Conservative Exclusion can be instanced very simply. A tribe hears that strangers are advancing to its hunting grounds. Paul calls upon his fellow-warriors to attack these invaders while John urges the people to meet the newcomers with presents. If then some pick up their spears for the ambush while others gather fruit for the bearing of presents, the Paulist attack will fail and the Johnists will suffer reprisals. Clearly the actions of the members cannot, without disaster, divide according to their preference for the Paul or the John suggestion. The actions of all members of the set must be consistent. And for that purpose, the two conflicting calls to action cannot be allowed to sound upon the social field: only one is permissible. What shall this call be? The call to bear arms or to carry fruit? The policy of Paul and that of John may both be advanced, provided only that they are not presented as direct calls to do, but as opposing propositions to make the call to action this or that.

This looks more like Politics as it is currently understood and described than does the *ABH* relation of which so much has been made in this exposition. For instance the proposal of Alcibiades to the Athenian Assembly is that the expedition to Syracuse should be undertaken while the proposal of Nicias is that it should not be. Conflicting proposals compete for selection; one is retained and becomes command, the other is altogether eliminated.

But even if we have come a long way round to state what is familiar, it was not a useless way. For indeed the understanding of the direct moving of man by man has brought us to realize that in cases where conflicting instigations to do would result in placing members of the set in attitudes destructive of the set as a working system, as an ordered field, then there must be elimination of conflicting instigations, one of which, and one alone, is elevated to the position of a "command," which alone can be uttered and which precludes the utterance of any conflicting instigation.

Now this immediately brings out three features fundamental to any political system.

(1) There must be some *selection* between possible instigations whenever it would not be tolerable to have more than one: that is, when two or more would prove incompatible at the level of the set. And therefore, there must be some *selective process*.

(2) When the selective process has been completed, there must be a *proclamation* of the result. This proclamation must be such that the "call to do" now uttered is unmistakably recognized by all as utterly different in nature from an instigation which they would be free to respond to or not. This is now a *command*, and the abstract difference must be brought home by a visible *majesty*.

(3) When the command has been proclaimed, there is no freedom to utter an instigation conflicting with it.

Remembering that what is here sought is to preclude a clash of conducts, we see clearly that the reception of the proclamation is all-important. This causes us to stress the majesty which must attend the proclamation. There must therefore be "a high place," from which the words of the proclamation are uttered in quite a different guise than words of simple instigation would be.

In most countries of the world, at most times, commands have been handed down from a throne, raised by steps: they have been spoken by a man sitting in state, clad in robes of majesty, bearing a crown, holding a sceptre. And his words have been heralded by a sounding of trumpets. All this, which may now seem to us empty ceremonial, proved necessary to impress upon the listeners that here was not instigation but a command. The raising of the speaker upon a throne was no more irrational than is the raising of a weight to a certain height, in order that it may fall with greater energy. The means of endowing an utterance with majesty change with time, but some means there must be.

Nor do they become less necessary if the previous discussions of the proposals vying for the status of command have been prolonged and public. The debate closed, many of us, members of the public, feel that the proposal selected was not the best, or indeed that it is bad. The same feeling may be found in, and voiced by, some members of the ultimate decision-making committee. If so, that will detract from the impressiveness of the pronouncement made by that committee. It is now necessary that proposals which it was proper to champion at an earlier stage but which have been eliminated by the selective process should be "rubbed out" of our minds. And the best way to achieve this is that the proposal finally selected should be proclaimed by an agency which had no part in the controversy. Failing this agency of majesty, the ultimate decision-making committee must change its tone from argument to proclamation.

Even with the seal of majesty, and *a fortiori* without, it may prove difficult to clear away, after utterance of the command, the proposals which have been its unsuccessful competitors. This is a requirement which, as far as I know, has not been considered.

Let us restate it: "When the command has been proclaimed, there is no freedom to utter an instigation competing with it." This follows logically from the very justification of command here repeated.

Premiss A: a diversity of instigations is intolerable when it would lead to a destructive conflict of behaviours.

Premiss B: Z is such an occasion.

Conclusion: therefore a diversity of instigations cannot be tolerated on issue Z.

Since the very justification of command is to preclude the diversity of instigations when such diversity would cause harmful clashes (and Z is *ex hypothesi* such an occasion), then after proclamation of a command C_Z on this issue, the revival or introduction of an instigation clashing with that command restores precisely that diversity which the command was meant to eliminate. Indeed it does more than this: challenging in this one instance the efficiency of the proclamation, it tends thereby to weaken such efficiency in general.

How can I justify such an instigation? If I subscribe to premiss A and to premiss B, if my proposal has been considered in the procedure of selection of the command, then my taking up as an instigation what has been rejected as a candidate to command is "political interloping." For instance the Paulists have opposed the proposal to levy a certain tax: it has been carried against their opposition and now they call upon taxpayers to refuse their contributions. Such political interloping is always a challenge to the political system and often to the very existence of the body politic. The extreme form of political interloping will be an appeal by a defeated peace party not to participate in a war decided upon in spite of their opposition, or conversely the committing of acts of war by a defeated war party.[3]

Political interloping seeks justifications and finds them in the statement that the selective procedure has not been observed, or again in the more far-reaching statement that it does not accept the selective procedure in use. It may seek a higher justification in the plea of conscience, holding that it is more important to act in conformity with one's conscience than to secure the body politic against the destructive effect of incom-

3. There are disguised indirect forms of "political interloping" of which Thucydides gives an instance. After Alcibiades had carried the Athenian Assembly with him on the matter of the expedition to Syracuse, and when the expedition was on its way with Alcibiades one of its generals, the worsted peace party taxed Alcibiades with having, before his departure, participated in or led a defacing of the Mercuries. And as his winning voice was lacking, as well as the support of the young and the sailors, all away in Sicily, a proposal could therefore be carried taxing him with profanation and bidding him return to purge himself of the accusation. It may well be that his recall lost Athens its sole chance of victory, which lay in a celerity natural to Alcibiades and altogether foreign to Nicias, his former opponent in the Assembly, on whose shoulders the burden of military leadership now fell.

patible behaviours: then it negates premiss A. But an altogether simpler defence is the negation of premiss B: that is, the interloper then pleads that the issue Z was not one on which the diversity of instigations is intolerable. And this raises a point of great interest.

Above I have quoted simple examples where, quite clearly, the call to do this and the call to do that could be uttered side by side without harm to the body politic. While the different actions called for are incompatible at the level of the individual (he cannot do both) they are compatible at the level of the set (it does not matter that some do one and some the other). Against those I have quoted simple examples displaying cases where two different calls to action, if uttered side by side and if followed, one by some and the other by some others, would create a disastrous situation. The examples have been chosen for their simplicity and forthrightness: there could be no doubt in some of the cases that there was no need to eliminate competing signals to do, and no doubt in some other cases that there was room only for one signal.

Generalizing, we come naturally to the notion that all conceivable *signals to do* fall into two classes: class 1 is formed of the cases where competing signals would be incompatible at the level of the set, and this defines the realm of command where one signal and one only is permissible; class 2 is formed of the other cases where competing signals are not incompatible at the level of the set, and therefore this is the realm of free instigation.

Such a division is meaningful: in zone 1, there may be competing proposals that the signal to do be this or that, but there must be a selection among these proposals and the elevation of one of them to the dignity of command. There must then be a selecting and dignifying agency, corresponding to the notions of government and sovereignty.

Such a division is useful, since it affords justification to command in zone 1 and denies it in zone 2. But is such a division in practice easily made? Can we draw a hard-and-fast frontier once and for all between zone 1 and zone 2? The answer is that we cannot. The frontier between the realm of command and that of free instigation shifts in time and is at any time itself an issue. And it is natural that it should be so.

Consider a Paulist team which seeks to promote on the issue Z the action H_{ZP}. At the moment t_o, the Paulist team feels that it can get some, but not many, members of the body politic to do the action H_{ZP}. The expectation "some but not many" leads the Paulists to present the issue Z as one which does not fall within the realm of command. If it fell within the realm of command, at this moment, t_o, the proposal that all members of the body politic behave in the same manner relative to the issue Z would lead to the adoption of some action other than H_{ZP} and therefore would exclude the instigation of this action desired by the Paulists. But at some later moment, t_n, the prospects of the Paulists have changed; now they can hope for a majority in favour of the proposal that the action H_{ZP} be commanded. So now they say that the issue Z lies within the realm of command.

Thus the same group of people on the same issue at two different moments of time may plead that this is a matter in which individuals should be left free to respond to competing suggestions, or that this is a matter in which individuals should comply to one command; the reason for their shift being that if they took the latter line at the earlier moment their instigation would be squeezed out by an adverse command, while by taking the latter line at the later moment they hope to ensure that their proposal, attaining the status of command, will squeeze out competing instigations.

This simple pattern goes a long way towards explaining the vagaries of the "liberty" battle-cry. Freedom of suggestion and response is highly valued by a group at present anticipating weak response, but the maintenance of such freedom becomes a disutility to this group if it comes to a position enabling it to enforce its proposal as mandatory for all. Consider for instance the history of the labour movement in the United States. At an early stage, what is claimed is the liberty to organize and to join; at a later stage what is emphasized is the requirement that any worker in an organized establishment should be required to join.

Such shifts do not display cynicism. If the Paulists deem an action or behaviour good, they naturally seek to obtain it from the greatest possible number; and for that purpose invoke tolerance when their expectations are low, coherence when their expectations are high. Since a given group's attitude towards the inclusion of a given issue in the realm of command or its exclusion therefrom is a function of its expectations, it is not surprising that the subjective appreciation of the ideal dividing line should be subject to change. But objective appreciation itself is difficult.

It is difficult simply because coherence is not only a question of men's actions, but a question of men's feelings about men's actions. It may be that actions H_{ZP} and H_{ZJ} are not in fact incompatible, but that action H_{ZJ} so antagonizes the Paulists as to provoke them to the action H_{ZPJP} which is incompatible with H_{ZJ}. In other terms, subjective appreciations are objective elements of the situation.

CHAPTER 3

Place and Face

In the museum at Corinth there are two statues, artistically worthless, which testify to the fashion under Roman rule of setting up in a place of vantage the standing figure of the governor. The sculptor has reproduced, with uninspired exactitude, every detail of the military costume borne upon occasions of state by the representative of the *civitas imperans*. Only the head is lacking, nor is it by accident: a hollow between the shoulders reveals grooves designed for the fitting of a removable head upon the massive body. Thus were the citizens spared the expense of putting up a new statue to honour a new governor: the old face was taken down and a new face was set in its stead.

This can serve to symbolize established Authority. The statue has been set up at some previous time and lasts through many generations; but the face must be that of a living and active magistrate. The end of a life, or of a term, removes the transient head from the enduring shoulders. There is now a void to be filled, an opportunity for a new man to lift his head on to the shoulders of the statue. The aspiring politician who seeks to raise his face on top of the standing statue undertakes an operation far different from the raising of the statue itself, which requires slighter efforts, and skills different in kind.

Therefore men who come to occupy positions of established Authority are seldom of the same type as the Founders. But if there have been founders in the past, as attested by the existing statues, there are also potential founders at present. The less likely they are to become occupants of established positions, the more prone they are to challenge the standing statues.

A new face can be raised on to the shoulders of the existing statue by four main procedures: heredity, nomination from above, co-optation, election from below. A complex political system comprises many statues, and the procedures for lifting heads on to them are diverse. Take Great Britain at the time of writing: succession to the throne is by heredity; seats in the House of Lords are filled by heredity but also by nomination from above (the new peers); offices with great powers of decision, civil or military, are filled by nomination from above; co-optation predominates in the selection of judges. Election to a position of Authority by those subject to that Authority, while it is the essential idea of democratic polities, in fact fills but a small minority of the positions of Authority. As it is the main idea, and applies to key positions, we shall concentrate upon that procedure.

Knowledge of the formal procedure is one thing, understanding of the efficient process another. To take a simple illustration, in order to obtain a seat in the House of Commons, it is necessary and sufficient to gain a relative majority in any constituency at the time of election. But if we say only that much, we afford no practical guidance to an aspiring politician. The very first concrete specification we must add is that he cannot stand with any chance of success until he has been adopted as candidate by one of three existing parties. As soon as this is said, we must go into some details regarding this adoption. Such details make it clear that before our man offers himself to all the people, he must have satisfied a small number of people, who control avenues of access. Suppose that we are dealing with a by-election. Our man's name must be placed on a list sent from party headquarters to the constituency. Party headquarters will not put in just any name which happens to be sent in: a first discrimination is made by a few people there. The result is still quite a long list sent to the constituency, where it is cut down to a shorter list, again by a few people. The men who remain on the short list are then called up before a constituency committee, comprising this time a few dozen people, who make the final selection.[1] All this occurs before our man can offer himself (with any chance of success) to the electorate. The two or three individuals who finally compete for the votes of the people have, in each case, been selected by "insiders."

It can hardly be otherwise. It is quite impossible to give the people a choice without narrowing it down. Take what is possibly the greatest position of Authority in our day, the American Presidency: if one wished to suppress any process of selection prior to the opening of the campaign, this would imply granting equal treatment to all individuals deciding to stand, and utter confusion would result. The logical necessity of prior selection can be simply proved by referring to the most democratic system ever worked, that of Athens in the fifth century B.C. All important decisions were taken by the Assembly of all citizens, called together for one-day sessions, ten to forty times a year. Even though only a small minority of the citizenry attended, obviously it was impossible to "give the floor"

1. David Butler states that the selection meetings are "typically attended by 30 to 100 members of the constituency [party]" (*The British General Election of 1959*, London, 1960, p. 122). Cf. R. T. McKenzie's *British Political Parties*, and his report on *The Political Activists and Some Problems of Inner Party Democracy in Britain* to the Fifth World Congress of the International Political Science Association.

to any one of the three to five thousand participants, each of whom had an equal right to speak.[2] Therefore there must have been some *ex ante* process of nomination of speakers, of which we are ignorant. It can be stated as a general proposition that *the greater the number of potential participants, the sharper must be the selecting process.*[3]

It is also true that the larger a decision-making body, the more necessary it is that the choice offered to it be narrowed down to a simple alternative (which incidentally gives a dangerous opportunity to slant the question if posed by a single man or team, not by rival teams). That is another subject, linked to our main theme in this chapter only because it again emphasizes the narrowing down which is always required when great numbers are called upon to make a choice.

Such narrowing down is an operational necessity. Going back to the bottlenecks through which our would-be candidate to the British House of Commons has to pass, these can be said to restrict the people's choice: but it is far more reasonable to stress that they make for an orderly choice. The more democratic the regime the greater their role.

The "straits" through which the aspiring politician must go are held by insiders, "screening" or "monitoring" groups. Obviously a great deal hangs upon the character of the insiders. If assembled on the basis of a special interest, they will bias the recruitment of competitors finally offered to the choice of the people. But more naturally they tend to be correlated with a high degree of individual preoccupation with the public interest.

---

2. The citizen body possibly comprised forty thousand people, probably a good deal fewer. Attendance at assemblies sometimes fell as low as two thousand, seldom reached five. Cf. G. Glotz, *La Grèce au Vᵉ siècle* (Paris, 1931).

3. Cf. B. de Jouvenel, "The Chairman's Problem," *The American Political Science Review*, vol. LV, no. 2 (June 1961).

Anywhere, at any time, citizens differ very sharply in the intensity of their preoccupation with public affairs. If we could measure this interest, we should find it at a high point in a few and falling off rapidly as we embrace successively greater numbers.[4] It is natural that those whose interest is high should gravitate to groups guarding straits, and thereby exercise an influence commensurate with their interest.[5] It is possible moreover that interest in public affairs takes various forms. People who mainly think about what should be done are less apt to occupy straits than people who care about who gets in.

"Getting in" is of course the immediate problem of the politician. We find it natural to say that a certain man "has gone into Politics," an expression quite shocking in terms of democratic theory, according to which every citizen is personally committed to the seeking of the public good. What we mean of course is that this man has entered the *cursus honorum,* is trying to occupy successively more important positions of Authority. There are many positions dotting the Hill of Command at various heights, there are a number of paths leading up and up. There are a number of men climbing up these paths (and some sliding down), and there are also on these paths a number of people who are not climbing but guarding avenues, those who have been called "insiders." All this consti-

4. Prima facie one may assume that such interest is, as mathematicians say, "lognormally distributed." On the causes which, in general, produce such a distribution, cf. J. Aitchison and J. A. C. Brown, *The Lognormal Distribution with Special Reference to Its Uses in Economics* (Cambridge, 1957).

5. R. T. McKenzie has estimated the number of those who are continually active in Politics (and whom he calls "political activists") at some 60,000 in each major British party. And he says, "The activists are in effect a tiny 'stage army' continuously marching across the political scene, encouraging as best they can the illusion that they represent the vast numbers of equally committed and interested millions who make up the paper membership of the great parties . . . [they] exert an influence vastly disproportionate to their numbers within the British political system." (From R. T. McKenzie's report on *The Political Activists* quoted above.)

tutes a population of hill-dwellers, and when we say that a man has gone into Politics, we mean that he has joined this population of hill-dwellers, which we sharply contrast in our mind with the population of plain-dwellers to which we belong. It is possible to be a plain-dweller with eager concern for the public good, and not all hill-dwellers are dedicated to it. The principle of distinction is different, and has been made clear enough.

Moving from the plain to the hill is moving into an Otherdom, which requires learning one's way, fitting in. I can here refer back to what has been said in part II. It is quite possible that the same man should fail to make his way up the Hill of Command and succeed in raising up on the plain a hillock of his own making.

Any established upward path is guarded by some group, usually quite small, which holds the pass. Some who come to the pass are admitted and some are turned down. In a complex system there are a number of paths held by quite different groups.[6] Each of these groups has its specific character and style, tends to perpetuate its being and to conserve its hue. In short, even where such a group controls promotion in a revolutionary party, its temper regarding itself is traditionalist and conservative. Thus in the case of the French Communist party, its younger men have of late bitterly complained about the conservatism of the "Old Guard" retaining control in aged hands and reluctant to move from the eulogy of Stalin and the

6. It is easy to observe, on a great many different occasions, the controlling influence exerted by a few. These few then loom large. But it is sheer fantasy to lump together the few found to exercise control at some point in society, with the quite different few who also exercise a similar control but at a quite different point. All these sets are much alike as to their technique but sharply contrasted as to their composition, style and principles. They are established, but they do not altogether form "an Establishment."

assertion of a progressive deterioration in the condition of the proletariat.[7] The "Old Guard" attitude of such groups has also been apparent in the case of the British Labour party, where a majority of the party insiders were unwilling to move from a doctrinal position which the Leader of the party and most of its members of parliament felt to be outmoded, and for which the bulk of the party's electorate cared little.[8]

It is characteristic of such groups that some persons quite bereft of any influence outside the group carry great weight within it. For this reason the control exerted by such a group is often called "esoteric." However, nothing is more natural than that a group which has a specific spirit should, in terms of this spirit, make much of people who seem its best representatives: these then are the group's own notables.

These "group notables" (often in France called *bonzes*) set the tone. They decide whether a newcomer will "do." They are prompt to detect the wrong style, the possibility of an unsuitable behaviour; and the arbiters of the most radical circle are apt to be far more severe than those of the most exclusive club. As we shall see, there is a great deal to be said for such canniness. However, it does tend to keep out or to keep down some vigorous personalities. Discussing such groups, which he called "political guilds," Max Weber said:

> It has been impossible for a man who was not of their hue to climb high in the circle of those notables who made their petty positions their lives. I could mention names from every party, the Social Democratic party of course not excluded, that spell tragedies of political careers because the persons had leadership qualities, and precisely because of these qualities were not tol-

7. This is the theory known to Marxists as "absolute immiseration."

8. Cf. the survey conducted by Mark Abrams, published in *Socialist Commentary* from May 1960 onwards, recently republished by Penguin Books as *Must Labour Lose?*

erated by the notables. All our parties have taken this course of development and have become guilds of notables.[9]

Having formerly referred to the British political system, I can point out that even the man who has found his way into the House of Commons may be excluded from any important role. In order to occupy any ministerial office, high or low, he must be called to it by the Prime Minister, who may see a menace in the man's very ability, or, if more generous, may be hampered from employing this talent by fear of frictions with other ministers. A famous example is afforded by the case of Winston Churchill, who was systematically excluded from ministerial office under the Coalition and Conservative Governments, from 1931 to 1939.

When the workings of the system tend to keep out or keep down vigorous personalities, these then are apt to seek the employment of their gifts outside the system, either in a different field (e.g. union-building) or in playing the political game outside the framework inhospitable to them (e.g. by forming a revolutionary movement). Debarred from an existing position of Authority, they build up a position of their own. And through this process every system of established Authority ultimately comes to grief.

Men of high position are often mediocre and we chafe under the obligation of obeying their commands; at the same time we readily respond to the promptings of an individual who lacks any established Authority. It therefore comes naturally to us to regard our relationship with the latter (Secundus) more favourably than our relationship with the former (Primus). Secundus is the better man: the proof thereof lies in our listening

9. Max Weber, "Politics as a Vocation," in Gerth and Mills, *From Max Weber* (New York, 1958).

to him, though he does not speak from the altitude of the statue, while we would not listen to Primus if he spoke from our own level. Further, we feel that our compliance to Secundus is an exercise of our freedom while our compliance to Primus entails an impairment of our freedom. I am not bound to do what Primus asks; if his suggestion is distasteful to me I need not follow it. It is not so when Primus speaks from on high: I am aware that I must act as he requires, like it or not. Therefore my balance of preference lies heavily in favour of informal authority.

This is an authority which I personally grant, day by day, on each several occasion. Such is our preference for that type of authority that we are invited to see the Authority of Primus in that light; but no amount of legal fiction will make it psychologically true that, because I have at some past moment participated in the election of Primus (possibly casting my vote against him) I now want to do what at this moment he prescribes. We know full well that this is not true; there exists no form of government under which we can feel just as free when obeying the bidding of Primus as when responding to the instigation of Secundus.

Informal authority is the better liked: it does not follow that it is the best. Informal authority is natural[10] and the power it gives is natural. But all power is dangerous, and natural power far the most dangerous. It is true that Primus has a hold upon us through an artefact, the statue. But because of this, the hold is defined and circumscribed. Formal Authority can demand obedience because it invokes a right: but the right which it invokes, because it is a right, has its legitimate scope and its assigned boundaries.

10. When I say that informal authority is natural, I should not be understood to say that it naturally inheres in the person who exercises it. It is the relationship which is natural, that is, I spontaneously respond to Secundus. Throughout this work, authority is not an attribute of a person but denotes the character of the relationship.

It is meaningful to say that an Authority is diverted from its proper object or exercised *ultra vires:* such statements are meaningless in the case of an informal authority. If the mayor of a town ordered the municipal police to forbid the delivery of goods to certain plants or shops, he would obviously be exercising his Authority *ultra vires*. But if the "boss" of a teamsters' union instructs all drivers to cease such deliveries, and if they comply, he thereby demonstrates that his authority stretches that far. It is absurd in his case to say that the action is *ultra vires,* just as it would be absurd to say that a stream is exerting a force beyond its force when it carries away a bridge. In the case of a natural force, we can never say that its force is less than its work proves it to be. Indeed our only way of measuring its extent is to test its utmost efficiency.

Herein resides the great difference between formal Authority and informal authority. Both are capable of moving men, and both therefore have the capacity to effect what the combined forces of the men they set in movement are adequate to achieve: and this ability to do, through the energies of other men, is power. But in the case of informal authority, anything and everything it is in fact capable of getting done is its power. Not so in the case of a formal Authority: it rests upon an idea which defines and limits its exercise, so that its legitimate achievements differ from its possible efficiency.

The point is well brought out in the following quotation from Locke:

> The power which a general commanding a potent army has, may be enough to take more towns than one from the enemy: or to suppress a domestic sedition; and yet the power of attaining those benefits, which is in his hands, will not authorize him to employ the force of the army therein, if he be commissioned only to besiege and take one certain place. So it is in a commonwealth.[11]

11. Locke's *Third Letter on Toleration.*

The thought is clear enough: the number of men who will march at the general's signal is adequate to take more towns than one, or to suppress a domestic sedition: thus the power he has in his hands is adequate for such objects. However, the soldiers owe him obedience by virtue of a commission which directs him to take only the one town: such are his powers. It would be convenient to find two different words to designate the two different notions. An attentive perusal of Cicero's works, and specially of *De Re Publica*, reveals that when he speaks of those who are powerful, he says *potentes*, and when he refers for instance to the powers which pertain to the consular office, he says *potestas*. This is a very helpful duality of words which allows us to recast the expression of Locke's thought as follows: though the *potentia* in the hands of the general is adequate to the larger or different purpose, yet his *potestas* is limited to the taking of the one town.

Potestas is a source of *potentia*: the men obey the general because he has a title to their obedience; but *potestas* also limits the use of *potentia* to its valid purpose. That it does not always do so in fact is attested by many historical instances: for instance the *potestas* of Caesar assuredly forbade him to cross the Rubicon at the head of his "power." [12] He did so none the less. But there must have been some hesitation in his mind, inexistent in the case of a leader of brigands who wields a pure *potentia*: in the case of the latter, who has no *potestas*, his companions are under no obligation to follow him, but as long and as far as they will follow him, he can do anything which the willing forces he commands are capable of achieving. And this is obviously dangerous. *Potentia* is so capable of harm that it seems safer where it is rooted in and limited by *potestas* than in its crude state.

---

12. Shakespeare quite often calls an army a "power"; thus in *Richard III:* "How far off lies your power?" (Act 3, scene 2).

The willingness of the followers does not make the *potentia* it constitutes more consonant with freedom than *potestas*. A man called Paul has aroused enthusiastic response from me and a number of others, we act upon his signals and behave as "Paulists" quite freely. Indeed we are apt to feel that our being associated under his leadership enlarges our individual freedom, because our strengths united can accomplish what we could not hope to do, one by one. But what is the impact of our Paulist association upon others? We would not follow Paul if we did not feel that it was in some way "good." And therefore it seems to us correspondingly "bad" not to follow him. We pity or despise the weak-minded, the faint-hearted, who prove irresponsive to Paul. Must we not hustle them into the fold? Thus the company of the willing presses hard upon the unwilling and drives them along by intimidation. Such a phenomenon can be observed in a society of boys where reluctant individuals are carried in the wake of an assertive band. Moreover, if it is already "wrong" in our eyes not to go along with us, it is even worse to oppose us: opponents should be battered into submission.

Thus every pleasant trait which our company has, when regarded by itself, has its unpleasant counterpart, when the impact upon others is considered. We follow Paul of our own will, freely, but, by so doing, we constitute a force which can coerce others into obeying Paul against their will, unfreely. Between members of the company there obtains a warm comradeship, which is surely far superior to the tepid sympathy which we show to our fellow-citizens in the ordinary course of things: here is real community revived. Yes, but this gain in affection within our circle is paid for in feelings of contempt towards non-joiners, in feelings of indignation, anger, rage, hatred, against opponents. What a pleasure it is to love and honour our leader, and how preferable that feeling to the formal deference we pay to the colourless John who happens to be established in Authority! Indeed; but the support we afford to Paul makes him to others a threatening, frightening, fiendish figure. Rooted in love, *potentia* bears fruits of terror. A company of volunteers gathered around a standard-bearer becomes a warring tribe, a conquering army, capable of subjecting some and dictating terms to others. And here we have a pattern endlessly repeated in history. It is most conspicuous when the company takes over a foreign country, as did that of William the Conqueror or Cortés. But the company more often operates within its country of origin for the wholesale capture of political power. Our own times offer all too many examples of this. Moreover, while Cicero is our source for the doings of a Catiline or a Clodius Pulcher, in our day we can refer to a variety of foreign observers for descriptions and evaluations of such phenomena. Appreciations tend to be favourable in so far as the observer contrasts the enthusiasm, activity and dedication of the Paulists with the political listlessness and "idiotism" (i.e. concentration upon narrow private concerns) of most citizens; and as he contrasts Paul's disposition to take bold steps with the timid avoidance of any hazardous steps by men established in Authority. The horror which the latter express for the dynamism of the Paulist faction is then readily interpreted as the defence of oligopoly against a vigorous competitor. And such indeed it is: but such defence may also be in the public interest.

One of the most obvious features of any system of established Authorities is an unspoken solidarity between the "hilldwellers," who tend to keep out exceptional personalities and also to impede the *extra muros* activities of the latter. It is easy to say that the system weakens itself by failing to recruit "born leaders" and thereby gradually "loses face," being filled with relatively faceless individuals. It is easy moreover to point out that keeping out in the cold the men of natural authority induces them to generate *extra muros* the warmth which may bring down the edifice of established Authorities. All this is no doubt true: but letting Paul in is even more immediately dangerous. Examples drawn from the life of Cicero prove the point.

Twice defeated for the Consulate, and thus denied *potestas*, Catiline built up a threatening *potentia*: but his lack of *potestas* made it relatively easy to destroy him altogether, with most of his faction. A far lesser man, Clodius Pulcher, went further because he obtained the *potestas* of tribune. With his *potentia* thus bolstered up, he could subject Rome to his gang-rule and drive Cicero into exile. Only his murder by Milo put an end to his mischief. It was thanks to the *potestas* he had enjoyed for five years as leader of the army in Gaul that Caesar could achieve his capture of Rome. The final undoing of the Republic and Cicero's own death were determined by the entrusting of *potestas* to Octavius. The record shows that dangerous men are more dangerous when admitted to *potestas* than when denied it: the Nazi challenge to the Weimar Republic was not successfully countered by calling Hitler to the chancellorship. Therefore while it is possible to speak derisively of "the eunuchs of the seraglio" keeping out the more vigorous personalities, there is a good deal to be said for it.

Our purpose here is not to discuss what is or is not wise policy. We meant to bring out the duality of Authority and authority and the natural tension existing in this respect, a feature of all political systems.

PART V

Decision

---------- CHAPTER 1 ----------

The People

Wherever there is a high place from which decisions are handed down, concrete questions arise: which man (or men) will occupy the high place, which of several proposals will be chosen as a command? There is a competition of men and a conflict of proposals, and these constitute the most familiar aspects of Politics. Behind these manifestations stand fundamental questions: what is the spirit of the men who compete for or occupy the high place? what is the specific character of the work implied in selecting one proposal out of two or more? what are the different attitudes which can be taken towards this function?

Before we come to these fundamental questions, it may be helpful to consider the limit case[1] of Perfect Democracy, of a body politic in existence without any established Authority; this may throw some light upon what is to follow.

Thus in this chapter we shall speak of the People as existing in a pure state, that is, when self-government is a reality. It does not matter that this is simply a model, provided we can learn something from it.

Let us proceed slowly and systematically. When we think of an established Authority, the very notion implies our thinking of

1. The situation obtained by pushing a certain tendency to the extreme.

three categories of people: *subjects* to whom commands are addressed, *agents* who carry out commands, *choosers* who decide the contents of the commands.

It is obvious that an Authority must have subjects: when we call it "established" we thereby imply that a given set of people acknowledge it as a source of commands, are in general prepared to receive its utterances solemnized by Proclamation. People who bear that relation to Authority are subject to it, and it is proper to call them its subjects. The term has gone out of favour, due to a long-prevailing substitution of flattering and vague terms for those which describe subordination. Be it noted that the situation of "subject to a certain authority" can be circumstantial and temporary: when driving a car, I am subject to the Traffic Authority. Further, even in relation to the most exacting Authority, it is understood that I am subject to it *ratione materiae*; for instance as a soldier what I write to my wife does not lie in the realm of obedience to the military Authority.

While a subject is defined as one who acknowledges allegiance to a certain Authority, it does not follow that each and every command is well received by each and every subject. There is a problem of reception of commands; there is also a problem of the carrying out of commands.

It is not obvious that an Authority must have agents, but it is increasingly uncommon that it should lack them. It is conceivable that, as a driver, once I am fully informed of the traffic regulations I should be left to observe them without any traffic agents to oversee my conduct; that, as a taxpayer, I should be fully informed of the scale of income-tax and left to assess myself and pay into the Exchequer, without any tax agents to revise my declaration and exact my payment. It is, in short, conceivable that the carrying out of commands should be left to each subject individually, operating as his own enforcement agent.

Such identification, one for one, of subjects with agents would be an ideal state of things. It would, however, be wrong to believe that there is an approximation to it in a condition of imperfect identification, where a large part of the subjects function as agents in regard to themselves, and moreover as overseers in regard to their neighbour. Subjects who function as their neighbour's overseer exert a lateral pressure which is apt to be far more oppressive than that of specialized agents. Before the command is proclaimed, its content must have been chosen. This brings us to the choosers: and again we can imagine identification of choosers with subjects; if it is a perfect (one-to-one) identification, then obviously established Authority is without purpose or justification: we have the self-governing body politic in pure form. Let us start from there.

We assume a body politic wherein every command addressed to all has been chosen by all together. The identification between subjects and choosers is perfect if it is one-for-one, that is, if, during the process of selection, each one has been in favour of the command chosen. Then obviously there will be no problem of reception, and no problem (other than operational) of carrying out the command. Each subject receives well the command in favour of which he decided as chooser, and is a willing agent to carry it out.

This seems at first sight a most improbable situation. We do not now think in terms of unanimous decisions but of majority decisions. If we have only a majority decision, then those who have stood against it as choosers will not take to it as subjects, or carry it out as agents, as willingly as the members of the majority. The inconvenience of imperfect identification between subject and agent, noted above, will naturally follow from the imperfect identification between chooser and subject.

However improbable the perfect identification between

choosers and subjects, it is not an inconceivable and not an impossible state of affairs. Rousseau described it as follows:[2]

> The first man to propose them[3] merely says what all have already felt, and there is no question of factions or intrigue or eloquence in order to secure the passage into law of what everyone has already decided to do provided he is sure that all the others will do it as well.

Within Rousseau's "Committee of All" there is no difference of opinion. Only one proposal is advanced and all agree to it. Indeed members agree not because they have been won over, convinced, persuaded, by the first speaker, but because their feelings run in the direction which the speaker's words advocate. It might be said that under such conditions no command is necessary: to this Rousseau would reply by pointing to the last words of the paragraph "provided he is sure that all the others will do it as well." Light is cast upon this sentence by Rousseau's discussion elsewhere of man's need for assurance that he will not handicap himself by complying with prescriptions which others will violate.[4]

Rousseau's model is imaginary: modern anthropology has, however, proved that it is not absurd. There is a "camp-fire democracy" which works on the principle of unanimous decisions, though they are not reached as spontaneously as Rousseau fancied. Let us hear about the Navahos:

> Navahos have no notion of representative government. They are accustomed to deciding all issues by face-to-face meetings of all individuals involved — including, most decidedly, the women. The native way of deciding an issue is to discuss it until

2. Social Contract, Book IV, ch. 1.
3. "Them" refers to new laws, but might as well apply to executive decisions.
4. See the so-called "suppressed chapter" of the Social Contract, meant as a reply to Diderot's article "Droit naturel" in the Encyclopédie.

there is unanimity of opinion or until the opposition feels that it is no longer worthwhile to urge its point of view. . . .
To the People [i.e. the Navahos] it is fundamentally indecent for a single individual to presume to make decisions for a group. Leadership, to them, does not mean "outstandingness" or anything like untrammelled power over the actions of others. Each individual is controlled not by sanctions from the top of a hierarchy of persons but by lateral sanctions. It will be remembered that decisions at meetings must be unanimous. To white persons this is an unbelievably tiresome and time-wasting process. But it is interesting to note that experiments with "group decision" in war industry have shown that the greatest increase in production has been attained when all workers in a unit concurred. Majority decisions often brought about disastrous results.[5]

We see here clearly that unanimity is required for a decision but that such unanimity is not spontaneous, as Rousseau imagined. It is arrived at by an exhaustive process of arguing things out, in the course of which there is a cumulative building-up of assent. This is probably what occurs far more rapidly in the case of communities smaller and less advanced than the Navaho. When we are dealing with the very small bands, such as the first political bodies must have been,[6] all naturally sit together in the evening, constituting an informal committee; this is what we hear about the Bushmen and the Bergdama.

In effect the affairs of a band are among both peoples managed by its men generally. They foregather every evening around the central camp-fire, and as the need arises to discuss what should

5. Clyde Kluckhon and Dorothea Leighton, *The Navaho* (Cambridge, Mass., 1946).
6. It has been argued that the size of "the People" is the smaller the lower the technology. See Ludwik Krzywicki, *Primitive Society and Its Vital Statistics* (Warsaw, 1934). The reasoning of this author and the evidence marshalled in support of his thesis seem to me impressive.

be done, they plan the following day's hunting, and periodically decide upon such other matters as moving camp or burning the veldt to stimulate the growth of new plants: among Bergdama they occasionally also plan raids upon nearby Herero cattle-posts, or prohibit food gathering in localities where the fruits are still green. From time to time they organize initiation ceremonies for boys; among Bergdama they consult with the women about selecting wives for the young men, and among Bushmen they occasionally have to decide upon abandoning feeble, old people when forced to migrate rapidly. They arrange trading and other visits to friendly neighbours and take steps to resist aggression or to retaliate against enemies.[7]

Unanimous decision and common action brought about by the cumulative effort of persistent advocacy seem to me strikingly illustrated, in the case of the most elementary body politic, by this scene, which a missionary among "Stone-Age men" recounts:

Late one day I came out of the bush to a camp where Yakangaiya and his married sons were sitting quietly in groups by the fire, cooking fish and waiting for their wives and mothers to come with fire and firewood. For an hour or more Damilipi, the oldest of Yakangaiya's wives, partially blind, stark naked and switching flies with a bunch of twigs, strode up and down haranguing and insulting her men, accusing them of cowardice and laziness in not raiding their hereditary enemies and continuing a feud which was dying out by mutual consent. Damilipi's campaign was continued for two days, and as other women joined her the horde was roused to the point of organizing a killing party. Weeks later the men attacked, and in the reprisals two of Damilipi's sons and a daughter-in-law were killed.[8]

7. I. Schapera, *Government and Politics in Tribal Societies* (London, Watts, 1956), p. 85.

8. Wilbur Chaseling, *Yulengor: Nomads of Arnhem Land* (London, 1957), pp. 63–64.

What we find here is not in fact a proposal laid before a more or less formal committee, but an instigation, which, by a process of cumulative stimulation, finally moves the body politic as a whole. It is quite plain that common action is taken not in response to a command issued by an established Authority, but because of the strong inner coherence of the body politic, a coherence such that its members cannot conceive of not moving together, and have no will to resist a mood which gains momentum within the group. We have here a form of consensus such as Rousseau desires, but which does not necessarily run to the wisest decisions as he seems to assume.[9]

Where the emotional coherence of the body is such, obviously the parts of choosers, subjects, and agents are not distinct, and, just as obviously, the notion of a majority is meaningless: there is a chain reaction, more or less rapid, each partner who successively responds positively to the suggestion adding to the demonstration effect, which pulls in with increasing ease the as yet silent remnant.

Observation of such phenomena is of extreme importance for the understanding of basic political processes, but in cases of this kind, while we certainly find a body politic, we do not find an established Authority. In fact the lateral ties within the body politic are of such strength that an Authority is not called for. Men are impelled to act with their fellows not because a majority has so decided and a proclamation has been issued to which the minority must bow, but because in such a social condition it comes naturally to go with the others.

9. "As long as several men in assembly regard themselves as a single body, they have only a single will which is concerned with their common preservation and general well-being. In this case all the springs of the Commonwealth are vigorous and simple and its rules clear and luminous: there are no embroilments or conflicts of interests. The common good is everywhere clearly apparent and only good sense is required to perceive it." (*Social Contract*, Book IV, ch. 1.)

It is hard for men coming from countries where an established Authority with a title to compliance from subjects is taken as a fact of nature to understand a body politic without such establishment; and therefore such explorers or conquerors have ever been inclined to believe that "chiefs" of more or less primitive folk were sovereigns. This is brought out very well in the case of Burmese people in the following quotation:

> Throughout this chapter I have stressed that the status of the individual whom I describe as chief (*duwa*) is primarily defined in terms of prestige symbols. One can say then that the office of chief is a ritual though not a chiefly office in the sense, for example, that the Lord Mayor of London has a ritual though not a priestly office. But how far is the Kachin chief's office also a political office of real power? Here the empirical situation (in 1940) was greatly confused by the fact that the British Administration had always taken it for granted that a Kachin chief *ought* to be an autocrat. He was expected to execute without question all instructions received from the British District Officer . . . by way of the Government Native Officer; furthermore he was made responsible for the collection of house tax and he was entitled to a commission on his collection; he was also responsible for the law and order of his community and for adjudicating upon matters of native law and custom. Nearly all these functions are quite alien to the traditional role of a *duwa* and most chiefs under the British found themselves in an awkwardly ambiguous position. . . .[10]

Under the British, the Government-recognized chief was responsible for making a great number of day-to-day executive decisions, but he did so simply as an agent of the paramount power. The executive decisions which had to be made by the Kachins themselves without waiting for orders from above concerned such matters as where to make a field clear, when to

---

10. E. R. Leach, *Political Systems of Highland Burma, a Study of Kachin Social Structure.* London School of Economics (London, 1954), p. 183.

burn the felled brushwood, when to make the first sowing, where to place a house site. The decision here rested not with the chief or with any particular individual but with the *salang hpawng* (i.e. council of the leaders of principal lineages) as a whole. Mostly this body of elders seems to act by precedent; where precedent gives no clear guide resort is made to divination or soothsayers. So again there is a conflict between theory and practice. Kachin *theory* is that the chief rules (*up*) with autocratic power; in my actual fieldwork, I seldom identified any instruction which had issued from a chief acting upon his own initiative. Where he gave an order it was as mouthpiece of the Government or of the *salang hpawng* or of some oracle which he had first consulted.[11]

In fact chieftainship in the case of the simpler peoples seems to have as its office essentially the preservation of the given coherence of the People, a coherence which is highly valued. There is no question of making decisions to which all are subject, but of solving conflicts which disintegrate the People.

The Pawnee (Nebraska) chief, far from being a Sovereign ruler, was above all a peace-maker and guardian of the village, his Hidatsa colleague was "a man of general benevolence who offered smoke to the old people and feasted the Poor." Their counterpart among the Plains Cree was not only expected to exercise generosity but to sacrifice his property for the maintenance of order, nay to forgo vengeance if one of his kinsmen was slain. Correspondingly, a Winnebago (Wisconsin) chief constantly distributed his possessions and interceded between evildoers and their revengeful victims; he went so far as to mortify his own flesh in order to arouse the pity of the aggrieved. In these tribes, then, *the chief was essentially an appeaser working by cajolery.*[12]

11. E. R. Leach, *op. cit.* p. 189.
12. *Lowie's Selected Papers in Anthropology*, ed. Lora du Bois (University of California Press, 1960), pp. 252–53; italics mine.

The Bergdama or Bushman chief has no legislative or judicial functions, nor are there official tribunals of any other kind. Among Bergdama, it is true, people sometimes ask elderly men to arbitrate their disputes, but such requests are not obligatory nor are the decisions necessarily accepted. Both here and among Bushmen, persons who arouse general hostility, for example by repeated acts of violence or by committing incest, may be punished by thrashing, expulsions from the band or even death. There seems to be no formal trial; the data indicate merely that the decision to act against the offender is reached casually round the camp-fire and if necessary the younger men are then told to enforce it. Private disputes, on the other hand, are usually settled by self help.[13]

Endless quotations of this general meaning could be amassed, persuading us that established Authority as we understand it must have been a late-comer in the history of mankind. We have seen already what makes it necessary; that is, the possibility of divisive instigations.

Before coming to discuss situations more familiar to us, I have deemed it important to bring out the basic moral content of the expression which we so commonly use — "the People." As I see it, this term is most properly used when we think of a set of people tightly bound together by lateral ties, so that each member of the set has a high propensity to go along with the others, will not only feel in honour or in duty bound to accept and execute the decision in which he has not concurred (a "later" attitude) but will in fact concur in the decision which at its first proposal did not strike him favourably, if and because the others rally to it. In every social setting we do find such phenomena of contagion, but they are surely weakened when we come to societies within which, by virtue of complexity, there are increasing differences of interests and attitudes.

13. I. Schapera, *Government and Politics in Tribal Societies* (London, Watts, 1956), p. 87.

Both Rousseau and Marx assume in primitive society a low degree of opposition of interests and a strong community feeling; both regard the course of history as an increasing departure from this initial situation, a heightening of interest-conflicts and a weakening of community spirit, attended by increasing strife. Rousseau regards this development as inevitably attending a larger and more complex society.[14] Marx regards it moreover as essential to the development of productive forces.[15] Rousseau regards the outcome of this development as irretrievable and calling for a Hobbesian government. Marx assumes a U-shaped political development: when the process of economic development has reached an adequate stage, the antagonisms which were aggravated in the course of development come to a crisis in consequence of which they are wiped out. Both, however, regard disintegration of the consensus as characteristic of the process of development. Hobbes of course is concerned to raise the status of established Authority in order to counter the conflict of interests. Alone among the great authors of the past, Machiavelli has found words of praise for internal strife, as a dynamizing factor in the body politic.[16]

But let us descend from great authors to familiar illustrations as I have sought to do throughout this treatise. I shall set the scene within a company of actors: this will be our body politic, and we assume that it is a self-governing body, that all its members have an equal voice in decisions affecting the company. As a young actor I join this company, which has been formed to perform Shakespeare's plays, and traditionally plays nothing else. Therefore I expect to play parts in Shakespeare's plays, the

---

14. Cf. *Social Contract*, Book IV, ch. 1, and the whole *Discourse on the Origin of Inequality among Men.*

15. This is most clearly brought out by Engels in the *Anti-Dühring.*

16. Cf. *Discorsi*, Book I, ch. 6.

other members of the company expect it of me: so far so good, we can speak of a basic homogeneity of expectations.

However, within the sharply defined pattern of *Hamlet* I may want to move from playing the part of Bernardo to that of Horatio, and thence to the part of Hamlet. This is promotion within an established structure, and we can range my efforts to obtain the role of Hamlet in preference to rival claimants under the terms: "politics of position." For the sake of simplicity let us assume that I have one rival only, thus my ambition will be fulfilled if the majority of the company will vote me into the part rather than the other man.

How shall I win? Let us look into the matter closely; I have some good friends in the company and so has my opponent. Can we base our respective expectations on these particular friendships? Not to any considerable degree. It is important to each member of the company that the part of Hamlet should be so played as to ensure collective success. Each member of the company has some idea of my ability to fill this role and of my opponent's ability. They are more likely to go by this judgement of capacity than by personal sympathy. Only those members who see no great difference between the ability of competitors are likely to be swayed by my campaign. The important thing to each and every one is that the play should not be a failure. If I happen to be defeated, and the other man plays magnificently, I may still feel aggrieved, but my strongest supporters of yesterday will rejoice that the play has gone well, and they certainly will not resent our defeat.

Now, still assuming that I am an actor of a Shakespearean company, let us suppose that I have a design quite different from that which has just been discussed. I want this company to give a play by Noel Coward. It does not matter why I want this. Possibly I feel that I am unlikely to shine in a Shakespearean role while I would be superb in a Coward part: in that case personal frustration is my motive. Or I may feel that we shall make a great deal more money by performing a Noel Coward play, in that case "collective welfare" is my motive. Or again I believe that one should be "modern," and this can be called loosely an ideological motive. Anyhow, "Not Shakespeare but Coward" is my battle-cry. Now it is immediately evident that in order to win over the company I shall have to work upon the members of the company a great deal more and in a very different manner than for the securing of the Hamlet part. The idea is far more surprising. The members have far more difficulty in picturing themselves acting a Coward play than in picturing me acting the role of Hamlet; there is far more uncertainty about the success of this much greater change and far more room for diversity of appreciation. This time it is quite another business to wrest a majority decision in my favour. Previously I was asking people to trust my ability (reasonably well known to them) to play a part (thoroughly well known); now I am asking them to trust my judgement that they should embark with me upon a hazardous venture and rely upon my capacity to procure the success of this venture. The job of majority-building is this time of a different kind. But further, the winning of a majority will not necessarily be as decisive or final as previously. Say that I have won a majority for the production of the Coward play. It is quite possible that the members of the minority will break away from the company.

We can easily imagine a spokesman for this minority saying: "We [meaning the members of the company] came together as performers of Shakespeare's plays. Now you [meaning the members of the majority] have decided to perform Noel Coward instead. But we [meaning this time the members of the minority] are not interested in this different activity. And therefore we secede from the company." Note in this imaginary speech the two successive and contrasting uses of the term "we." The former "we-all" has been split up and now there is a "we" applying to the minority, another applying to the majority. This is not at all the same division as that occurring when the point at issue was whether I or another would have the part of Hamlet. If the issue is merely "Who will have the part of Hamlet?" then those who did not fancy me for the role, when beaten in a vote, will submit to the decision. The probability of any one of them refusing to stay with the company is very slight: except in the case of my rival, the preference given to me makes no difference to their individual performances. Thus if an opposition to my taking the part manifested itself in the vote, its existence is fugitive, it constitutes no team of "bolters" ceasing to "belong." The "we-all" of the company is not permanently affected. If, however, the issue upon which I have carried the majority is that of a change-over to performing Noel Coward, the minority is very likely to leave the company.

In the case of the Coward vote, what is demanded of the members of the company is not that they should allow me, rather than another, to take the part of Hamlet while leaving them individually playing the same parts as before the vote; what is demanded is that they should agree each and all to change their own individual performances. That the majority does agree by no means entails that those in disagreement will, after the vote, meekly accept the roles allotted to them in the new play. So while they belonged to the "we-group" or "people" of the Shakespeare company, they may well break away from the we-group of the Coward company, cease to belong to that people. It is easy to imagine circumstances precluding them from a physical break-away: for instance, there are no alternative jobs open to them. In that case a physical break-away will be replaced by a moral secession. The minority remains visibly "of the company" but psychologically it does not remain "in the company"; or in larger terms, it is still in the people but not of the people.

The point of the foregoing tale is that a "politicking" individual affects the social body in a very different manner when he seeks a given position within an existing pattern from when he seeks to change the pattern. In the former case he aspires to play a part known in advance, and all the participants in the election have only to ask themselves whether they regard him as the most suitable to fill this role. They may well differ in their judgements but each elector is engaged in the same operation, that is, measuring the man against the part. It is to this operation that Montesquieu refers when he states: "The people are admirably fitted to choose those to whom they must entrust some portion of authority." [17] Montesquieu develops his thought as follows:

> The people can then base their decision wholly upon things they know and facts of which they are aware. They know that this man has gone to the wars and acquitted himself successfully, and knowing this they can pick him as general. The people know that a certain judge is painstaking and that many of those who have appeared before him have lauded his judgement while there has been not the slightest rumour of corruption: this is enough information to elect a praetor. . . .

Obviously what our author says here is entirely relevant to the election by a dramatic company of one of their number to play the part of Hamlet. What makes a difference to each and every member of the Company is how well the part will be played. The case is very different indeed if a change of pattern is suggested. A change of pattern means that each and every

17. *The Spirit of Laws*, Book I, ch. 2.

member must now consider whether the part to which he may be called in the new play is more or less to his advantage than before; and more than that, whether he likes or dislikes the new play.

All members of the company gain by choosing the best Hamlet. But by going over to Noel Coward some will gain (have a more important part) and some will lose (have a less important part). Thus the very nature of the suggestion causes each to look to his own interest. Nor is it a matter of interest alone but also of meaning. The word "interest" is ambiguous, but we shall follow custom if we use it to designate the advantages which are objectively measurable. For instance, we can tell an actor that the change is in his interest if he has more lines to speak in the new play, or again we can argue that it is in his interest if we can show him that even while speaking less lines, he will get far more pay as his proportional share in overall increased receipts. If that is the sort of thing we mean by "interest," it is plain that there are other powerful considerations here subsumed under the word "meaning." To a certain actor it means something to perform Shakespeare and he is robbed of that meaning when made to perform Noel Coward. Thank God it is not true that men evaluate a general change wholly on grounds of their personal safety and perquisites; their affections are deeply involved in the shape of things around them, in the nature of the play. Who would deny that some Romans were deeply hurt by the fall of the Republic, some Englishmen by the beheading of Charles I, some Frenchmen by the beheading of Louis XVI? Who doubts that national independence is regarded as a positive value to which men willingly make sacrifices? Who questions the chagrin caused by a national humiliation? Who would argue that an officer in a prison camp, secure from danger and well taken care of, is then better off than in the toughest campaign? The very zest for living may vanish if people are torn from what means much to them.

The Tasmanians bravely resisted the Whites, till, having been reduced to hundreds from thousands, they submitted. The remnants that remained were presented with sheep and received annuities. In a word, in comparison to the uncertain life of a hunter, these remnants were surrounded with plenty and secured as to their morrow. And yet they kept dying out! In order to understand the inevitability of their dying-out, we must take into consideration the breaking up of their inner life by the changed conditions of existence. For many centuries the Tasmanians had lived on their island, sometimes exposed to famine (when, probably, they saved themselves by devouring children) and always subject to various anxieties, but for the most part their life was a happy one. Those migrations of theirs, when moving from one forest clearing to another, from one forest fastness to another, doubtless gave rise to a host of impressions of the most various kinds and to many pleasant thrills. Their hunts together, their assemblies and corroborees, their initiation ceremonies, and many other events, broke the monotony of their lives, awoke their imagination, touched the strings of their sentiment and gave a charm to life. But the white settlers came, and after years of struggle they transported the little groups which remained to Flinders Island. They were surrounded with the outward semblance of material well-being, but they were deprived of their former abundance and vitality of impressions and emotions. The Tasmanians, restricted to a small area, had parted with all that had made up the life of their forebears for ages. A more and more dominant home-sickness began to afflict them. Sometimes they would assemble on an eminence from which, in favourable weather, they could see the indistinct outline of their native island, and they would gaze at it helplessly. When a poor gin, with eager look and pointing finger, asked a gentleman if he saw the white, snowy crest of the towering Ben Lomond, then just looming in the distance, the tears rolled down her swarthy cheeks, as she exclaimed: "that-me-country!" Life lost its charm for them.[18]

The attitude of the Tasmanians offers in extreme form the reaction which may in some members of a social body result from a change of pattern which, on the other hand, may exhilarate other members of the same group, thereby creating a moral schism.

Such changes of pattern therefore are harmful to that psychological cohesion which Rousseau deemed so important: such changes being on the other hand inherent in the history of an evolving society, it follows that its institutions cannot rest upon the basis of that psychological cohesion. This is indeed what Rousseau argued: the body politic comes to depend increasingly upon established Authority. It is only in a small, rustic, and conservative community that the role of established Authority can be slight or insignificant.

The role of established Authority must inevitably increase as the body politic grows in size, complexity and heterogeneity. This is a "Dimensional law" which has been stated in various terms by all classical writers, and with especial clarity by Rousseau."[19] But another point should be stressed. In a "State" as distinct from a "People" (described above), decisions of Authority imply instructions to act which are addressed immediately to agents of Authority rather than to the people at large. Take the decision to carry out an afforestation programme: this implies great activity on the part of the Department of Agriculture, none from the citizens, some of whom will be subject to the taking-over of land for the fulfilment of the programme.

18. Ludwik Krzywicki, *Primitive Society and Its Vital Statistics* (Warsaw, 1934).
19. Cf. *Social Contract*, Book III, chs. 1 and 2.

In the modern state no one citizen is aware of every decision taken by established Authorities, nor need he be, since the very great majority of such decisions imply instructions to specific agents. In fact the whole modern trend is away from direct instructions to citizens: for instance, in the recovery of taxes, the practice of "withholding" transforms what would have been a demand addressed to a great many taxpayers into a demand addressed to a far smaller number of employers, who find themselves for the occasion in the position of "agents."

Political analysis at the level of the State—which we are not concerned with here—involves asking the question: "Who is requested to carry out this specific decision?" The importance of the question can be brought out by a simple example: suppose that a popularly elected government decides to develop biological warfare, and suppose even that it obtains for that purpose the backing of a majority of the electorate; but suppose also that the biologists refuse to carry out this work: the government is stymied. This extreme case brings out what is too often forgotten: that any government is naturally dependent upon those whose actions are required to carry out its instructions. How right was Hume to say:

> As FORCE is always on the side of the governed, the governors have nothing to support them but opinion. 'Tis therefore on opinion only that government is founded; and this maxim extends to the most despotic and military governments, as well as the most free and popular. The soldan of Egypt, or the emperor of Rome, might drive his harmless subjects like brute beasts, against their sentiments and inclination: but he must at least have led his *mamalukes* or praetorian bands like men, by their opinion.[20]

---

20. David Hume, *Essays and Treatises on Various Subjects*, 2 vols. (London, 1757), essay IV: "Of the First Principles of Government," p. 31.

This statement is perhaps the most important of all political science. It helps us to understand the true basis of oppressive government, which is to be found in the intense solidarity with its head of a minority whose organization and activity allow it to intimidate every other subject. It sharpens our awareness that, in a simple body where decision-makers have no specific agents of execution or enforcement—such as the People described above—it would not much matter in fact if formally decision-making rested with One, called Absolute: because in such a situation, the execution of decisions devolving upon each, the formal decision-maker is entirely dependent upon their willingness to execute and can therefore command only what the "subjects" will be willing to carry out. It is not so when a state apparatus is developed. Decision-makers are always naturally dependent upon the goodwill of those who carry out decisions; but as this carrying out shifts from members of society to members of the apparatus, so does this dependence. As ideas are of practical efficiency, such a shift, which lies in the nature of things, can be checked to some degree by emphasizing that subjects are "citizens" and calling agents "instruments": but the underlying facts may break out.[21] Further, the established Authorities who want some decision carried out must naturally attach a major importance to the co-operation of any individuals or groups in society whose help can be decisive. If there exists a social condition wherein local lords carry great weight, the government will seek to enrol them as special agents for the enforcement of its decisions, and in order to involve them will invite them to participate in the making of decisions. If a social condition exists wherein trade union leaders carry great weight, then they

21. E.g. the political pretensions of the army.

will be consulted in order to procure their involvement and co-operation.[22]

Tell me to whom authorized decision-makers look for the implementation of their commands: from this I shall derive my idea of the State considered, and my assessment of the forces with which the Authorities must bargain. The character of a State changes with the agencies and procedures whereby what has been said gets done.

22. An illustration comes to hand at the time of my final revision. The convening of trade union and business leaders in the newly formed National Economic Development Council corresponds to the same governmental need as the first convening of parliaments. People who are well placed in society to procure the carrying out of a policy are invited to participate in its elaboration (i.e. "Come and let yourselves be convinced").

The Committee, I
(Judicial or Political?)

Wherever there is an established Authority, the decisions it utters must first be chosen. Whenever more than one person does the choosing, differences can arise. These differences form the subject of the present chapter. To clarify my intention, I shall explicitly exclude what I do not propose to discuss at this point: (1) to what set of people should a certain category of decisions be entrusted; (2) whether there is perfect coincidence between those entitled to participate in the decision-making and those effectively participating; (3) by what method (majority or other) the decision is made, differences notwithstanding; (4) how the decision is to be carried out.

The picture of the decision-making set which I have in mind is one which comprises more than one person but not a large number. For the sake of convenience I shall call this set "the committee." It seems reasonable to think in terms of a small set. Even when the decision belongs to many, the debate must in fact be limited to a few.[1] On the other hand, when decision belongs to one, he will be apt to seek the views of a few advisers; and even if he does not, the several courses he contemplates in solitude can be regarded as several opinions.

---

1. See my paper: "The Chairman's Problem," *American Political Science Review*, vol. LV, no. 2 (June 1961).

The theme is thus delimited. Several men are engaged in choosing a decision to be issued authoritatively. In what various ways can they differ? To answer this question, we shall begin by considering different kinds of decision.

I am a juryman sitting with eleven others throughout a trial. What is the nature of the decision I am called upon to make? Formally speaking I am not called upon to decide what shall be done in the future to Smith, the accused, but to say what Smith has done at some moment in the past. My decision bears upon the truth of a bygone occurrence: "Did Smith, on such a date, commit a certain action?" This I do not know as I first take my seat. But the matter has been looked into (this is of course the literal meaning of *inquisitio*): there has been an inquest, inquiry, investigation, thanks to which "evidence" is laid before the jury. As etymology testifies, evidence is designed to manifest what was hidden, to make me see what I have not seen. When all the evidence has been produced, marshalled on both sides and summed up by the judge, I should be able to recognize the truth; which is what I am here for: the function of the jury is *recognitio veritatis*.

Clearly such *recognitio* is not equivalent to a *cognitio*. However much the evidence accumulates against Smith, I can never know for certain what he has done. I can only hold the opinion that Smith is guilty and feel that the chances of its being mistaken are negligible.

What now can be the nature of the difference arising between me and a fellow-juryman? It is not a difference in the understanding of our function: he and I are jointly engaged in a *recognitio veritatis*. Also we are both convinced that there is a truth to be known. Even in our time when it is fashionable to say with Pilate *Quid est Veritas?* it is hardly doubted that a question of fact is capable of a "Yes" or "No" answer.

What then is our difference? The evidence which has convinced me has failed to convince him. The opinion of "guilty" seems to him doubtful.

What sort of feeling should his doubt evoke in me? Unless I account his judgement for zero, which is presumptuous, his contrary view must make me less sure that my opinion is true. I have no good reason to be angry with him for failing to share my views, but reason rather to thank him for saving me from a precipitate judgement.

In this case it seems obvious that I must practise *tutiorism*, a term of moral theology which denotes a preference for the safest course. *Tutiorism* is the general rule in criminal law. It is displayed in the maxim that the accused should have the benefit of the doubt, in the English requirement that the jury should be unanimous to "find for" guilt validly,[2] but above all in the leisureliness of criminal procedure. The inconvenience of delaying a decision, the cost of gathering more information, are disregarded as against the danger of incomplete information: "expeditive justice" is no justice.[3]

2. Though in fact the unanimity rule in England seems due to the antiquity of the institution. The jury system, indeed for other purposes than those of criminal law, was at work in England long before the idea occurred that a majority could stand for consensus. This is a modern notion, hard to justify in logic. It is because this modern notion had come to be established that the countries in which a jury system was introduced at a late date (such as France) have a majority rule. Statistically speaking the majority rule affords less guarantee to the accused (see below), but of course a greater reluctance to find guilt can compensate for this.

A full discussion of the guarantees afforded respectively by the unanimity and the majority rule can be found in Condorcet's *Essai sur l'application de l'analyse à la probabilité des decisions rendues à la pluralité des voix* (Paris, 1785). If one wants the chance of condemning an innocent man to fall below one in a hundred thousand, this can be achieved in a majority system only if each individual juryman has less than eight chances in a hundred of going wrong, but it can be achieved with a unanimity system if each juryman has less than thirty-seven chances in a hundred of being wrong, as anyone can find out from tables of the cumulative binomial. Simple answers such as this one can be given only on the unrealistic assumption that the jurymen do not influence each other.

3. It is noteworthy that the "safest course" maxim which works in favour of the accused in normal times is reversed in favour of "the State," "the People," "the Party,"

The most extreme example of *tutiorism* in decision-making is afforded by the process of canonization in the Roman Catholic Church.[4] There we have a quite remarkable case, because established Authority is in the position of denying a recognition of saintliness demanded by the people. A number of centuries may elapse before ultimately sanctification is obtained for a memory which has been constantly cherished. Established Authority waits, to see whether the popular fame increases over time: *expectat ut videat utrum fama ista sanctitatis et miraculorum evanescat, an incrementum capiat.* If so, no less than three successive procedures are required, lengthy and separated by great stretches of time. In the case of each, established Authority stands as it were on the defensive, raising doubts. The question is repeatedly asked: "*An . . . tuto procedi possit?*" Is it possible to proceed safely, with full confidence?

Now for a violent contrast let us consider an army in a tight spot (the "Blue" army), and suppose that its general calls a council of war, in which I am included. Whatever is to be done must be done quickly and therefore it is impossible to decide *tuto*.

There are "hard facts" of the situation such as the present positions of the various Blue forces and of the various opposing Red forces. I call these hard facts because they are accomplished facts, by nature capable of being thoroughly known. But they are not at present known to me as the positions of white and black pieces on the chessboard are known to a chessplayer. Regarding these hard facts I have information which I deem reliable for some items and more or less doubtful in the

---

"the Revolution," "the Cause" in troubled times. Then what is called "safest" is what is most apt to strike terror in the hearts of the actual or potential opposition: the condemnation of the innocent will do as well as that of the guilty.

4. Cf. Vacant et Mongenot, *Dictionnaire de théologie catholique*, Fasc. xv: "Canonisation dans l'Eglise Romaine," with an extensive bibliography.

case of others. I cannot wait to improve my information since this implies staying in the same positions while the enemy moves and this may turn out to be the most disastrous course. Even if I had perfect knowledge of present Red and Blue positions, I could not with any considerable degree of assurance foretell the effect of a certain decision now made, because I cannot tell how it will be carried out by the various Blue forces nor what Red will do in the meantime. Thus even with perfect information my decision would be a gamble. But I am gambling even more wildly because my information is so incomplete.

In such circumstances, proposals to the council of war are a matter of character more than mental speculation. The first to indicate a bold course is apt to rally those of similar temperament and to be opposed by those of a more timid disposition.

Our council of war, its situation characterized by the necessity of making a momentous decision in the course of a single sitting, is of course an extreme case. Even so, if we think of a spectrum at one end of which we set our criminal procedure, with our council of war at the other end, executive decisions stand nearer to the latter than to the former. They are more like the latter, not only because they cannot be long delayed, but also because delay is not necessarily conducive to the increase of information and therefore to a safer decision. The decision to be taken is meant to affect the future and the best way open at the moment t_o may well have closed by the time it has been investigated. While politicians are discussing what the situation calls for, the situation is in fact changing. No doubt there are many cases in which the situation changes slowly enough to justify an interval spent in the collecting of more information; while it may be true that the decision taken at a later moment implies action from a worsened position, the improvement of information may be such as to improve the odds in favour of getting good results from the action decided. But all too often the case is different: the need for full information is felt only when the situation is worsening rapidly, so much so that the information called for is doomed to obsolescence before it can be used.

Whoever has given a good deal of attention to the course of events knows how things are apt to go. There is a long, slow subterranean progress to a problem. You point to this mole-track and you are told: "There is nothing there"; or perhaps they will admit: "Yes, there is a problem there which we may have to deal with some day, but there is plenty of time. Things have been that way for a long time and they are not moving, you know." It is true that "things" have a deceptive trick of moving slowly, giving the lie to Cassandra. But however long this may last, one day, suddenly, there they are in the open.

Now they are discovered, discussed, there is a scurrying and people come triumphantly bearing as their great idea some suggestion which was made about the problem a long time ago, when it might perhaps have been effective. While people are discussing this, matters move at a pace which is forever accelerating towards a real crisis. This is the time when the stewards of the public interest come to make a decision. And they are in the condition of our council of war. They need not have been, but there they are.

A chess-player who has been dilatory in his first moves is apt to find himself in time-trouble just as things come to a crisis: much the same usually happens in Politics. It is of great interest to discuss how decisions should be made: not least for purposes of contrast with the actual manner of their making.

We have compared sitting on a jury and sitting in a council of war. The immediately striking contrast lay in the attitude of the decision-maker to time: in the former case time can be freely spent to buy more information; not so in the latter case. This contrast regarding time turns upon the fact that the same decision produces the same effect, whatever its date, in the first case, not in the second. This constitutes a fundamental difference between a judicial and an executive decision. It is related to "the behaviour of facts" relevant to the different processes. The facts upon which the juryman (or the judge as the case may be) passes judgement "stand still" while the decision is being elaborated. The facts in respect of which the military or political committeeman (or sole executive) must make a decision are "on the move" while the decision is being elaborated. The "standstill" of facts is so essential to judicial decision-making that the only precipitate measures taken in judicial procedure are directed to immobilizing the facts: measures of conservation tending to preserve the evidence or to secure that the object claimed does not disappear or suffer irreparable alteration.

Over the centuries a continuing effort has been made to improve the administration of justice. Its excellence we regard with good reason as an admirable trait in a body politic. We are prone to take it as an ideal model, and would like political decision-making to imitate judicial decision-making. This imitation is very apparent whenever we formulate our requirements in the political realm: we feel that the deciding political body should carefully possess itself of all the facts and that it should patiently hear out arguments on both sides, freely developed.[5] Time-pressure, however, is likely to impede the fulfilment of these requirements. For instance, when Presi-

5. Other analogical requirements could be mentioned but are not relevant at this stage.

dent Truman, in 1950, decided upon intervention in Korea, had he waited for an exhaustive collecting of the facts, and for a full-dress discussion of the reasons for and against intervention, this would in fact have amounted to a decision of non-intervention. This is indeed what happened in March 1936 when the question arose for France whether to answer by military intervention the German remilitarization of the Rhineland.

Many political decisions—and those the most important—cannot be made according to a procedure as careful as that which is required in the administration of justice. They can be reviewed afterwards, but whether this review approves or condemns the decision taken, it can never undo its effects. And indeed because the political decision has produced effects, subsequent approval or condemnation of the decision will not turn upon a reconsideration of the same facts or arguments which the decision-makers considered at the time or which were available to them: the approval or condemnation will depend essentially on the *new* facts produced or deemed to have been produced by the decision.

And this brings us to a difference between judicial and political decision-making far more essential than those previously recapitulated. The one looks back to the past, when, it is alleged, Primus committed a certain criminal action or, if it is a civil suit, injured the rightful interests of Secundus. The other, on the contrary, looks forward to the outcome of the decision now being formed. Practically everything that is said in the course of a trial or lawsuit is couched in the past tense; not so in the case of a political debate: here the future tense is sure to be used.

In essence a judicial decision is a finding that some person or persons did at some past moment unduly affect the then existing state of the world;[6] while a political decision is an endeavour to affect the future state of the world. Such an endeavour implies surmising how the decision will work out, and therefore taking into account facts yet to come, contingencies.

If facts, lying in the past, have been properly ascertained, and if the relevant rule is duly applied to them, then a judicial decision is correct. Here the decision-makers are not required to consider the practical consequences of their decision;[7] it can even be argued that they should not consider these consequences; at least it is clear that they must not choose their decision according to the various consequences they could foresee as flowing from this or that choice.

Let me illustrate. I am a juryman sitting in 1956 in Smith's trial for a murder allegedly committed in 1955. The evidence regarding Smith's character is unfavourable, but the evidence regarding the alleged action is very inadequate. I would act in a most improper fashion if I decided for Smith's guilt on the following grounds: "I cannot tell whether Smith has committed murder in 1955, but I regard him as likely to do so in the future, and therefore I shall so speak as to preclude a future evil." My correct behaviour is to say "not guilty" and should Smith commit a murder in 1958, my 1956 decision will not thereby be proved incorrect. My business was not to foresee the

6. The purpose of restoration (*redde*) pervades the administration of justice. Any future effects of a judicial decision, punishment, restitution, etc., follow from the finding of an illegitimate perturbation.

7. An instance comes to hand during final revision of this chapter. The United States Supreme Court, finding that the holding of a large portion of General Motors shares by Du Pont is against the law, requires the latter company to divest itself of them, and regards the harm which may accrue to General Motors' individual stockholders from the consequent dumping of shares upon the market as beyond its purview.

future and I was not to take my present decision on consideration of its future effects. It is quite the contrary in the case of a political decision.

For instance, as Secretary for War I consider the case of General Smith, a worthy man with an excellent record. Let us suppose that his seniority now calls him to a position of major responsibility and that I have no choice other than thus promoting him or retiring him. The latter course seems unfair in view of the evidence collected about his past. It is, however, my feeling that the man's mind is not elastic enough to adjust to rapidly changing forms of warfare. I may then quite correctly retire General Smith because my concern is to provide for the future. Should I regard myself as bound by all the past facts in favour of Smith, and give him the major position, and should Smith at some later date perform incompetently, my decision will then be attacked and my defending it on the ground that his past record called for the nomination will be irrelevant and immaterial. My business was to do the best for our future defence.

The contrast here drawn is of major importance. It seems undesirable to allow the Secretary for War a great deal of discretion in the promotion of generals. He may then abuse his power to advance men towards whom he has a personal leaning, possibly independent of their merit. Therefore one wishes to bind him, setting rigid rules of advancement. If so, every promotion becomes a judicial decision of the simplest kind: "What are the facts regarding Smith? Do they qualify him according to the rules?" But in that case the War Secretary cannot be held, and cannot hold himself, responsible for the outcome. The feeling of responsibility for the outcome permeates and characterizes political decision-making.

This seems to set a natural limit to the binding of public decision-makers by rules. If the field covered is one within which many decisions will have to be made over a period of time, each of which by itself can cause little harm to the body politic, then it is convenient to submit of the whole field to a rule designed to minimize the frequency of harmful decisions. But where a single decision can produce a major harm, then it seems inevitable that it should be taken with discretion on the basis of surmises regarding its outcome.

The contrast between political and judicial decision-making can be further stressed by reference to international affairs during the period between World War I and World War II. A new hope had then arisen that international disputes could be settled by quasi-judicial decisions, and international crimes put down by a quasi-judicial process. Of course neither the Assembly nor the Council of the League of Nations was formed of decision-makers wholly disinterested;[8] it is easy for a jurist to point out, besides this major difference, many other important differences between the decisions of such bodies and true judicial decisions. None the less the basic idea was that the international committee could go beyond the role played by former conferences, that is, attempts to reach workable compromises, and, if necessary, could utter verdicts based upon consideration of facts and application of principles. For our present purpose the interesting feature is that once such a quasi-judicial decision was made, it fell to the individual governments to make a political decision towards the implementation of the verdict. And this helps to bring out the contrast.

For instance in 1935 the question arose whether Italy had engaged in military aggression against Abyssinia, whether this was a violation of treaties, of the Kellogg Pact, and of the League Covenant; whether the occasion was one which called

---

8. This point, however important, is left aside here: it will be dealt with in another chapter.

for the application of sanctions by members of the League. Opining in a judicial capacity, representatives of the several Powers could not honestly give any other answer than affirmative on each point. But actual moves in the case called for arrangements to be made individually by the several governments. Before making such arrangements, each government considered the consequences. The French government, for one, felt that Italy should not be antagonized; much trouble had recently been taken to tie her up in a military agreement against Germany:[9] if Mussolini were angered he might be driven to alliance with Hitler. This consideration, based on the future, stopped the French government from any active implementation of the judicial decision. History has passed an unfavourable judgement upon this political decision (or indecision). But failure to follow up a judicial decision is not always a political mistake. On 13 December 1939 the Assembly of the League of Nations found: (1) that the Soviet Union had made a military attack upon Finland; (2) that this was a violation of a Russo-Finnish agreement, of the Kellogg Pact, and of the League Covenant; (3) that the Soviet Union was a delinquent under the Covenant. Clearly this was a decision of a judicial nature. But now the Western Powers had to make a political decision: the Assembly had explicitly invited members to aid Finland: therefore Britain and France would not have done wrong, had they sent troops to bolster the Finnish defence. This was quite seriously contemplated in France.[10] Indeed, means of so doing were prepared. Such a decision would, however, have been foolish; Britain and France, already at war with Germany, would have disastrously impaired their position by adding Soviet Russia to their enemies.

9. Signed in January of the same year.
10. Cf. Paul Reynaud, *Au coeur de la mêlée* (Paris, 1951), pp. 364–69. The same occasion has been referred to by Hans J. Morgenthau.

The contrast between the two kinds of decision can again be stressed by referring to Munich. Let us leave out the shameful aspect of this episode, the desertion of Czechoslovakia by two friendly Powers, Britain and France. Let us assume that the Munich decision was taken by neutrals.[11] In our "revised history" of Munich, Lord Runciman's mission to Czechoslovakia has for its sole purpose the ascertaining of the true facts about the inhabitants of the Sudetenland: and the "true facts" in our version are a very strong demand from the Sudeten Germans for secession from Czechoslovakia and reunion with Germany.[12] Now, our four neutral decision-makers apply the rule of self-determination. And they make the very decision which history recounts. In our revised version, the process is far more honourable than was the case, since the four neutrals have been concerned to make a correct judicial decision on the basis of ascertained facts and of an ascertained rule. But while now judicially correct, the decision is still politically bad. Czechoslovakia still (as was the case) loses her fortified area, the Skoda works, the means and spirit of defence. Such consequences have to be contemplated in making a political decision. Resorting to judicial decision-making, when the occasion calls for political decision, is a grave political mistake.

"What will come of it?" is the question which the political decision-maker must have in mind.[13] Note that this question

11. It is of course a feature of political decisions that they are very seldom, if ever, taken by neutrals. And this is another very important contrast with judicial decisions. But it is not a feature which I wish to deal with in the present chapter.

12. Such a demand had indeed been aroused.

13. I do not forget that in some cases moral duty so forcibly requires a certain decision that it would be wrong to weigh the consequences. For instance, the White State harbours refugees from the far stronger Green State. Green demands "that these refugees be handed over . . . or else." The obvious reply of White is: "No . . . and damn the consequences!" But I do not have to consider such cases here since whenever moral duty immediately dictates the decision, there is no problem.

can never[14] be answered with complete certainty. However plausible it may now seem to me that the I_a decision will lead to an O_a outcome, this depends upon many factors, some of which I have taken into account and some of which I have not. If I am careful, I shall have thought of the behaviour of agents, the reception by subjects, the reaction of opponents; to all these I can only attach probabilities: but moreover the advent of outcome O_a may be balked by the unforeseen impact of another chain of events. Every outcome is uncertain. We decide on the basis of expectations.[15]

14. Before using so strong a term I cast about for possible exceptions. I did not find them.

15. Shackle gives an excellent definition of the term: "By *expectation* I mean the act of creating imaginary situations, of associating them with future named dates, and of assigning to each of the hypotheses thus formed a place on a scale measuring our belief that a specified course of action on our part will make this hypothesis come true." (G. L. S. Shackle, *Expectation in Econonics*, Cambridge, 1948.)

CHAPTER 3

The Committee, II
(Foresight, Values and Pressures)

It has been stressed that we have to deal with forward-looking decisions. Let us start with a simple instance: "the President's deficit problem." The imaginary situation is as follows. In January a recession is in progress; the President must now decide upon a balanced or unbalanced budget for a period beginning six months hence and ending eighteen months hence. We assume that the budget is his only means of action upon the economy and that no subsequent correction will be possible.

Two circumstances independent of the President's will may present themselves: in the course of the budgetary period an economic recovery may spontaneously occur, or it may not occur. If recovery occurs early in the period the President's "soft" budget will produce inflation. If no recovery occurs the President's "hard" budget will leave the recession to its downward course.[1] Thus the President may fall into two evils: inflation if he budgets for a deficit and the circumstance "recovery" appears, and depression if he budgets for balance and the circumstance which appears is "continuing recession." On the other hand he will do well if he budgets for balance and recovery

---

1. We are not here dealing in economics, we do not have to consider the eventuality of a deficit occurring through the very progress of the recession.

appears or if, recession tending to continue, his deficit happens to be timely for the restoration of prosperity. Calling the three possible outcomes inflation, depression and prosperity, we can group the eventualities in a simple "pay-off" table.

		Future circumstance	
		Recession	*Recovery*
Present	*Balance*	depression	prosperity
decision	*Deficit*	prosperity	inflation

Now the President calls four advisers: *A, B, C* and *D*. Let us take them in pairs. *A* and *B* both regard the evils of inflation and depression as equivalent. They disagree, however, on the likelihood of circumstances. *A* regards spontaneous recovery early enough within the budgetary period as highly unlikely while *B* regards it as very likely. Thus *A* will recommend deficit financing as adequate to the more likely circumstances, while for the same reason *B* will advocate a balanced budget.

C and *D*, asked to assess the relative chances of spontaneous recovery and continuing recession, refuse to commit themselves: they cannot tell; in other words recovery and recession seem to them equally likely. Still they differ very sharply in their recommendations to the President. Why? Because *C* deems inflation much worse than depression, while *D* regards depression as far the greater evil.

Thus the President's advisory committee divides equally; both *A* and *D* recommend deficit financing though for different reasons; both *B* and *C* recommend balance, again for different reasons. *D* is willing to admit that the deficit he advocates has even chances of producing inflation, but this, in his view, is the lesser evil. *A* is willing to admit that the evil produced by deficit financing is as bad as the other, but he deems it less probable. Thus the positions taken by our four advisers are determined by their ranking of the evils to be feared and their assessments of circumstances.[2]

Finding a deadlock within his advisory committee, the President decides to hear out what the advisers have to say, first on the relative evils of inflation and depression (a discussion of values), secondly on the relative likelihoods of spontaneous recovery or continuing recession. On the value issue A and B are silent, C stresses the evils of inflation, D the evils of depression. The President is swayed to the side of D: he now feels that depression is the greater evil, not perhaps by a large margin. There remains to discuss the relative likelihoods of spontaneous recession and continuing recovery. This time C and D are silent, A denies and B affirms that spontaneous recovery is the more probable alternative. The President is swayed by B, and comes to believe that continuing recession is the less likely circumstance.

After these two discussions how does the President stand?

Depression is the greater evil: therefore let me make sure that it does not occur, and for that purpose I shall choose the deficit budget. But before I settle for it definitely, let me consider the consequences. I hold spontaneous recovery to be the more likely circumstance and I know that its coincidence with a deficit budget is inflation. Therefore the most likely outcome of my deficit decision is inflation.

At this point the President may regard it as "irrational"[3] to take a decision which has more than even chances of producing an

---

2. It is customary to speak of "subjective utilities" (in this case disutilities) and "subjective probabilities." Subjective probabilities are nothing other than "degrees of belief," as Shackle puts it.

3. An expression very loosely used.

evil result, he may shift back to the balanced budget which has more than even chances of producing a good result (since spontaneous recovery is the more likely circumstance): but he must admit to himself that in making that choice he runs the risk of the greater evil, and he turns back again. . . .

Situations of this type are quite frequent in politics (as they are indeed in private lives). An important literature has developed on "rational" choice in conditions of uncertainty, and, more recently, experimental research has been undertaken to find out how men are in fact likely to choose under such conditions.

Such speculations and investigations are very attractive to me and I believe that they will come to play an important part in political science: this will, however, require a great deal of adjustment to the specific requirements of the discipline.

The President's problem, as outlined above, is an extremely simple "gamble" situation, where the maxim for rational choice is almost unquestioned: he should "maximize expected utility."[4] In our elementary instance the maxim leads to a simple comparison of the ratio of likelihoods to the ratio of utilities. But the President's evaluation that depression is worse than inflation does not entail his formulating a numerical ratio between the two; nor does his evaluation that recovery is more likely than recession entail his formulating a numerical ratio. He will appreciate differences only if one is large and the other small, in which case he will neglect the small one.

---

4. Putting it roughly, any given course can give rise to a number of outcomes (in our simple example only two). The chooser sets a value on each outcome (subjective utility) and attributes to it a likelihood (subjective probability). He multiplies for each outcome its subjective utility by its subjective probability and adds up the terms thus obtained for all the outcomes of a given course. That course which produces the higher sum is to be preferred.

Now let me note the hidden assumptions relative to our committee. These are indifference to outside pressures, a common concern for general prosperity, agreement as to what is bad,[5] and honesty in statement. Let me start with the last point. Suppose that the advisers have been called upon to give their views in alphabetical order; each of A, B, and C has stated what is to him the likelihood of spontaneous recovery and how he feels about the evils of inflation and depression: he has thus justified his counsel. D has listened throughout, and he is deeply worried. Remember that he dreads the depression as the greater evil and regards continuing recession as just as likely as recovery. The situation after A, B and C have spoken seems to him glum. The three preceding speakers have left a majority (of one to zero) for the value-judgement that inflation is the worse evil.[6] D knows that he can balance this. But he wants to do better than that. Now the three preceding speakers have left a tie as to the relative likelihoods of recovery and recession.[7] If D speaks honestly on that point, he will leave the committee tied as to likelihood. If, however, he takes the line that continuing recession is the more likely circumstance, then he establishes a majority on likelihood.

Then if the President makes up his own mind on the basis of statements by his advisers, the President will recapitulate as follows. First, as to the evils to be feared; one is to be feared just as much as the other.[8] But secondly, as to likelihood of

5. All members agree that both inflation and depression are evils, even if for C inflation is the worse evil and depression is the worse for D.

6. C regards inflation as the greater evil, A and B are neutral in this respect.

7. A regards recovery as less likely, B as more likely, C accepts that they are equally likely.

8. A and B: they are equally bad; C: inflation is worse; D: depression is worse. Result: equal division.

continuing recession, there is a majority which regards this as the more likely circumstance.[9] Therefore, the best policy is deficit financing.

Thus, by making a dishonest statement on likelihood, D will have achieved his purpose of ensuring against the evil he fears. Such behaviour not uncommonly arises out of patriotic concern. D may not even be aware that he makes a dishonest statement. While he himself had no views on the likelihood of recovery or recession, he was impressed by A's exposition of the likelihood of continuing recession. Because that is what he fears, the prediction of A made a greater impression upon him than that of B, and now he has worked A's opinion into his mind.

Whatever the differences between the members of our committee, we have assumed that they have the same object in mind, national prosperity. They do differ in their ranking of evils, but they agree that both inflation and depression are evils. This being so, we can say that they have a general will in common, or that they have a common concern, or that they display moral homogeneity. Never mind what form of words we use, it is clear that the situation will be altered if, for instance, C not only has a strong conviction that inflation is bad for the country, but positively desires a depression, because, in his view, "it will break the unions"; it may be that breaking the unions is for him a means to an ultimate patriotic end, it may be that he has come to desire it with such a passion that it is now a goal in itself. Not only in the second case but also in the first, C has in mind some other object than national prosperity in the fiscal year to come, and this disrupts the moral homogeneity of the committee.

This disruption is completed if the various advisers do not

---

9. A: more likely; B: less likely; C: equally likely; and now D calls it more likely.

have the same interest in mind, but the interests of various parts of the body politic.[10] Then of course the members of the committee display what would be a fault in members of a tribunal and what is also a fault in members of a political committee: partiality.

But such a fault is more natural in a member of a political committee. In the example which has served us up to now, the President has freely recruited his four advisers and therefore he could choose men owing no special allegiance to any one section of the community and prejudiced in favour of none. But if we substitute for our model a committee of five Ministers equal in decision-making power, these men may feel special concern for that section of the public from which they draw their support or with which they are in sympathy.

In the foregoing chapter, judicial and political decision-making were sharply contrasted. Yet I left out the main difference between them. The judge is deemed to be impartial and independent. I have briefly suggested that the political decision-maker is less apt to be impartial. What I now wish to stress is that he is never independent. The judge is deemed exempt from any outside pressure, and should he be exposed to such pressure he is expected to withstand it. The condition of the political magistrate is utterly different.

His being subject to outside pressure is not abnormal but natural. The judge decides an issue which affects only one or few,[11] by application of principles which are generally received. He stands in a position of intangible majesty relative to the parties affected, and saving some exceptions their reactions

---

10. Cf. Rousseau's *Social Contract*, Book IV, ch. 1.

11. Except in the case of so-called judiciary decisions which have the value of precedent, but in that case this becomes a political decision. It would be hard to deny the political character of some Supreme Court decisions in the United States.

are insignificant.[12] The political magistrate, on the other hand, decides issues which affect great numbers; as he must decide them with a view to their outcome they cannot always be presented as a mere application of principles. He does stand in a position of majesty, but a precarious one because his authority rests upon opinion and is apt to vanish if opinion turns against him. He cannot be indifferent to the reactions evoked because these are a part of the decision's outcome, and may indeed determine the outcome.

It is possible to write a play centring either upon a judicial or a political decision. But in the first case the curtain falls when the sentence has been passed: the drama resides in the conflicting motives whose interplay results in the decision; this, however, constitutes no more than the prologue in the second case: the drama here consists in the reactions to the decision, and the consequences arising therefrom. Obviously the story of prohibition in the United States does not come to its end with the passage of the "dry" law. What followed is essential: the rise of a whole profession dedicated to the violation of the law, the habit of illegality bred in subjects, the cases of corruption among enforcement agents: these constitute the drama.

A political decision may indeed fail to achieve the object sought by decision-makers even if dutifully accepted by subjects and carried out by agents: but such miscarriage falls outside our present purview. We have to consider the trouble attending a decision resentfully received by some subjects or agents. The outside pressure to which the deciding committee finds itself subject at the decision-making stage deserves notice

---

12. This will not be true if great excitement has been generated. But if for instance authors of a lynching are being judged, even popular emotion in their favour should be disregarded by the judge. If it is necessary to bow to popular fury, this will be a matter for the political authority.

as the premonitory shadow of the resistance to which the decision, once made, may give rise. The committeemen must therefore consider whether the good result they expect from the decision may not be balked by such reactions. But discordance between the judgement of the committee and existing dispositions is even more likely, in a democratic form of government, to occur the other way round: that is, there may be a strong demand for a decision which the committeemen regard as ill-advised or harmful.

Only a dearth both of imagination and experience can lead to a simple view of the relationship between a governing body and opinion. It is a rank absurdity to believe that any governing body can ever afford indifference to the dispositions of subjects and agents, because it must depend upon them for the actualization of the commands it utters: and this remains true whatever the form of government.

But it is no less unrealistic to assume that the governing body, acknowledging the power of opinion, can live in harmony with it, letting itself be guided by its demands. This could be done of course if the people were consistently of one mind, or even if there were a continuing majority for a coherent set of decisions. But in fact demands for a certain decision are usually minority demands, and different minorities may on different occasions be strong enough to "swing" decisions inconsistent with each other: nor should this be taken as implying that one and the same majority is incapable of demanding successive inconsistent decisions. But we need not consider this, since in fact outside pressures are, at the decision-making stage, almost always minority pressures. Let us consider them.

Let us picture the polling of a population for and against a given decision. Such polling results in a threefold classification: "for," "against" and "don't know." It is conceivable that some method be devised to measure the intensity of feeling of those who take a stand: [13] if this were done, all the members of one camp could be ranked according to the intensity of their feeling. We can imagine a simple graph where the intensity of feeling is measured on the Y axis and the number of those having an intensity of feeling equal or superior to Y^1 is measured along the X axis. Indeed we can imagine both camps represented on the same graph, with those *for* the measure counted in the positive right-hand quadrant and those *against* in the negative right-hand quadrant.

What such a graph would show, in all but exceptional cases, is that those with a great intensity of feeling, either for or against, are but a minute fraction of their camp, while intensity of feeling falls off very rapidly as greater numbers are taken into account. Those people who feel very strongly on the subject are therefore likely to exercise the outside pressure at the decision-making stage. They may be well- or ill-placed to obtain a hearing from the committeemen, to make an impression upon them. But prudent decision-makers will bear in mind the "multiplier potential" of these few. Suppose that the committee disregards strenuous opposition to a measure because it comes only from a few. And suppose that the measure once passed, these opponents, goaded to exasperation, find it possible to raise the tepid disapproval of their fellows to a great pitch of intensity: the government is now in great trouble.

Let us stress that the "majority" notion is of no help here. Possibly there were somewhat more people mildly for than against the measure before it was taken; possibly even after the opponents have stirred up many followers, there still are more people favourable to the measure than hostile: but if they are

---

13. For instance, one would seek to find out the degree of sacrifice which those interrogated would personally make to ensure the passing or shelving of the decision.

mildly favourable, while a very important minority is energetically hostile, the government is hardly helped by such feeble support. While if it excites those favourable, bringing them also to fever pitch, then the community is split. Prudent governors will therefore, when faced by a very vigorous opposition to a measure — even if it comes from a small number — seek to estimate the potential multiplier of this small number. Similarly, when faced by pressing demands which are uttered with great energy by only a small number, it must consider the possibility that this wind will grow into a hurricane.

Let us find a name for our small number of people who feel very strongly on a given issue: call them "issuists." They can be said to enjoy a natural multiplier if they happen to be the most intense members of a large natural group. For instance, they are farmers violently contesting a measure inimical to farmers, it is not improbable that they will arouse the whole farming group.

But we may also have a small number of people who have intense feelings of a more general nature; for instance they detest the present political regime. Such people have no natural multiplier but they may build an artificial multiplier by strong internal organization and efficient propaganda. It will obviously be to their interest to join on every occasion with those excited issuists who are endowed with an important natural multiplier. And the trouble which each issuist group is capable of causing by itself will then become not a succession of unrelated troubles but a consistent building-up of ever-increasing trouble from crisis to crisis.

PART VI

Attitudes

CHAPTER 1

Attention and Intention

Our thinking is actualized in our speaking: looking at our words therefore is a good way of looking at ourselves. The Latin *tendo* denotes both effort and orientation, that is, the basic properties of any living organism. A child knows that while a stone can be picked up in shallow water, a fish which the hand seeks to grasp will escape: it mobilizes its energy for flight. While energy is *available* in physical systems, only the living organism can be said to *possess* energy. The difference is striking: in the case of the former, stored energy can be released at the time and in the direction chosen by an outside operator; in the latter case the timing and orientation of the release come from within the organism, which also controls its degree, making a lesser or greater effort. Man is immensely superior to other living organisms in the control of owned energy: under the telling name of "self-control," we praise a high capacity of refusing the release of energy under outside provocation and of administering this release purposefully.

Our generalship of energy release involves *attention* and *intention*. Lacking both, the human organism would be passively responsive to any pressure exerted upon it. Attention is a "presence of mind" whereby we take cognizance of a situation, conceive it as a problem and try to solve it. Intention might be called a "futurity of mind" whereby we picture a future situation and seek to actualize it. These attitudes pertain also, in far lower degrees, to animals. For instance, if we observe a sleeping dog bothered by a buzzing insect we first notice its merely mechanical reactions to each contact of the fly: but then the dog awakes, becomes attentive to the fly, and then becomes intent upon catching it.

While Man is eminently capable of attention and intention, these capacities are very unequally developed. Anyone who has raised children — or indeed looked at himself — knows the difficulty of steadying attention or intention: attention shifts or vanishes, intention flags. Men manifest great inequalities in these capacities, essential to achievement.

Let us consider attention and intention from an ethical angle. We would hardly hesitate to say that greater capacities of either attention or intention are better than lesser capacities. But the likeness stops here.

Attention can never do any harm. If a man attentively follows a game of bridge while aware that at the same time he could listen to the admirable rendering of an opera, I will opine that he has ill-chosen the object of his attention; he has missed something but he has not done anything injurious. If a man devotes his attention to games of dice, this seems to me wasteful: but that is the harshest adjective which I can apply; indeed attention is so inherently good that a great good has on occasion come from this most "silly" application of attention.[1]

Of intention, we cannot speak as kindly. It is telling that the adjective "bad" has quite a different force when qualifying intention than it has when qualifying attention. "Bad attention" will mean no more than "weak attention"; but "bad intention"

---

1. Probability calculation arose out of Chevalier de Meré's observations upon games of dice. Von Neumann and Morgenstern's famous *Theory of Games* is said to have been fostered around the poker tables of Princeton.

does not mean "weak intention"; indeed the term is most apt to be used when the intention is strong. Now if we are dealing with a strong attention we shall never call it bad: however unworthy its object may seem to us, this mis-direction of attention may in our eyes bring the utility of attention to a negligible value; but never to a negative value.

It is otherwise in the case of intention. The core of the contrast lies in the fact that the several attentions of several men cannot conflict with one another, while their several intentions can do so. My attention to the problem in hand is in no way impaired by my neighbour's attention to a quite different object. But my intention to get on with this chapter is impaired by my neighbour's intention to have a conversation with me. This familiar example makes it clear that there can be no reason to attribute a negative value to the other man's attention while there is often reason to attribute a negative value to his intention (even if objectively innocent or indeed praiseworthy).

Scholars discussing Politics labour under a most heavy handicap. They are men blessed with the delights of attention and who experience practically no other intention than that of persevering undisturbed in their attention. The best of possible worlds for them would be one whose every inhabitant would be wrapped up in attention to some subject, whatever it might be. No conflict can arise from these different exercises of attention. In the midst of such a society, the occasional inattentive and therefore bumbling fellow can be a slight nuisance but no more.

The picture, however, is completely changed with the advent of the intentive man: his intention affects and involves others, clashes with other intentions: intention is the great breeder of conflict. Incompatibility of intentions fosters a Manichaean view of society. The man who intends to build a dam cannot but be regarded as an enemy by the villagers whose homes are to be submerged, and their intention to preserve the village cannot but be regarded as an obstacle by the engineer.

I have spoken of attention up to now in a way which suggested its concentration upon some one object, problem or task. But obviously attention differs again from intention in its transferability. *What* is intended seems essential to the idea of intention, not so to the idea of attention. We can think of "attentiveness" as a general disposition to attend to unspecified objects. It is revealing that the word "intentiveness" does not exist: it would denote an absurdity, a disposition to intend, empty of content.

Attentiveness is a readiness to devote attention: more than that, a disposition to respond with attention to any problematic situation arising within a field. This is a functional obligation of anyone who finds himself responsible for the welfare of others. As it is my policy to pick the most trivial illustrations, I shall point to the tourist agent in charge of a guided tour:[2] any kind of difficulty may arise, he must cope with it. But his position implies a fundamental contradiction: our man must give his attention to any one of his wards who needs it, and yet his attention must remain available to others. Here is a fundamental contrast between the attention of the intellectual, which, committed to one object, becomes unavailable for others, and the attention of the warden[3] which must always be available, even though it is always engaged.

It is most illuminating to call upon an inexperienced Min-

---

2. Had I chosen the more obvious example of a parent, I should have had to dispel misunderstandings which go back to Filmer.

3. I use this word to denote a man whose acknowledged role it is to "take care" of a given group, in some respect.

ister. While he tries to focus his attention upon the problem one expounds, his telephone calls to his attention other matters, assistants also rush in with portentous mien and urgent whisperings. This variety of demands which utterly balks the poor fellow's honest attempts to attend represent the "natural" condition of the warden. Of course a capable statesman gives his visitor undivided attention for the time period allotted, the telephone does not ring, no doors open, but this implies a system of damming up and channelling claims on his attention.

Wherever there is power, demands for the use of it pour in, and the statesman needs many ears; but these demands cannot be relied upon to guide the allocation of attention: the din of paltry requests may well blanket the faint cracking, ominous of landslides. The statesman needs many eyes to follow the course of things all around him.

It is pleasing to picture a committee of wise men vigilantly over-seeing the whole life of the body politic: so wide-awake that nothing escapes their notice; so discerning that they do not allow minor issues to draw them away from the major; so prudent that they are not only capable of meeting critical situations but also able to deal in time with situations which might become critical. These wise men practise attentive statesmanship: we can call them Attenders. And they have indeed no intention, besides the general purpose of warding off difficulties and evils.

The task of these wardens will be heavy in proportion to the conflict of intentions within the body politic.[4] This is so obvious that all the plans for an ideal commonwealth have ever been addressed to precluding the conflict of intentions. The requirement is perfectly met if you can substitute for the clashing diversity of unpredictable individual intentions, an *ex ante*

---

4. If we omit consideration of external relations.

coherent pattern of intentions driving individual men to behaviours harmonious with one another. This you will have,
said the ancient philosophers, if citizens are taught from an
early age to intend "a life of virtue," if this is so clearly delin-
eated that no one can mistake his path and if each person's self-
respect is so stimulated that he would feel ashamed to stray.
While the habit of virtue will prevent the worst, the reinforcing
desire for honour will lead to supreme achievements: all this
within a pattern of basically coherent intentions.

This of course constitutes a Utopian model. But it cannot
be accepted even as a Utopia if one sets a high value upon
the originality of individual intentions. That men's intentions
bring them into conflict is a fact accepted by all minds. But it
can be accepted in different ways: at one extreme it will be
regarded as a measure of the community's moral derangement,
at the other extreme as the natural outcome of a desirable ac-
centuation of individuality. Hobbes stressed the latter view, but
on account of this he was also led to picture the task of coping
with conflicts as very hard and calling for very great authority.

We have said something of the attentive statesman. His attitude
could be summed up as follows: "Who knows what may happen? But when something happens I must quickly find out
what to do about it." Let us now turn to the intending politic.
His attitude is very different indeed and could be summed up
as follows: "I know what I want to bring about. My business is
to devise and procure its actualization."

The intending politic can more easily capture men's imagi-
nations than the attentive statesman: "he knows what he
wants." True, and therefore his task is a very much simpler
one. Not for him the renewed worry of seeking the best answers
to problems arising out of circumstances. He has but one problem and that a purely operational one: procuring the victory of
his intention.

He wills a definite achievement and pursues it, with single-mindedness. Occurrences irrelevant to his purpose leave him indifferent, unless they can be exploited for his end. While the attentive statesman wears himself out repairing everything which goes wrong, the intending politic addresses the whole of his faculties to the furtherance of his one project. Let us picture, with some allegorical trappings, the encounter of our two men. The attentive one sits in a high place; he has eyes all around his head, like Argus, and he mutters to himself, thrashing out the problems which come pouring to his feet. The intending one strides boldly at the head of his followers, wearing blinkers which allow him to see nothing but his goal, which he restates in a loud, clear voice. In this encounter, the attentive statesman is obviously at a disadvantage; the other man is wholly concentrated on this one definite issue, and easily looks like a hero.

The attentive statesman cannot well cope with the vigorous Intender who has proved an efficient instigator. A great variety of intentions, arising more or less evenly throughout the body politic, are apt to create only minor problems of adjustment: some part of this various intending finding its way to completion, some wasting away in friction, and only very little of it turning to congestive points calling for treatment. It is quite otherwise when the intending politic successfully musters energies for his political enterprise. This then is a concentrated drive which creates disturbances, and towards which the attentive statesman must take a definite line, opposing it or accepting it. But the latter alternative puts him in an unhappy position; this drive causes perturbations to which he attaches far more importance than the driver is willing to. The association of the intending politician with the attentive statesman is bound to be an unhappy one, because the statesman must want the driver to relax his drive so that adjustments can be made, while the intending politic is eager to press on, regardless of the perturbations which are a by-product of his enterprise.

Hence these two types cannot work together; one must squeeze out the other. At a glance, it appears that these two types dominate alternately in political history. Indeed one is tempted to distinguish quite short-term swings from attention to intention and back to attention, swings of much longer duration between the same poles, and possibly a long-term trend from attention to intention—but that may be a delusion due to our present position.[5]

The bold sweep of imagination of the intending politic, his strong visualizing of a shape to come, his passion for this creature of his mind, his will to make it come alive, his courage in pursuing that purpose—all this catches our fancy. Here is a hero for us, a man who casts his spell upon the future, a creator. This is the supreme politic: personally I do not like him very much, it is better to encounter him in history books than in real life.

Be that as it may, the intending politic is the man upon whom a study of political dynamics must focus: because he is the provider of movement in the body politic. For this purpose, he need not be a Great Intender. It is not very difficult to be an effective Intender; it is far easier than to be an effective Attender.

Consider that attending effectively involves attending to everything which can affect the body politic or its parts, while intending effectively implies only intending something. While the Intender is concerned only to clear the road to his goal, the Attender is concerned to keep the whole communications sys-

---

5. "Driving" and "targets" are characteristic expressions of an intentive attitude.

tem working so that many different people can attain their many different destinations: this is a far less spectacular feat but it is far more difficult.

Therefore it is not surprising that the perfection of attentive statesmanship should be so rare. Where it is approximated to as nearly as human fallibility allows, it is not recognized; the benefits which then accrue are not attributed to the statesman, since he has not directly procured them but has only fostered the conditions of their occurrence. Human foresight being limited and uncertain, our man sooner or later will fail to see the cloud "no bigger than a man's hand" out of which the tempest will come. Trouble may arise from any point; and it is the handicap of the Attender that he is expected to abate any trouble; while the Intender promises nothing of the sort: he turns people's minds to his goal and away from any intervening troubles. Indeed he represents any trouble arising as one more reason to drive towards the goal, however illogical the connection.

As the pace of change increases, it seems that the world of politicians is increasingly caught unprepared by events, its *mores* and procedures having undergone no tightening up, perhaps the reverse: perception is not more acute, reaction to impending events goes in a more dilatory manner through more sprawling channels. With this increasing lack of efficiency in attentiveness, intending comes to the fore as the most visible political attitude.

CHAPTER 2

The Team against
the Committee

A certain small group of men (hereafter called "the team")
share an intention, the implementation of which requires at
least a once-for-all decision of some public authority.[1] The
most obvious procedure (hereafter called "first") is to plead in
favour of that decision with the holders (or holder) of the competent authority. The next most obvious (hereafter called "second"), is to win over people who have easy and habitual access
to the decision-maker or makers. These first and second procedures can be practised under any regime.

In the United States of this day the first procedure consists
of calling upon the President, or Secretary, or upon Senators
and Congressmen, and putting the case for the decision. The
second procedure consists of mobilizing people who "have the
ear" of these important people and may bring up the matter.
The same methods can be practised in a despotic regime. The
despot is seldom inaccessible: the case can be put to him; also
he lives surrounded by courtiers, and these may mention the
request at favourable moments. Of course some requests have

---

1. It may require as much as the complete taking-over of public authority, but we
start out with the narrower requirement.

no chance at all of being listened to by the despot: but the same is true in any regime.[2]

The case which interests us here is that in which the decision-makers ("the committee") cannot be persuaded directly or swung over by the mild nagging of their immediate circle. The team then turns to a third procedure, the organization of an outside pressure upon the committee. This is a current procedure in a regime of liberty: indeed its being held legitimate defines political liberty.

What is this third procedure? Through propaganda, the team recruits partisans of its intention who join with it in demanding the decision. How does this affect the committee? Here we must distinguish two possibilities. (a) When the team first uttered its demand, the committee failed to consider it, owing to the abundance of other business or to sheer negligence. Anyone at all familiar with government knows how often demands fail to pass the threshold of attention. If such was the case, then the volume of support now afforded to the demand forces it through the threshold, and it may be that the committee, now impelled to pay attention, will find that the arguments advanced in favour of the decision are sound and convincing. But there is a second possibility; (b) the committee had seriously considered the request, heard the reasons given in its favour, and had found against the decision. Let us concentrate on this latter case. If the decision demanded by the team is wrong in the eyes of the committee, it is still wrong now that there is notable support for it. How then will this support swing the decision? In this case the support obtained by the team works as a threat.

2. E.g. in the United States: that all unions be dissolved and declared henceforth illegal, or that all corporations with a capital exceeding a million dollars be nationalized, or that no citizen with a German grandfather be eligible to public office, etc.

First, committeemen may have a selfish regard for their own political future: for example, "I might not be re-elected if I antagonized this determined group." But secondly they must have a patriotic regard for peace and order, and may dread the trouble which the faction now arrayed in support of the measure is capable of causing.

We have seen that instigating support for the team's intention may well be necessary to force its request through the committee's threshold of attention. If the proposal then and therefore receiving proper attention is deemed receivable, well and good: the mobilizing of support has been effective and salutary. If, however, the committee, having given due consideration to the proposal (whether before or after the mobilization of support), has condemned and rejected the proposal, then support can "swing" the committee only through its nuisance value. This is what we shall now go into.

Let us restate the assumptions unmistakably:

(1) There is a team which demands of a committee a certain decision.

(2) The committee has fully heard the reasons given in favour of the decision, and after deliberation has found them wanting.

(3) The team has mobilized outside support for the decision.

The situation can then develop in various ways, which I shall classify from the angle of the team, on which my interest centres here.

(*a*) The team is confident that it can muster ever-increasing support, expects that such backing will in time become overwhelming, and is content to wait for the reaching of this situation.

If so, then the team logically turns its back upon the negative attitude of the committee and addresses its attention solely to generating positive attitudes in the public. It makes converts who then join their voices to those of the team, and the outcry in favour of the wanted decision grows exponentially.

What is the committee to do? It may stand fast because it forms an estimate of the team's potential support very different from the team's own sanguine expectations. If the latter seem likely to be verified, the committee may suddenly cave in, seized by a fit of political cowardice; or it may stand fast come what may, and then the surge of public opinion will wash it away. But in any of the eventualities envisaged, the process involves no breach of the peace. Not so if we turn to another system of behaviour of the team, following from its alternative premisses.

(*b*) The team regards it as unlikely that it can over a period of time mobilize adequate support to carry the wanted decision by sheer weight of numbers, or it is unwilling to accept the implied delay, either because the critical date is too distant, or too uncertain, for its patience, or because the decision called for would be stultified by the passage of time.

Then the team's problem is to overcome with its present means, a mere minority support, the stubborn refusal of the committee. This is not a matter of winning over indifferent or near-indifferent members of the public but of breaking the deliberate will of men in authority, who enjoy the obedience of agents, and at least the passive support of the majority. How can this be achieved? We need only look around us to answer the question.

In such a position, the team avails itself of its dedicated supporters to generate nuisances for the committee. Nuisance policies are the natural resort of a team which relies upon intensive rather than extensive support. Its efforts are addressed to subverting the committee rather than to converting the people. The word "nuisance" is here used relative to the committee: it is not implied that the actions so denominated are in themselves "wrong," but that they are meant to badger the committee. There exists a vast range of nuisance tactics. Ethically speaking, going on a hunger-strike and throwing a bomb are poles apart: yet both are demonstrations of intense feeling, meant to break the will of the committee.

All forms of action here dealt with tend to dissolve the assurance of the committeemen, to make them feel insecure in one way or another. The milder forms of action (such as picketing, demonstrations, marches), peacefully conducted, bring home to the rulers that here is discontent: and it must generate in them some doubt whether they have done all they should. A feeling of compassion and possibly shame is excited by the self-inflicted suffering of a hunger-striker.

There are many means of pressure which raise a question-mark in the minds of the committeemen, without offering them a direct challenge. But it is tempting for the intending team to go further. If its militant members turn to obstructive practices, then the committee is forced to choose between enduring the disturbance caused by the team, giving in to the demand backed by the agitators, or using the means of force at its disposal to put down the perturbation. The first course is acceptable only if the perturbation is limited in time. The government for instance may put up with the blocking of roads by the farmers if it lasts only a day or two, not if it is kept up. On the other hand, breaking up the barricades by force is also a disturbance, the moral costs of which the government must weigh. Or supposing that a group which petitions Parliament mulishly bars access to it, the authorities must clear the way; but if this clearing is pertinaciously opposed it can involve considerable moral costs to the committee.

In such cases much depends on just how far demonstrators are prepared to go. A march peacefully begun may turn ugly.

Pressure designed as a show of feeling may evolve into an exercise of power. It is all too readily assumed that an assembled crowd embodies the feelings of "the people"; this is obviously a confusion. A group quite incapable of mustering an electoral majority can be quite capable of mobilizing a marching crowd at a strategic time and place and to endow it with such impetus as to place the committee between the alternative of shooting or fleeing.

Terrorist strategy unfortunately calls for special mention. It requires only a small number of adepts willing to commit acts of violence to place the committee in a position of extreme embarrassment. Especially if the terrorist blows are dealt at random, it will almost inevitably happen that reactions will fly wide of the mark and affect the innocent. Goading the authorities into hurting innocent bystanders is essential to terrorist strategy. Its efficiency lies mainly in evoking blind anger and blundering retorts: if pea-shooting at a policeman can induce him to run after a harmless little girl, that is farce: on the same pattern, major tragedy can be enacted. A course of terrorism can be guaranteed to call forth from the authorities reactions which displease public opinion and worry consciences within the government itself. Any innocent who happens to be hurt by repressive action benefits the guilty, to whom compassion extends. The trick of combining the manners of gangsters with the moral benefits of martyrdom has been developed throughout the twentieth century.

This is the century of the terrorist technique, fittingly opened by Sorel's *Réflexions sur la violence*.[3] If a team feels very strongly about an issue and communicates this strength of feeling to others, there is always a risk that some one of these others will commit an act of violence. If this occurs, those who have inspired the feeling should now experience a sense of

---

3. Georges Sorel, *Réflexions sur la violence* (Paris, 1908).

guilt: that is an ancient and natural pattern. Very different is the modern pattern. The acts of violence are positively desired by the team not only for their immediate impact upon the adversary, but for the reactions to which they will goad him and the harm they will do to his reputation. Devising such a strategy requires the complete abolition of moral sense which can be obtained in Man only if and when he becomes possessed by an "idée fixe," an intention, deemed moral, which he pursues at all costs. The most immoral of all beliefs is the belief that it can be moral to suspend the operation of all moral beliefs for the sake of one ruling (supposedly moral) passion. But this precisely is the doctrine which has run throughout the twentieth century.

It has led to a form of Politics which first admits that what is waged is a form of war, and secondly admits that there are no ethical rules in this sort of war. This dreadful evolution has been prepared by the thoughtless admission that Politics is institutionalized conflict. If it is essentially conflict, why respect the institutions?

There are "our people" and "others." With others, we may be at peace or at war. We Oceanians may be at war with the Ruritanians for a variety of reasons roughly falling into five classes: (1) we want to do them some harm in reprisal for the harm they have done to some of us: this is *avenging* warfare;[4] (2) we must oppose the present exercise of their power against us: this is *defensive* warfare;[5] (3) we dread[6] the future exercise of their power against us: this is *preventive* warfare; (4) they stand in the way of something we want,[7] their opposing will and power constitutes an obstacle which has to be overcome: this is *purpose-*

---

4. A very ancient category.
5. This has ever been adjudged a *just* war.
6. Whether rightly or wrongly.
7. Whether we want it purely and simply, or deem ourselves entitled to it.

ful warfare; (5) their behaviour offends our moral feelings and we must force them to desist from it: this is *moralizing* warfare. I set no great value on this classification: it is merely expedient for what follows.

No century has been more concerned than ours to do away with war: it has proved signally unsuccessful. All too little attention has been given to the phenomenon that internal politics have become increasingly more warlike.[8]

War is a condition which may obtain with foreigners, but peace is the condition which must obtain between compatriots: that is a most ancient maxim of Politics. The idea of peace implies that I wish my neighbour well, rejoice or grieve with him, take notice of his needs and wants, help him into success or out of failure, bear with his faults, am slow to take offence and ready to forgive, do not grudge him his good fortune, do not suspect his intentions, and would rather excuse than condemn his vagaries.

While this peaceful and friendly attitude is unanimously accepted as proper in a private man, strangely enough, as soon as I address other men, all is changed. It is easy to compose a political oration which brings in the five war motives spelled out earlier:

My friends, you are Blues. It would be wrong of you to forget the harm which was done to our fellows by Greens on X day. [Motive one.] This was indeed nothing but an instance of the immoral behaviour of the Greens, which cannot be tolerated in a proper city, and must be curbed. [Motive five.] Indeed, how can you let them at this very moment exercise their powers in a manner injurious to you? [Motive two.] Will you then allow them to build up this power still further? Should you not act before it has become irresistible? [Motive three.] Think of the

8. Not irrelevant to the observation above.

gain if you constrain these Greens to concede what, on any reasonable view of the matter, should be yours! [Motive four.]
Therefore, my friends, awake, arise! [etc.]

Which of us has not listened many a time to speeches built
on this model? We hardly notice that the pale horses of war are
evoked therein, fully confident that the speaker means a great
deal less than he says, and that the hearers take it at an enormous discount. It therefore comes to us as a shock that sometimes an orator does mean just what he says and does convey
an emotion corresponding to the face-value of his utterances.
The speaker is not, in that case, using big words to drum
up mild support for a mild measure mildly opposed by the
Greens, but he is actually mobilizing the Blues for war.

When some part of a people is joined together in a bellicose
spirit against some other part, that is a "faction."[9] All great

9. For American readers, it may be proper to point out that the present definition
is different from Madison's, simpler and—I believe—more convenient. Madison says:
"By faction, I understand a number of citizens, whether amounting to a majority or a
minority of the whole, who are united and actuated by some common impulse of
passion or of interest, adverse to the rights of other citizens, or to the permanent and
aggregate interests of the community" (*Federalist*, x). I quite agree with Robert A. Dahl
(*A Preface to Democratic Theory*, Chicago, 1956) that such a definition is equivocal.
Say that I am a member of a group "united and actuated by some common
impulse . . . ": I shall not grant that our action is directed against "the rights of other
citizens" but only against rights abused or usurped, or which, while they may at this
moment (under present law) be positive rights, have no basis in equity and should
"rightly" be cut down by a change in the law. In like manner, I shall not grant that our
action is directed against "the permanent and aggregate interests of the community"
but only against a caricature of these interests invoked by our opponents. A difference
of opinion regarding what rights should be, and what are the aggregate interests, must
then produce a difference in the denomination of our movement: a faction to those
who disagree with us, but not to ourselves.
    On the contrary, the far simpler definition offered above rests upon two ascertain-
able facts: that some are banded against others, and that their spirit is bellicose; and of
course it can be more or less so. This banding and bellicosity is what classical writers
have ever had in mind when speaking of factions.

political authors[10] have condemned factions and that for an obvious and fundamental reason. What constitutes a People is a general feeling of amity which faction turns to enmity. Militant members of a faction regard some of their compatriots with hostility, that is, as strangers.[11] Thus forming a faction is estranging some members of the commonwealth from others, which stands in direct contradiction to the classical understanding of the statesman's function, deemed to be the establishment, preservation and increase of amity between citizens. Therefore the founder of a faction plays exactly the opposite role to that which legend attributes to mythical founders of states. Hume expresses it very strikingly:

> As much as legislators and founders of states ought to be honoured and respected among men, as much ought the founders of sects and factions to be detested and hated; because the influence of faction is directly contrary to that of laws. Factions subvert government, render laws impotent, and beget the fiercest animosities among men of the same nation, who ought to give mutual assistance and protection to each other. And what should render the founders of parties more odious is the difficulty of extirpating these parties, when once they have taken rise in any state. They naturally propagate themselves for many centuries, and seldom end but by the total dissolution of that government in which they are planted. They are, besides, seeds which grow most plentifully in the richest soils; and though despotic governments be not entirely free from them, it must be confessed that they rise more easily, and propagate themselves faster, in free governments, where they always infect the legislature itself, which alone could be able, by the steady application of rewards and punishments, to eradicate them.[12]

10. With but one exception, and that one Machiavelli.

11. "Hostility," from *hostis* which means "enemy" but meant originally nothing other than "stranger," "he who is not one of us."

12. David Hume, *Essays and Treatises on Several Subjects* (London, 1742), vol. 1, part 1, essay VII, p. 52.

The urbane Hume speaks here with unwonted and significant intensity. Historical experience entitles him indeed to feel that warring factions first ruin the climate of civility and ultimately bring down the form of government under which they have arisen: thus did the Roman Republic perish, thus too the Italian Republics of the Middle Ages. But what can he mean when he calls for their eradication? He is too much of a realist to deny that men are prone to band together for a common purpose, and too far from being an authoritarian to recommend that such banding should be forbidden and contraveners persecuted. What then does he have in mind? The key is given, I believe, in the definition proposed above.

It is natural that men should band together in pursuit of a common intention; it is deplorable that the *animus* which unites them should turn to "animosity" against those who do not favour their purpose; it is detestable that they should develop "bellicosity" towards these compatriots. If such bellicosity defines the *faction*, then what is more reasonable than to desire the eradication of factions—which then clearly means that whatever groupings may occur within the people, none should wax bellicose? But how to prevent it?

Hume advances the view that it can be prevented by the legislature through "the steady application of rewards and punishments." The thought is not developed: had it been, it would have afforded precious guidance to the Weimar Reichstag. It is to me a wholly pleasing principle that political activity which waxes angry, pugnacious and threatening, thereby forfeits its legitimacy: but how to carry out the principle—that is an unsolved problem. Where is to be found the neutral authority, capable of uttering a fair judgement on whether a movement so behaves as to be called an enemy to the peace? The leaders of the movement will be arraigned because they induce their followers to violent conduct? So far so good. But how easy it is for them to argue that the true responsibility for such violence devolves upon the Authorities who obdurately resist just demands and obstruct a noble purpose: that it is the very resistance of the Authorities which generates the heat of anger: and in short that violence, incidental to their purpose, is a pretext invoked to disable them from achieving it.

Such a plea never fails to touch many hearts, to worry many consciences. Scrupulous people ask themselves whether their disposition to condemn has not some root in their enmity to these men's purpose. Sentimental people stress the sincerity of these men: and it is true enough that they sincerely want to attain their goal. The discussion shifts from what these men have done or caused to be done, to the cause which inspires them. And one fails to condemn them as wrongdoers for fear of condemning them as martyrs to their cause.

The attitude described has unimpeachable motives but disastrous consequences. Violence thrives on faint-hearted attempts to suppress it. And soon the situation evolves in a manner very favourable to the violent movement (call it A). At the other extreme of the political spectrum, a group (call it Z) clamours for exemplary punishment. This allows the A people who are committing an aggression against the body politic as a whole, to overshadow that fact by pointing to the hatred of the Z group directed against them. They can then ask moderate people: "Do you then join with the Z group?" The desire not to be identified with the Z group introduces a new factor of paralysis. Another stage is reached if the Z group itself resorts to violence. Now confusion reigns. The Authorities will have to hit right and left, with unseemly vigour and uncertain success. Violence is poison to the body politic, which, once introduced, spreads and leads to convulsions. It must never begin. How to avoid its appearance is not well known to us. What we do know is that it can disappear altogether where it was formerly frequent, and that it can also appear where it was quite unexpected.

I like to ask which of the states enduring to this day has the most lurid record of political violence, the most numerous instances of authority won at the point of the sword, and the longest list of murdered princes and ministers; the answer is: "England!" The frequency and brutality of English convulsions throughout the Middle Ages and right into the seventeenth century is unparalleled. It is the triumph of the British genius that its country's tempestuous politics have changed to an exemplary mildness, rightly admired throughout the world. This marvellous achievement cannot be adequately appreciated if one assumes that change in political manners must inevitably go in the direction of improvement. Unfortunately, this is not so. A striking contrast is offered by the history of Rome, where political disputes, however vigorous, were for many generations conducted with formality—up to the evil day when raving Senators assaulted Tiberius Gracchus and caused the blood of the newly re-elected tribune to be spilt on the very Capitol. This opened a horrible century, marked by the fury of Marius and the ruthlessness of Sulla. Rent by such ferocity, Rome was to seek peace at the hands of Octavius; but political criminality was to reappear at the very court of the emperors. This is classical proof—borne out, alas, by modern instances—that the change in political manners can also occur in the wrong direction.

Words receive their weight from experiences, which can be very different. The words "overthrow of the government" fall softly upon the ear when they call to mind a defeated President driving to the Capitol with his victor, and then retiring to enjoy henceforth high moral status, assured that respectful notice will be taken of his occasional pronouncements. Or again when one pictures the defeated Prime Minister "expelled" from the Treasury bench no further than to the bench opposite, or perhaps, as happened in France, "tumbled" from his leadership of the Cabinet to the Ministry of Finance or of Foreign Affairs.

The man whose memory harbours nothing but pictures of this kind cannot imagine that defeat may mean exile, imprisonment, execution or murder. Possibly, during the campaign he has now lost, he has said of his opponents: "They are a danger to the country." But whatever tone of conviction he may have brought to such a statement, certainly it did not imply that their victory places him in jeopardy. The new management may take some decisions he disapproves, do things somewhat offensive to his feelings, or somewhat injurious to interests he supports or shares. But he will not be despoiled of his property, deprived of his livelihood; his liberty, life and dignity are not at stake. It is to him unthinkable that he might be hunted as game, herded as cattle. But to a man who has witnessed *saeva jussa, continuas accusationes, pernicium innocentium* [13] Politics bears quite another appearance.

Such a contrast of experiences fosters an opposition of views. The man who was born into mild Politics cannot imagine it ferocious: and historical instances are to him fantastic tales. But he who has once seen men unmanned by victory and unmanned by defeat, who has watched how blood flushes the face of the one and drains from the face of the other, who has heard the blustering laugh and the pitiful cry, that man feels that the mildness of Politics is not so well assured, that its maintenance needs to be contrived: that this indeed is the first and foremost of political arts.

---

13. Tacitus, *Annales*, Book IV, xxxiii.

CHAPTER 3

The Manners of Politics

Let us indulge in a piece of make-believe. Ruritania is endowed with a computer which infallibly gives the optimal answer to every question, including those which refer to the choice of its attendants. All Ruritanians know *ex ante* that the prescriptions issued by the computer will be the most conducive to the good of the whole; and indeed *ex post*, when each prescription has been published, it becomes apparent to anyone who takes the trouble to check that this is the wisest decision. Assuming such a magic machine, what follows? However convinced that a decision coming from the computer is the best for the whole, an individual Ruritanian, Ego, may still dislike and infringe a prescription, because it does not suit his egotistical rationality[1] or, even more simply, because he will not bow to reason.[2]

1. Rousseau powerfully made this point: "Basing virtue on reason alone is giving it a shaky foundation. They say that virtue is the love of order. But should and can this love dominate over the love of my own well-being? Let them give me a clear and sufficient reason to prefer it. At bottom their supposed principle is a pure play of words: because I can in turn state that vice is the love of order taken in a different sense. The difference is that the good man refers himself to the order of the whole and the bad man sees the whole in relation to himself: he makes himself the centre of all things, while the good man sees himself at the circumference and looks to the centre of the whole." This is from "La profession de foi du Vicaire Savoyard" in *Emile*, and it is noteworthy that Voltaire jotted against this paragraph on his copy of the book: "These horrors should never be discovered to the public."

2. It is profoundly unsafe to assume that men act rationally in Politics.

If however Ego, under the conditions stated, revolts against the prescription of the computer, he will be handicapped in recruiting associates or followers. Those he will seek to stir up will be aware, *ex hypothesi*, that their action, behaviour or demand goes against the reasonably assessed good of the Whole. Such recruitment must therefore be limited to those who share a special interest, or who are fired by some blinding passion. Now let us add a second assumption (and here we move up from the mythology of science into philosophic anthropology). Suppose that Ruritanians have a nature so different from that with which we are familiar that the view of what is good for the whole invincibly determines their will. Now the problem is entirely solved: what is good for the whole will always be published to all and will always be done by everyone.[3]

This two-tiered fantasy serves to stress that in fact: (1) men are not irresistibly swayed by certain knowledge regarding the-good-of-the-whole (the second assumption does not correspond to reality); and (2) there is no such certain knowledge available to them (the first assumption does not correspond to reality). What follows? Primus advances what may be called "the imperative syllogism of political obligation" as follows:

Major: It is certainly good-for-the-whole that (all or certain) citizens do H;
Minor: All citizens should do what is good-for-the-whole;
Conclusion: Therefore (all or certain) citizens must do H.

Now Secundus feels strongly that the Major in this case is false, and therefore he sets himself against Primus. Tertius has no personal opinion about the Major and might perhaps be persuaded that it is right; but he strongly dislikes the conclu-

---

3. Obviously when we move to the second assumption, it is tempting to do away with the computer and replace it by the supposition that "right reason" brings each Ruritanian to reach the conclusions regarding the public good which are achieved in the first model by the computer. But this correction is not relevant to my purpose.

sion as it applies to him; he dares not deny the Minor, therefore he is relieved to find that he can justify his refusal of the conclusion by following Secundus in denial of the Major. Thus in Politics we find a mixture of disagreements about the common good and of personal wants. According to the temperament and experiences of the onlooker, he is likely to emphasize the former or the latter. There are cynics who affirm that any Major referring to the common good is only meant to lead to a conclusion wanted for self-regarding reasons, but this is untenable: such camouflage would be ineffective if there were no effective concern for the common good, lending prestige to propositions referring to it, and therefore making it worthwhile to resort to such camouflage.

The common good is indeed a powerful notion, but of indefinite content:[4] its uncertainty, together with the variety of personal wants and wills, gives rise to a number of disagreements. Who should fill this position? What should be the decision on that occasion? Such is the daily stuff of Politics, inflamed from time to time by disagreements regarding the very structure of institutions.

Politics is conflict. To be sure, far the largest part of governmental activity is removed from the field of conflict: that part is performed by professional agents. The necessary and sufficient condition for "de-politization" of a government activity is that the agents entrusted with it should know for certain what is to be done. This knowledge is afforded by standing rules, and therefore what has been done can be assessed judicially: it is a matter for a "judge" to find whether the relevant rule has been applied, and for a "jury" to appreciate whether the agent's performance has been as good as can be reasonably expected. Need I say that the distinction here made is conceptual

4. Cf. my *Sovereignty* (Cambridge, 1957).

rather than realistic? If my business here were (as it is not) to describe the political system of modern states, I should start with the body of public servants, regarding it as the very core of the system. The growth of professional Government far beyond the performance of specific sets of instructions, indeed with a capacity to generate new sets, is both remarkable and inevitable. But this is not my subject.

My purpose is to stress that Politics refers to "unsolvable problems": that is, situations where no effective computational procedure (or *algorithm*)[5] is available by means of which a solution can be found, which *dissolves* the problem, carrying irresistible conviction.

A "solution" is an answer which fully satisfies all the requirements laid down: when such a solution is found by anyone, everyone else acknowledges it. When, however, all the requirements cannot be met, then only a "settlement" is possible, which does not meet the requirements of some parties and therefore leaves them unconvinced and, while legally bound, psychologically dissatisfied. That is the sort of thing we find in Politics, and which imparts to it the character of a ceaseless conflict.[6]

But what sort of conflict? That is the important question.

Politics is often called a game. This implies that conflict is conducted according to unbreakable rules. Let us follow the metaphor. The best games are those of amateur athletics where winner and loser congratulate each other at the close and chatter gaily on their way to the changing-room. Some of us (as is my case) strongly disapprove of money games; while this is not the attitude of the majority, there are few people who would

5. Cf. Martin Davis, *Computability and Unsolvability* (New York, 1958).
6. This is developed below in the Addendum, "The Myth of the Solution."

not regard it as deplorable that a man should hazard his family's keep at a card table.

Now imagine a player so foolish and sinful as to wager the liberty of his children, to be slaves if he loses. Should we be astonished to find this madman cheating to win, and upturning the table if he seems to be losing? Such disregard of rules must naturally follow from inordinate stakes. We therefore conclude that to keep the game of Politics within the rules, the stakes must be kept moderate.

But here is the difficulty: in the case of a game, a man is free to play or not; and, if he does, he can limit his stake. Not so in Politics. In a card-room, a few people are enjoying a game incapable of ruining them or of bringing misery to third parties. There enters a newcomer who raises the stakes: the old players cannot refuse the higher stakes and, if they leave the table, the intruder wins by default. This is Politics. The "old" parties of the Weimar Republic certainly never agreed to stake civil liberties and the lives of German Jews on a game of dice with Hitler: but that in fact was what they lost. As this instance illustrates, it is not even necessary for the intruder to name the stakes: "You must play with me," he says, "and if you lose, you will find out in my own good time what you have lost."

The game of Politics in its parliamentary guise obtained a good reputation thanks to its manners in nineteenth-century England. Neither the players nor third parties stood to lose from the game. Whatever its fortunes, the governance of England altered very little and always in the direction of improvement. Citizens had no cause for alarm: they feared nothing from Government, whatever category they belonged to; neither did they look to Government for any sudden change in their condition. The public was not much concerned with Politics. Leonard Woolf describes this state of feeling prior to the nineties of the nineteenth century:

In my father's generation, very few people were occupied professionally or permanently with politics. . . . When I was a child, except at the time of Mr. Gladstone's Home Rule Bill, politics were rarely or never mentioned. In those days politics was something which took place in parliament; it was something carried out by a special class of persons; it entered the life of the ordinary person on very rare occasions, principally when he paid his income-tax (at 6*d*. in the £) or at the time of a general election.

Anyone who can look back, as I do, to a childhood lived in the eighties, and adolescence in the nineties of last century, will remember the remoteness of politics to their fathers' generation compared with the nearness, urgency, and devastating impact in the lives of all later generations.[7]

As for the players themselves, mere admission to the gambling rooms of Westminster was honourable and enjoyable, it committed the entrant to decorous conduct. This was an opportunity to achieve office and distinction, to be useful and to feel important. Defeat was no tragedy: the loss of office was not irrevocable and even if the player left the scene, he was certainly not worse off than on entering it, and that was usually good enough. Trollope describes a very relaxed participant:

Throughout his long life he had either been in office, or in such a position that men were sure that he would soon return to it. He had taken it, when it had come, willingly, and had always left it without a regret. As a man cuts in and out at a whist table and enjoys both the game and the rest from the game, so had the Duke of St. Bungay been well pleased in either position. He was patriotic, but patriotism did not disturb his digestion. He had been ambitious—but moderately ambitious, and his ambition had been gratified. It never occurred to him to be unhappy because he or his party were beaten on a mea-

7. Leonard Woolf, *Principia Politica* (London, 1953), pp. 9–10.

sure. When President of the Council, he could do his duty and enjoy London life. When in opposition, he could linger in Italy till May and devote his leisure to his trees and his bullocks. He was always esteemed, always satisfied, and always Duke of St. Bungay.[8]

Trollope used this picture to contrast the attitude of his hero, the Duke of Omnium. Of this latter, we are told:

But with our Duke it was very different. Patriotism with him was a fever, and the public service an exacting mistress. As long as this had been all, he had still been happy. Not trusting much in himself, he had never aspired to great power. But now, now at last, ambition had laid hold of him, and the feeling, not perhaps uncommon with such men, that personal dishonour would be attached to political failure. What would his future life be if he had so carried himself in his great office as to have shown himself to be unfit to resume it?[9]

As our author has wanted to draw a contrast, it is all the more remarkable that the chapter which describes the fall of the Omnium Cabinet is entitled: "Only the Duke of Omnium" (the same note as "always the Duke of St. Bungay"), and contains this dialogue between Lady Glencora and the defeated Prime Minister:

Glen. Don't you feel like Wolsey, Plantagenet?
Duke. Not in the least, my dear. No one will take anything from me which is my own.[10]

How true! And how right is Trollope to point the lesson by reference to the persecution of the fallen Wolsey! The Duke of Omnium has won and lost the Premiership; but as he goes

8. Anthony Trollope, *The Prime Minister*, ch. 72 (Oxford University Press edition, vol. II, pp. 367–68).
9. *Op. cit.* p. 368.
10. *Op. cit.* vol. II, p. 388.

out, he is assured of retaining his liberty, property and status. And this safety of *res privatae*[11] from the vagaries of Politics is enjoyed by every inhabitant of the realm: no one is going to suffer from the fall of the government just as no one suffered from its advent.

To a man of our day, impregnated with class-war concepts, it comes easily to say that Politics could well be mild when retained in the hands of a very narrow class, with huge vested interests. These happy few had not much to quarrel about. The tone could not help changing with the awakening of the exploited, when their urgent demands would strike fear in the hearts of the privileged: Politics, then and therefore involving high stakes, would become a violent business.

Surely there is truth in this now commonplace view, but far less than one is wont to think. Many instances can be adduced of Politics growing violent in the wake of class demands. But how many more instances can be quoted of political violence occurring without any such class-conflict associations!

Social clash can be pointed to as responsible for the climate of violence which coloured the last century of the Roman Republic, but thereupon followed well-nigh fifteen centuries of Roman Empire,[12] replete with political crimes which cannot, by any stretch of fancy, be interpreted as manifestations of class war. A brave and interesting effort has been made to stress the social-revolt element in the German Reformation:[13] the net result of this effort is to show how limited in time and space

11. Cf. Cicero, *Pro Domo* XVII: "Vetant leges sacrae, Vetant XII tabulae leges privi hominibus irrogari: id est enim privilegium. Nemo unquam tulit."

12. This formulation of course implies that the Byzantine Empire is the continuation of the Roman Empire.

13. L. G. Walter, *Thomas Munzer (1489–1525) et les luttes sociales à l'époque de la réforme* (Paris, 1927).

was the intervention of this factor. Of course each outbreak of political violence affords to some the opportunity of appropriating the belongings of others: but robbery by the few can hardly be represented as falling into the pattern of demands by the many. We have witnessed the advent of violent Politics in a country where they had been unknown since the Wars of Religion: they were certainly not evoked in the service of the Workers against the Capitalists, nor the other way round.[14]

A *contrario*, the land where industrial Capitalism and the Proletariat first expanded, and which Marx regarded as their field of Philippi, has to this day remained free from political violence. Lloyd George was not bludgeoned to death at Westminster for having introduced progressive taxation: no crowd of angry Peers surged out from the Upper House, with a mob of servants unleashed upon this new Gracchus. Nor have the corpses of beheaded dukes been dragged infamously through the East End. Without any expense of ferocity or anger, what a change has been achieved![15] Surely it is less a consequence than a cause of such smooth progress that Politics has retained its ancient systems of manners: the perfume of eighteenth-century civility clings to Westminster.

It is easy to think lightly of manners. Whoever is so disposed should read what Necker had to say on the subject in 1792.[16]

---

14. Book-length efforts have been made to represent the Nazi party as "a reaction of defence" of the steel industry. It takes great naïveté to imagine that such passion can be fanned into flame by company directors.

15. It is often pointed out that two great wars have hastened the process. This is quite true since on such occasions the most fortunate were willing to accept sacrifices made at that time for the country rather than for a section of the people (however large). But, moreover, it should be remarked that whatever tendency the "social conflict" might have had to disrupt, the standing together to meet an alien challenge fully remedied.

16. *Du pouvoir executif dans les grands états* (2 vols., 1792).

Here is no feather-brained dandy bemoaning lost struts and sweeps of the leg. "Le bonhomme" was all stodgy and virtuous earnestness, quite bereft of sympathy for exquisite futilities. But this essentially good man was deeply shocked by the brutality which developed at an early stage in the course of the French Revolution, however irrelevant to the achievement of its positive reforms. An unimpeachable witness,[17] Necker describes the proscription of civility,[18] he stresses that polite forms forever call to the mind the feelings whereof they bear the outward appearance.[19] He points out that, conversely, a flaunting of brutal language, loutish familiarity, and gross irreverence,

17. Surely unimpeachable, since all the positive achievements of the Revolution, he had sought to obtain by reforms: since he was the author of the calling of the States General, the author of the doubling of Third Estate representation, and the chief minister during the initial period of the Revolution.

18. Necker speaks of "les égards," a wonderful expression which denotes an attitude of respect by no means exclusively addressed to the superior: e.g. "les égards dûs aux faibles." A man polished in "les égards" will be a respecter of everyone.

19. Since Necker's works are not easily available, a substantial quotation may be in order: "Il restait encore pour égide à la douceur des moeurs de la Nation Française, cette Législation des égards et des manières, qui n'était point écrite sur les tables de bronze ou d'airain, mais qui, par la seule force de l'opinion, rappelait les hommes aux sentiments dont ils étaient contraints d'emprunter les formes. La politesse et les manières, en acquérant comme toutes nos idées une sorte de raffinement, par l'effet du temps, sont devenus, dans leur perfection, l'apanage particulier des hommes bien nés. Il n'en a pas fallu davantage pour rendre ces sentiments suspects; on a cru qu'ils tenaient, par quelque point, à la gradation des rangs, et l'on s'est hâté de les comprendre dans la proscription générale, exécrée contre toute espèce d'Aristocratie. On n'a pas vu qu'ils remontaient à des principes absolument différents; on n'a point vu qu'ils tenaient, par leur origine, à des idées d'égalité; on n'a pas vu, qu'imaginés pour défendre la faiblesse contre la force, c'était aux idées les plus généreuses qu'ils se trouvaient associés. On s'en servit d'abord pour environner les vieillards d'une enceinte propre à les garantir des insultes d'une jeunesse, imprudente au moment où son règne commence; on donna ces mêmes sentiments pour sauve-garde au sexe faible et timide que les loix de la nature avaient soumis à notre orgueilleux empire; enfin les mêmes sentiments furent encore destinés à soutenir la puissance de l'imagination, et à maintenir ainsi l'autorité des Chefs des Nations, contre la force du nombre et contre les excès déréglés de la multitude" (op. cit.).

fosters actions of the same type: the man who prides himself on not sparing the feelings of his fellows in his language will pretty soon not mind inflicting more concrete injuries. The subversion of civility in the French Revolution is surely the true explanation of so violent a reaction as Burke's.[20] This subversion came as a staggering surprise to Europe. All expected political change; none the new expressions on faces, the new tone of voices. Indeed, members of what was to be the Constituent Assembly came in no such mood: they were all men of learning, grounded in the classics, whose modes of speech had been shaped by Ciceronian periods. They saw themselves as displaying the *gravitas* of Roman senators, to whose example their minds had been directed by the reading of the ancients, by the representation of tragedies, and by their early admiration of the robed magistrates who had stood up to the king.[21] Moreover the lighter literature which they had absorbed, from l'Abbé Prévost, Rousseau, Marmontel, and so many others, was all a display of sensitivity, an invitation to the ready shedding of tears on every occasion.

With such initial inclinations to dignity on the one hand and to the softer emotions on the other, it is indeed a wonder that events should have taken so brutal a course, especially since the reforms they demanded met with insubstantial opposition only. Episodes are telling: when the mob marched to Versailles and carried the Royal Family with it by mere pressure of force, when the heads of guards, carried on spears, were kept bobbing up and down at the windows of the Queen's carriage, this outrage, both to formality and to sensitivity, was one which the deputies dared not condemn, and it is apparent in Burke's writing that such a scene and its condoning by the Assembly swayed him altogether.

20. I.e. his attack on *principles* was moved by his emotion concerning *behaviour.*
21. The most popular form of opposition under the Ancien Régime had been that of Les Parlementaires, i.e. the members of the Courts of Justice.

It has weighed heavily upon the subsequent history of parliamentary government in France that the first National Assembly was incompetent to discipline itself,[22] improvident against lawless behaviour at the very time when it sought to be omniprovident in its renovation of all laws;[23] dared not condemn disorderly behaviour,[24] allowed itself to be dictated to by bold self-appointed deputations which were forever coming to harangue it, and thus opened the door to a successive coarsening of official manners in the course of the Revolution.[25]

The French Revolution has played no mean part in world history. Whatever boons have been conferred by many of its principles and laws, it has also left another inheritance: it has hallowed violence. The generation of Benjamin Constant and Lafayette, its memory replete with echoes of howling hordes, and mourning murdered friends, was concerned to separate the positive achievements of the Revolution from its violence;[26] but this attitude was soon regarded as squeamish, the "sound and fury" came to be regarded not only as inseparable from the

22. For instance as early as 1 August 1789, when the Assembly had been sitting for less than three months, Thouret, elected to the Chair by an absolute, although narrow, majority, was forced to resign immediately by the tumult which arose on proclamation of the results. Only six weeks later, by a mere show of hands, without any prior deliberation, the Assembly passed a resolution enabling it to censure and thereby remove any member whom it should deem unworthy, a resolution which took no immediate effect but laid down a principle which afforded a prior blessing to the purges of the subsequent assemblies.

23. This may be thought the more surprising in view of the enormous preponderance of the legal profession in the Assembly. It is worth noting that in a discussion on the form of promulgation of laws, Robespierre was almost alone in stressing the necessity for impressing upon the people the sense of the majesty of law.

24. Circumstances of course explain a great deal: the Assembly was so rife with rumours of a danger to it from the military that it was disposed to accept that the rioters were acting in its interest.

25. The only statesman of the Revolution, that is Robespierre, never bowed to this fashion of coarseness.

26. Which was all the easier in view of the fact that all the saner principles were laid down in the very first weeks.

tale but as essential to it, and indeed as necessary to make it sublime. The actions of the revolutionary figures came to be admired not by virtue of their beneficence, or even their good intentions, but because they were extreme.

The history of political messianism has been well written,[27] but we lack a parallel history of the sanctification of political violence. After mature consideration, I would deny that excessive hopes by themselves move men to ferocious conduct: there is some radiance in hope which does not tend to inspire the inflicting of harm. What most easily moves men to destructive conduct is the unpleasant emotion of fear.[28] While this is valid for the rabble of followers, the leaders of violence must have overcome the natural sense that it is wrong.[29] I purposely use the verb "overcome" because it adequately describes the subjective attitude of the man who "elects" violence. He feels that he "rises above" the prejudices of his fellows, defies their vulgar opinion, and, the most difficult and truly sinful feat, does not allow his conscience to "make a coward" of him. This evil attitude is far more harmful than any false ideas, and it is not fostered by intellectual error but by aesthetic suggestions: slipping on the ludicrous panoply of "Spartan Brutus," revolutionary leaders saw their cruelty as heroic virtue. And in turn their atrocious deeds provided a new set of pseudo-heroic masks, to be worn by others.

The new "sublime of extreme actions" has been immortally illustrated by Stendhal in the micro-portrait, the medallion, of Julien Sorel. What characterizes the hero is that in a succes-

---

27. Cf. J. L. Talmon, *Political Messianisim* (also *The Origins of Totalitarian Democracy*).

28. I do not base my opinions on reading. Unfortunately, I have not lacked opportunities to observe the course of violence.

29. Whoever doubts that there is such a natural sense is referred to the anthropologists who have described men "working themselves up" for a killing.

sion of small incidents, Julien overcomes both his timidity and his decency, which he satanically confuses, to do the bold thing. Faguet acutely remarks that, towards the end of this great novel, the hero has it in his power to sate all his wants of wealth, title, and position, by marrying the girl he has wanted, humiliated and won: quite reasonably, Faguet underlines that Madame de Rênal's denunciation of Julien, while embarrassing, does not really alter his prospects; it is therefore quite incredible, says the critic, that Julien should run off and quite literally lose his head in killing his previous mistress.[30] But if there were no such extreme action at the end, then all the smaller acts of daring with which the novel is strewn would sink to the condition of means for a profitable consummation: the story would then carry only an unethical lesson; it would not be what in fact it is, an apology of criminality for its own sake.[31] Crime its own reward, that is the lesson of *Le Rouge et le noir:* it is in crime that man truly rises above himself, an idea echoed more or less ably by so many others after Stendhal.[32]

Obviously this is no place to sketch out, however roughly, a history of attitudes towards violence: but it would be the height of absurdity not to mention at least Georges Sorel, who stands at the beginning of the twentieth century as its herald.[33] Here the praise of violence is starkly Puritan. Violence is not a

---

30. Emile Faguet, *Politiques et moralistes du dix-neuvième siècle* (3 vols., Paris, 1900), vol. III: "Stendhal."

31. The same would be true of Dreiser's *American Tragedy,* if the hero drowned the girl and then achieved his social ambitions. In Dreiser's book crime does not pay, nor is it endowed with any aesthetic quality. The novel is "a moral tale," unfortunately of no great artistic merit.

32. See, for instance, Gide's pernickety treatment of "l'acte gratuit" in *Les caves du Vatican.*

33. Mainly in *Réflexions sur la violence* (Paris, 1908). An American edition (Glencoe, 1950) is available, translated by T. E. Hulme and J. Roth, with a notable introduction by Edward Shils.

means to a desirable end, it is not a grand operatic fulfilment, it is an ascetic exercise performed by the Chosen[34] to maintain and develop a separateness from the Corrupt. There is perhaps no more revealing sentence in the whole book than this: "Let the proletariat shun the evil which befell the Germanic invaders of the Roman Empire! Ashamed to see themselves barbarians, they sought lessons from teachers of decadent latinity: how much better their fate, had they not wanted to be civilized!"[35] Such language offers a faint echo of Ezra: "The land, unto which ye go to possess it, is an unclean land, with the filthiness of the people of the lands, with their abominations, which have filled it from one end to another with their uncleanness."[36] Sorel also bids "seek not their peace," and he pours his contempt upon the peace-mongers, those who, as he accuses, mediate between the working-class and the bourgeoisie, obtaining, now from fear, now from goodwill, this or that advantage. Strangely enough in the eyes of a rationalist, Sorel is not really interested in the spoils of victory: what obsesses him is the image of the sacred battalion which develops its virtues in the fight—courage, temperance, solidarity. He even goes so far as to hope that the fight will revive some virtue in the opponents. All this would have seemed fantastic to men of the eighteenth century, but in the twentieth there have been bands of "militants" which saw themselves more or less in this light, however differently they appeared to others.

No deep understanding of the twentieth century is possible, I believe, unless we grasp that violence has received psycho-

---

34. The "Chosen" were to Sorel the proletariat, but he showed by applauding successively Lenin and Mussolini that what truly interested him was the "team of warriors," the form rather than the specific content.

35. My translation from the French, p. lx; American edition, p. 62.

36. Ezra ix. 11.

logical promotion.[37] Basic to the Saint-Simonian idea[38] that
the ethos of industrial society inevitably outmodes the ethos
of military societies are two propositions, one of which is a postulate, the other a historical surmise. The postulate is that violence cannot be anything but a means to the acquisition of
material goods; the historical surmise is that such means become increasingly irrational relative to their end. The historical surmise seems well-founded. Within a given society of advancing wealth, the improvement of organization will yield
more, over a period of time, to any *large* group than will pil-
lage.[39] This finding logically leads to the conclusion that optimal organization of the whole is, in the long run (and not so
very long), the best way to advance the material interests of any
large section of the public. If so, any rational politician, even
if he is wedded only to the interests of a section of the public
(provided it be large enough), can logically seek nothing other
than optimal organization and policies for the whole.[40] It will

37. Among the works which lead to such understanding figure, of course, Dostoevsky's *The Possessed,* and Malraux's *La condition humaine.*

38. Which readers of the English language are wont to attribute to Herbert Spen-
cer, who popularized it.

39. Nobody was better aware of this than Marx. He regarded capitalist domination
as necessary for the accumulation of capital, the condition of increasing production.
If he foresaw a revolution, it was because he assumed that the capitalists would bring
the wealth-producing system to a standstill by their refusal to distribute to the workers
increasing claims on increasing potential output: irrational conduct, calling for violence to establish a rational distribution consonant with the progress of productive
capacities. It is immaterial for my present purpose that the supposition of this irrational
conduct was tied to the supposed will to maintain a constant rate of profit, challenged,
as Marx believed, by the supposedly declining efficiency of capital (an erroneous assumption he had borrowed from Ricardo). The point which is relevant to my purpose
here is that Marx conceived violence as necessary to overcome irrational behaviour.
So far, he had what may be called a bourgeois mind.

40. Or, in other terms, if citizens are rational, no large following can be assembled
on any other basis.

then follow that the area of conflict about public affairs will be confined to disagreements about optimal organization and policies.

Under such conditions Politics must logically be peaceful: my opponent wants the same thing that I want. Optimal management is not so determinate as to remove any occasion for dispute, but it is not so indeterminate as to impede discussion. Where there is full agreement about the purpose,[41] there must be some underlying sympathy between those who pursue it, a conviviality which tempers their disagreements; and their mutual attempts to convert each other to what each deems the best way must take the form of a conversation, which can hardly fail to be fruitful. The procedure of settlement of an issue is greatly mellowed by the hope, if not conviction, that some algorithm might be found in common, which provides a *certain* answer to the same question which haunts different minds.[42]

A man of our day is entirely justified in stressing optimistically that a large part of public affairs now comes under that description;[43] and strangely enough, the divisions which Madison, after Plato and Aristotle, deemed the most dangerous for the commonwealth, seem amenable to such treatment.

We could indeed be wholehearted optimists, if we had no doubts about the postulate stated at the beginning of this section. The postulate was that violence is nothing but a means to

41. In our day, Economic Growth is such a purpose. It generates a true partnership between the men who are durably engaged in framing, proposing or discussing policies addressed to this purpose.

42. In the case of Economic Growth, an agreed language and an agreed mode of measurement of results are of course most helpful.

43. What is sketched in the preceding paragraph corresponds to my personal experience in the Conseil Economique et Social of France, also in its Commission des Comptes de la Nation.

acquire worldly goods. This is essentially a bourgeois postulate, unfortunately quite unfounded. Innumerable instances can be adduced of men fighting for some material possession, but they do not prove the contrary: that men never fight for any other reason; in fact innumerable instances can be adduced of violence resorted to where a material possession was not the motive (even if it was often a by-product).

It is then idle to believe that fighting can be removed as it becomes apparent that there are more efficient ways of achieving material advantages.[44] An ethos of peacefulness has precluded resort to violence where violence would have paid off.[45] A contrary ethos may bring violence where it is not likely to pay off. It seems to be borne out by observation that only small minorities are likely to have a "militant" ethos (which really means an ethos of war). But that is quite enough, because then the motivation of fear (which is very common) can intervene for great numbers. Clodius and Milo who brandish swords at one another do not remain alone, because Clodius can convince many that Milo's sword is pointed at them and by the same argument Clodius also can rally many around him.

This simple image, which explains the spread of violence, suggests two simple remedies. Let Clodius and Milo fight it out by themselves amid general indifference; or disarm them. Neither remedy is easy to apply. You will get general indifference if you can persuade people that whoever wins, it will not affect

---

44. This has become reasonably apparent in the wealthy countries of the world. The many have little to gain in taking over the property of the few (we are concerned here with net gain from appropriation, not with the quite different question of the gains which may be realized by a change in management). But what is true within one country is not so obviously true as between a poor country (say China) and a rich one. The Chinese people would have much to gain from taking over the United States.

45. An outstanding example is afforded by India, where the peasants quite obviously would have gained by throwing off their landlords.

them. This result was pretty nearly achieved in the international affairs of the eighteenth century, when which king won a province mattered not at all to the local institutions and the condition of the people. This gave rise to the expectation that wars could be done away with altogether. The reasoning ran as follows: (*a*) the people have nothing at stake in our present wars; (*b*) these are only the wars of kings; (*c*) therefore do away with the kings and you will do away with the wars.[46] It was stressed in favour of this view that already wars were very tame, which was taken as a clear indication that little remained to be done for their total elimination.

We see already that wars are milder than among savage and ignorant populations. Legions shoot each other with politeness; heroes salute each other before fighting; soldiers of the opposite camps visit each other before battle, as people sup together before a game of cards. It is no more nations which are locked in battle, nor even kings, but only armies, and mercenaries at that; these are games with limited stakes; at last wars, which were frenzies, have shrunk to nonsense (LVIII).

We, who are only people . . . we shall not tire of telling the kings that the wars are meaningful only to them [LIX]. . . . The stupid hatreds of nations will wear out when kings no more excite them one against the other [LX]. . . . We can rigorously forecast the progress of reason [LXI]. If the robust body of France digests its revolution, we shall never more see these so great armies, with which so little is accomplished. The example of the French will be imitated; and from this angle as from so many others, the revolution of France will have achieved a saving in human blood [LXII].[47]

46. Among the many presentations of this view, that which I pick upon is entitled *Réflexions politiques sur les circonstances présentes*, by J. P. Rabaut; and while it bears no date it was obviously published at the beginning of 1792.

47. The author's final remark (LXIII) was: "The history of the revolution of France is a book of prophecies."

All this was quite persuasively stated. Unfortunately the booklet appeared hardly a few months before the French Revolution developed into a war which was, with a number of intermissions, to rage for twenty-three years.[48]

There is much to be learned from the argument which I quote. Its facts were undeniably correct; truly the wars had become tame[49] and truly they were only the wars of kings. But the prognosis derived from these facts was, as events proved, quite unwarranted. Which proves that the facts, however correctly stated, were not understood; a suitable explanation leads to a correct prediction, a blatantly incorrect prediction reveals an inadequate explanation.[50] The people had no stake in wars

48. France declared war on Austria and Prussia on 20 April 1792. The author from whom I quote, a Protestant pastor and throughout his life a most worthy man (who, among other acts of courage, tried to save the king's life), was beheaded on 5 December 1793.

49. The reasons which ensured so many military successes of the French armies against those of European monarchies during the French Revolution and Empire are almost all derived from the customs of "tame warfare" belonging to the Ancien Régime, which France abandoned while the monarchies still adhered to them. (1) The French forces were superior in numbers because the Republic had instituted conscription, unknown in monarchies. Prussia was the first to imitate it. (2) The French forces moved more easily and rapidly because they were allowed and expected to live from the plundering of the lands traversed, while Ancien Régime soldiery were strictly forbidden to do this and therefore tied down by heavy convoys, and even so often underfed (cf. Clausewitz, *On War*, Book v, ch. xiv). (3) The French forces formed in heavy columns which broke through the thin lines into which the Allied armies were formed, according to Ancien Régime habits. The column had been recommended as early as 1724 by the Chevalier de Folard (cf. especially his military commentary on Polybius, 6 vols., Paris, 1727–30). But it had been rejected as too costly in human lives, and it took the "cannon-fodder" procured by conscription to bring it into practice.

50. Alfred Marshall stated that explanation "is simply prediction written backwards; and, when fully achieved, it helps towards prediction. A chief purpose of every study of human action should be to suggest the probable outcomes of present tendencies; and thus to indicate, tacitly if not expressly, such modifications of these tendencies, as might further the well-being of mankind." (From *Industry and Trade*, 1919, p. 7; quoted by R. C. Tress in "The Contribution of Economic Theory Prognostication," *Economica*, August 1959.)

because the royal governments of the eighteenth century were so alike that it could make no difference to live under one or the other,[51] each of them moreover being a great respecter of existing establishments. Yet the latter statement is true even of that archetype of absolute kings, Louis XIV. A warlike, conquering, overbearing, illiberal monarch: that is beyond doubt. It is therefore the more striking that annexation of a province to the kingdom of France meant no change for the inhabitants, who were henceforth ruled in the name of a different sovereign but in the same manner, as stressed in a letter from the *intendant* newly installed at Douai to Colbert: "As I understand it to be your intention to bring no change at all to existing usage, be it dangerous. . . ."[52] Now, in sharp contrast, it did make a great deal of difference for the Czechs to come under German "protectorate" in 1939. The transfer of sovereignty over Algeria from France to the Front de Libération Nationale was not regarded by the European settlers as a matter which would bring no change in their lives. The inhabitants of West Berlin have displayed great emotion whenever it has seemed to them likely that West Berlin would be absorbed in the Republic of East Germany.

A change of sovereign in the eighteenth century was an affair which interested alternative sovereigns far more than the subjects, because any sovereign would exercise sovereign rights (in fact conceived as very limited) in much the same manner. All this is changed when the emphasis is upon *national* sovereignty, that is, when each national government determines at

51. As Burke stressed in his eulogy of the uniformity of manners throughout Europe before the French Revolution: *Letters on a Regicide Peace, Works* (London, 1808), vol. VIII, pp. 181 ff.

52. Cf. Marquis de Roux, *Louis XIV et les provinces conquises* (Paris, 1938); also a major work of scholarship by Irenée Lameire, *Théorie et pratique de la conquête dans l'ancien droit* (3 vols., Paris, 1903, 1905, 1911).

will the rights of those incorporated in its realm, so that passing from one realm to another means being subjected to quite different rules and bound to quite different manners.[53]

It is ironic that in times when so much is said about an "international community" it should have become a greater hazard than ever to find oneself incorporated in a different parish.

Just as the fear of our fate should the "other" army win is enough, whatever other motives may intervene, to make us put our hearts into a war as we had no reason for doing in the eighteenth century; in the same manner if a militant band threatens to seize power in our own country, the fear of what we would suffer under its rule is enough to make us respond to the other band which forms against it. We cannot leave them to fight it out "alone" because we are aware that the winner will not leave us alone. Therefore the shutting up of Clodius and Milo with their respective followers in well-hedged lists will not do.

When I first mentioned these obstreperous champions, it was suggested either to let them fight it out by themselves (and that, we find, will not do), or to disarm them. Let us disarm them. Let us turn to this possibility. The question arises: "Who is to disarm them?" Another man with a stronger weapon? That is the Hobbesian remedy. Let there be One Ruler, strong, and quite intolerant of any faction. This is not a pleasant solution; the other which offers itself is that the whole circle of onlookers, a vast majority in comparison with the gangs of Clodius or Milo, should intervene to overpower them. However, the chances are that some will be more concerned to disarm Clodius and others Milo, and we are back with a general fray.

---

53. B. de Jouvenel, *Quelle Europe?* (Paris, 1947), "Questions de frontières, questions de vie et de mort."

It would seem therefore that one should hasten to extinguish the fire of angry bellicose Politics whenever and wherever it is lighted. But this is likely to be practised only by those who themselves have risen through violence, not by those who, rightly abhorring violence, underestimate it; and they expose themselves to the fate of Priam: " . . . hic exitus illum Sorte tulit. . . . "

The Myth of the Solution

We commonly say "this is a political problem" and go on to ask for its "solution" and complain that it is not found. This is a way of speaking so well-established that it cannot be changed, or indeed avoided, but it should be realized that it is highly misleading. The word "problem" is loaded with memories of our studious childhood, when problems were set to us by the master. We concentrated our attention to understand the terms of the problem, and then bent our backs over our desks, striving to discover the answer. Many a time we floundered helplessly, but while failing we were aware that some of our fellows were finding the solution. On some occasions we rejoiced that we had solved the problem, and found out afterwards that we had given a faulty answer. Whether we had failed to find any solution or had handed in a spurious solution, when the master afterwards expounded the treatment of the problem on the blackboard and set down the solution, there was no shadow of doubt in our minds that that was what we should have found: if we had produced a different answer, we would not dream of taking up the cudgels in its favour. Such ready subservience to the answer written out by the master was in no degree a submission to his personal authority. It followed from our now perceiving that that answer, and that answer alone, satisfied the terms of the problem. And while we might feel some chagrin that we had missed or mistaken it, some annoyance at our own stupidity, on the other hand we would experience a joy of seeing things clearly.

This then was the answer which was waiting for us all the time. It is a pity that we did not find our way to it, or that we took another way which led us astray. It would have been pleasing to have won this answer by our own efforts: but in surrendering to it, now that it stands to reason, there is also a pleasure; and the answer, henceforth, is no less our own than if we had reached it alone. We are just as ready to champion the answer against any doubter, we have no doubt that he will be brought to see its rightness, and be grateful to us for his own acquired conviction. Such is the psychological attitude of Man to "the solution."

Now can we observe anything like this attitude when a "solution" has been given to a political "problem"? Do we observe that those who have opposed this solution rally to those who advocated it, feeling a bit ashamed that they had not previously perceived the rightness of this solution, but delighted to be now aware of it? Do we observe that the opponents of the solution at once become its champions? Surely nothing like this happens in politics.

Should it happen? Is this difference in attitudes due to the fact that in the classroom we are reasonable beings, willing to see the truth when it is offered to us, while in the Forum we are affective beings, with minds clouded by prejudice and passion? This view was widely held by the *philosophes* of the eighteenth century. They were prone to compare political problems to problems in geometry:[1] great disputes do arise between geo-

---

1. Cf. Mercier de la Rivière, *De l'ordre naturel et essentiel des sociétés politiques* (London, 1767), especially Book I, ch. IX.

metricians in the case of difficult problems whereof no one quite finds the solution; but when it has been found by one, and he has shown that his solution stands to reason, then all others cease their opposition and all enjoy in common what has become a common good.

Why then, they went on to argue, should it not be the same in the case of political problems? No doubt, here also we have difficult problems, on which opposing views are tenable, and indeed their clash may lead on to finding the solution. But as soon as the solution has been found, then only the prejudiced, the stupid, the selfish, the wilful, can deny it. They should see that it stands to reason; if they do not, either they are incapable of seeing the light of reason (an illness of which education can cure them) or they refuse to see it, because they are fractious, mischievous, self-centred and evil-minded.

The assumption that political problems are of the same kind as those set to us in the classroom, or as those which exercise the minds of geometricians, is optimistic in so far as it carries the implication that there is a right answer to every problem. But it is obvious that it justifies disciplinary measures against those who do not acknowledge the solution when presented to them, and indeed measures of persecution against those who continue to argue against them, and who are the more guilty the more educated they are, since they should then "know better" than to plead against what should have become to them self-evident.

It is not my purpose here to stress the dangerous consequences of regarding political problems as implying solutions, which should compel our assent with "the irresistible force of self-evidence" as Mercier de la Rivière puts it. Our concern is merely to find out whether political problems are of such a nature that they may reasonably be regarded in that light.

Let us go back, not ambitiously to the problems of geometricians, but modestly to those of the classroom. What was our task as schoolboys? Terms were stated and we had to find an answer which met them; or, in other words, a number of conditions had to be fulfilled and we had to find the *locus geometricus* which satisfied them all. One thing we knew for certain—that the problem had a solution. We might not find the best procedure for reaching the solution, or we might not find any, but what was beyond doubt was the existence of a solution. Now it is of course extremely easy to set problems incapable of solution (for instance, "Find a prime larger than 13 but smaller than 17"). Our teachers never played upon us such pranks: life, however, does. When the British held the mandate over Palestine, they had to find a solution to "the Palestinian problem" which could be stated in the following terms: "Find an arrangement whereby all of Palestine shall form an Arab national State as required by the Arabs, and whereby at least a large part of Palestine shall form an Israeli national State as required by the Jews." It is immediately apparent that the terms of the problem admit of no "solution." In the same manner, the French governments have been exercised for a number of years by "the Algerian problem" which could be stated in the following terms: "Find an arrangement whereby Algeria shall remain part of France as the European settlers require and shall become an independent sovereign state as the Front de Libération Nationale movement demands."

Obviously such "problems" are unsolvable. It is not here a matter of failing to find the solution: it just does not exist. The terms of a classroom problem can be thought of as *claims which can all be fully satisfied by the right answer.* Now in the case of the political problems which have just been quoted, the terms of the problem conflict: there is no answer that can satisfy them in full; there is no solution in the proper sense of the word. Admittedly the clash of terms is extreme in the instances adduced. But in the case of any political problem there is a clash of terms precluding a solution in the proper sense of the word. Else one might have "a problem" but not "a political problem." What makes a problem "political" is precisely that its terms admit no solution properly so-called. There are no doubt some matters coming up for decision by public authorities where the conditions to be met are somewhat complex, and where the finding of a solution is an intellectual task. But such problems, capable of solution, are quietly solved off-stage by experts. What constitutes "a political problem" is the clashing of terms, that is, its unsolvability.

Nor is it worthwhile to say that but for the passions of the parties concerned, the problem would easily be solvable, because these passions are the very data of politics. It is all too easy for an outside observer to say that there exists a solution which people would accept if they but knew their true interests: what the outside observer then means is that the people concerned would all accept what seems to him desirable if they all agreed with him as to what is desirable: which is true enough, but trivial and irrelevant. Of course the outside observer, who deserves no attention if he passes an armchair judgement by merely overlooking what constitutes the problem, merits more consideration if he turns himself into an inside operator seeking to win the people concerned to his view: but then he himself and his followers become an element of the problem.

What characterizes a political problem is that no answer will fit the terms of the problem as stated. A political problem therefore is not solved, it may be settled, which is a different thing altogether. By settlement, we here mean any decision arrived at, by whatever means, on the question which gave rise to the political problem. While it is the very definition of a solution that it satisfies in full all the terms of the problem, the settlement does not do so. It cannot do so, since, as in a bankruptcy, there is no possibility of meeting all the claims in full. Some must be denied altogether or all must be reduced. What method or procedure will be used for this adjustment? Three procedures can be adopted. First, the parties who formulate the demands creating the problem may pare down their demands, thanks to attrition or mediation or both, and the heretofore incompatible demands will then become compatible. The political problem will have changed into a problem admitting a solution. It will seldom be transmuted altogether in this way. It may be, for instance, that the spokesmen who had made incompatible claims will finally come together on some compromise. But in this process they may find themselves disowned by some few or many of their followers; even if not, the latter will be apt to express chagrin at the outcome. Certainly the compromise will not be received in the same spirit as a solution. There will be many on both sides who will go on thinking that their terms could have been satisfied more completely if only they had held out more. The best settlement by compromise therefore will not cause that feeling of enjoyment which comes with the offering of the solution to a problem. The solution as it were dissolves the problem: it will never be a problem any more. The compromise settlement leaves the issue in being. It may be reopened at any time.

The compromise settlement is not as good as a solution but it is far and away the best form of settlement. If not a solution, it has some kinship to it. To be sure the initial demands stated, constituting the terms of the problem, have not been met. But a sort of feedback process has been somehow set in train, whereby the unsolvability of the problem has reacted upon its terms and the conditions to be met have been so relaxed that they have become compatible. No doubt such relaxation is a temporary phenomenon — it is quite possible that after the negotiation, there will be renewed demands of a more exacting nature on one or more than one side — it is also possible, however, that the mood which has made the compromise settlement possible will not fade away, but, on the contrary, will be sustained by the favourable consequences of the compromise.

What are the other procedures for settling a political problem? In essence, they are the application of a principle, or the dictate of an authority. In practice the two may be joined together: that is, when the dictate of an authority is based upon a principle. Indeed while it is conceivable that the principle by itself may adjudicate between the demands, it is seldom possible to apply the principle without some authority which decides how it is to be understood in the particular case, and which fills the voids which the mere working out of the principle would leave.

I shall here refer to a historic instance which made a great impression upon my youth, and which perhaps served to make me feel how far the most elaborate settlement must necessarily differ from a solution.

After World War I, the victorious Allies having resurrected Poland, the question arose whether Upper Silesia should be attached to Poland or left to Germany. The former was the French view, the latter the British. President Wilson prevailed upon the Allies to have the matter decided by consultation of the populations. This was the application of a principle: self-determination. The plebiscite occurred on 21 March 1921 and gave 707,000 votes to Germany against 479,000 to Poland. Did this settle the matter? No. Incensed at the thought that the whole province would be attached to Germany, Polish insurgents rose in arms and took control of a great part of the country. Given that the voting had shown two strong blocks to exist within the territory, and that feelings ran very high, there was a clear case for dividing the province. This task was assigned to the Interallied Commission for Upper Silesia.

Theoretically, it was simple enough. Plot on the map the localities which have given a German majority, denote them by a black spot; plot those which have given a Polish majority, denote them by a white spot. When that is done, draw a line which leaves to the east (in Poland) all the white spots, and to the west (in Germany) all the black spots. This line constitutes "the right frontier" according to the principle adopted (at the cost of disregarding local minorities). This was all very well in theory. But in practice the intermingling of dots precluded the drawing of such a line. Therefore the deciding authority was not sufficiently guided by its initial principle, and had to adopt some supplementary principle such as:

A. Draw the line so that no white spot remains in Germany (but then a quantity of black spots will be included in Poland).

B. Draw the line so that no black spot goes to Poland (but then a quantity of white spots will remain in Germany).

C. Draw some line which leaves some white spots in Germany and some black spots in Poland.

Obviously sub-principles A and B both gave definite instructions, which, however, just as obviously favoured respectively Polish and German wishes. Sub-principle C gave no determinate answer, the line might be attracted more or less to the A or B lines. In the event, the line drawn, on the basis of the self-determination principle, complemented by the C sub-principle or instruction, was arbitrary. It was arbitrary by definition, that is, some freedom of decision had to be exercised by the authority; maybe it was also arbitrary in the narrower and unfavourable sense of the word, in the sense that it was partial. If we would speak a precise language in Politics, we should presumably reserve the qualification of "arbitrary," without any value-connotation, to a decision which is not dictated by principles, and political decisions all partake of this character to some (usually very limited) degree, and we should say, for instance, in this case that within the bounds of its arbitrariness the decision is more or less partial. But whatever the language, which is far from unimportant, here are the facts to be considered. In the event, there was some partiality to Poland. But no matter what the partition of Upper Silesia might have been, in any case, it would not have been accepted either by Germans or Poles as a solution of a problem is accepted. It will be remembered that when Hitler had come to power there occurred an agitation among the German minority of Polish Upper Silesia, and that Hitler in 1939 set the boundary very far to the east, while in 1944 Stalin pushed it very far back to the west.

This highly schematized historical instance displays the character of a political settlement. Whatever the principle invoked, there cannot fail to be some arbitrariness in its application. It is not inevitable that all concerned should accept the principle invoked, and the inevitability of some arbitrariness in its application will always serve those offended by the settlement to represent that the invocation of the principle is a lie.

Mankind has been wonderfully served by the instinct implanted in us to do things with the least possible effort. In the intellectual realm this leads us to seek general principles by means of which we can decide particular cases. However, we are prone to delude ourselves about the clarity with which principles speak in particular cases. Take the principle of self-determination. In its light it is immediately obvious that the Thirteen Colonies were entitled to their independence from England; but in its light, it is far from clear that the Eleven Southern States were not entitled to secession. According to circumstances we shift from invoking one principle to invoking another, nor is this shifting the manifestation of hypocrisy: Eduard Beneš was a man of the highest moral character, he invoked self-determination to obtain the setting up of Czechoslovakia; he did not like it when Sudeten and Slovakian leaders invoked it to obtain their independence from Prague.[2]

Finding that such men as Lincoln and Beneš were unwilling to apply the principle of self-determination should give us pause before we proclaim the absolute value of any principle taken by itself independently of circumstances. Or it should, at least, cause us to wonder whether there are many, or perhaps any, political principles which honest men are at all times, in all circumstances, ready to abide by. And if it is so, then obviously when it comes to settling a political problem by resort to principles, there may be a question as to what principle or principles should be applied in the event. If so, this removes the political problem one step further. Suppose that a political problem arises because of disagreement as to what the factual decision should be; suppose, however, that there is a vague agreement that the decision should be taken on the basis of principle. Then a secondary problem arises: there is disagreement about the principle to be applied. Suppose further that there is a vague agreement that a procedure should be adopted to select the relevant principle. Then a tertiary problem arises:

2. Neither did I like it, and I remain convinced that *The Times* article which pleaded that after all the Sudeten were entitled to self-determination, was, before Munich which it prepared, an important factor in setting off the disastrous course of events.

there is disagreement about this procedure of selection. We could go on like this, but it would be an idle exercise, because in fact what is apt to guide men in their choice of a procedure to select the relevant principle, and in their preference for the application of a given principle here and now, is simply the bearing it will have on the factual decision which is of immediate interest to them. From World War I to the fall of the Fourth Republic, France has many times changed the voting system for the election of deputies. It is pretty hard to follow the logic of the arguments offered for different systems: it becomes easier to understand them if one keeps in mind that the arguments were subordinated to specific ends, that is, to obtain or avoid a certain composition of the Chambre des Députés or Assemblée Nationale.

Obviously I have not here moved forward from the last chapter, which is properly the final one. I have instead gone back to emphasize and elucidate the statement made in the body of my exposition, that political problems give rise to settlements, not solutions.[3] Other statements no doubt call for similar elaboration; why then single out this one?

It is because the myth of the solution dulls our understanding of Politics, which is quickened by the recognition that we come only to settlements, which are inherently precarious. A solution makes no enemies and requires no defenders: it is otherwise in the case of a settlement. Its permanence cannot be taken for granted; its chances of enduring depend upon its fostering forces which will work to uphold it.[4]

A specific settlement may contribute to the strengthening or

---

3. Cf. pp. 228–29.

4. This is one of the reasons which require that political decisions be taken in a forward-looking spirit, as stressed in part v, chs. 1 and 2.

weakening of the public order wherein it occurs; this order or "settled state" is itself not incapable of unsettlement, a thought which should haunt us, to make us more effective guardians of civility.

That this is no easy task, an image attests: the head and hands of the great guardian Cicero, nailed to the rostrum.

Conclusion

This book preaches no doctrine, advances no recommendations. Its purpose was to pick out certain elementary and pervading traits of Politics. Nothing was further from my mind than to paint on a large canvas a complete picture of Politics: I doubt whether this is feasible; I am sure that, were it successfully accomplished, the picture would represent Politics at a given place and moment. One would have to take a microscope to discern on this large canvas certain traits and articulations also to be found in pictures representing Politics at different times or places. This is what I have wanted to do. Thus whatever criticisms the present attempt deserves, it would, I feel, be unwarranted to hold against it that much has been left out: this would be a misunderstanding of the intention, which implied concentration on certain simple and ubiquitous aspects. As it seemed possible to reduce Movement to elementary forms, these were taken as a starting-point, in preference to Order, which is always complex, never quite the same, and therefore does not lend itself to analysis into unambiguous components. It is my hope that, after discussion, the simple concepts which have been hammered out here will prove useful in the statement of the far more complex situations obtaining in the real world.

Index

Abrams, M, 161 n. 8
Abyssinia, 202
actions: extreme, 254–55; military,
195–96, 201; *ut* and *quia*, 8–9; *see*
also "actor"; instigation;
intention; political activity
"actor," political, 8–10; defined,
43 n. 14; as "entrepreneur," 13; as
instigator, 13, 93–94; as operator,
13; in politics, 159–60
advisors, in decision-making, 119–
20, 206–12
affections, exploitation of, 71
agitation, political, 93; *see also*
instigation; intention; nuisance
policies; "team"
Aitchison, J., 159 n. 4
Alcibiades, 18–21, 148, 151 n. 3
Alcibiades, *see* Plato, *Pseudo-*
Acibiades
Algeria, 262; "Algerian problem," 268
algorithm, 245, 258
Allais, M., 43 n. 11
America, *see* United States
A-motivation, 98–101, 106, 130–31,
143; defined, 100; *see also*
"authorship factor"

anarchy, 143–44
appraiser, role of instigations,
117–19
appreciation, subjective and
objective, 154
argument, 150
Aristotle, 3, 258
Assembly, Athenian, 23, 24, 27–28,
32–33, 157
Assembly, French, 252–54, 275
Athens; and expedition to Syracuse,
5, 6, 20, 23, 24–28, 33, 148,
151 n. 3; law of citizenship,
52 n. 34; and Sparta, 20, 23
attention, 219–27; defined, 219;
transferability of, 222
Authority (formal), 163–64, 171–72;
agents of, 172–73, 189–91, 244–
45; challenge to, 162–63, 167–68,
231–41 (*see also* revolution; sedition; "team"); and change, 133,
167–68, 188; and character, 133,
139; decisions, 193–233; defined,
131–33, 164; duties of, 139; and
elections, 140–41; and entrepreneurship, 137–38; and instigation,
132; and justice, 274; need for,

This book is set in Electra. Introduced in 1937, the typeface was designed by William Addison Dwiggins for the Linotype machine and is characterized by its subtle irregularity and simple, crisp italic. Dwiggins was a graphic artist and skilled calligrapher who began designing type at the age of forty-four at the invitation of the Mergenthaler Linotype Company.

Printed on paper that is acid-free and meets the requirements of the American National Standard for Permanence of Paper for Printed Library Materials, z39.48-1992. ∞

Book design by Erin Kirk New,
    Athens, Georgia
Typography by G & S Typesetters,
    Austin, Texas
Printed and bound by Worzalla Publishing Company,
    Stevens Point, Wisconsin